The Sexual Victimization of Children

The Sexual Victimization of Children

by
Mary de Young

McFarland & Company, Inc., Publishers
Jefferson, N.C., & London
1982

Library of Congress Cataloging in Publication Data

de Young, Mary, 1949–
    The sexual victimization of children.

    Bibliography: p.
    Includes index.
    1. Child molesting. 2. Incest. 3. Pedophilia.
    4. Child molesting — United States. 5. Incest — United
    States. 6. Pedophilia — United States. I. Title.
    [DNLM: 1. Child abuse. 2. Incest. 3. Paraphilias.
    WM 610 D529s]
    HQ71.D32 1982   362.7′044   82-17197

    ISBN 0-89950-063-3

This book is dedicated to my parents, Kenneth and Doris De Young, and to my sister, Karen, and to my brothers, John and David, with deepest thanks for a lifetime of love and laughter

CONTENTS

ACKNOWLEDGMENTS

I have thanked you all informally; now I would like to formally share my thanks. To all of the incest and molestation victims who re-experienced the pain and anger of their victimization in telling me their stories, my deepest thanks. So many of you stated that you hoped your story would make a difference; I hope so too. To the incest offenders and pedophiles I also give thanks for sharing your feelings and describing your behavior.

My thanks also to my friend Irene Nash for typing this manuscript and to my friend Presh Oldt for reading it and for offering helpful suggestions and encouragement. To my colleague and friend Dr. Jonathan White a special thanks for his valuable contributions to the chapter, "The Social Origins of the Sexual Abuse of Children."

Even though it was formed after the manuscript was completed, I would like to thank my "support group" — Suzanne Perkins, Virginia Kuzniak, Betty Hayes, Justin Wilson and Deb Smith — for caring and for helping me keep things in perspective.

Finally, I would like to thank my family to whom this book is dedicated. You gave me all the advantages that love can give, and I am deeply grateful to you.

Part I. Incest

CHAPTER 1: AN INTRODUCTION

The very word "incest" conjures up a host of contradictory feelings for most people: repulsion, fascination, anger, and curiosity, to name but a few. As any serious student of incest behavior also will come to realize, it conjures up some amazingly contradictory research conclusions as well.

Take as an example the speculations which can be found in the literature regarding the rate of incest in society. Is it truly a one in a million phenomenon as Weinberg (1955) suggests; or is its rate closer to Kroth's (1979) estimate of one in ten thousand? Perhaps these two researchers have seriously underestimated the rate of occurrence of incest in society as Burgess *et al.* (1978) believe, and that it actually does occur in one out of every ten families.

There is also a great deal of contradictory data in the literature regarding the effects of incestuous relationships on the children involved in them. Are these children only minimally affected by incest, as researchers such as Rascovsky and Rascovsky (1950) and Yorukaglu and Kemph (1966) so adamantly state? Or is it more likely that their trauma will be more overwhelming and even long lasting, as Meiselman (1978) and Reich and Gutierres (1979) among others have found? Perhaps incestuous relationships actually have positive effects on the children as De Mott (1980) has discovered so many "pro-incest" researchers believe.

Researchers also have vehemently argued the role the child victim plays in the incest. Some, such as Lukianowicz (1972), believe that the child is a willing temptress, therefore culpable for her or his own victimization. Others, like Schultz (1980), would insist that most child incest victims are naive seducers, and still others, such as Gruber (1981), would characterize these children as innocent victims.

If researchers so obviously disagree about these three fundamental aspects of incest — its rate, its effects, and the role the child victims play in it — there is not likely to be a consensus on the finer points; and there certainly is not. The student of incest behavior will be both amazed and frustrated at the plethora of blatantly contradictory research conclusions which have been reached over the past fifty years. Lest the frustration overtake the amazement, one must realize that there are at the very least four reasons why these contradictory conclusions are so common.

First, different researchers use different definitions of incest in their respective studies. Some require that the criterion of sexual intercourse with a blood relative be met to establish a case of incest, while others define incest as

1

sexual contact, short of intercourse, between blood relatives. A few researchers will include in their studies of incest those cases in which there have been sexual advances or even sexual interest between blood relatives. Now it is obvious that there is a great deal of difference between sexual intercourse and sexual interest, yet at one time or another cases in which either one of these has occurred have been labeled incest cases and, therefore, have been included in incest research. It is also obvious that the rate of those incest cases characterized by sexual intercourse will vary greatly from those characterized by sexual interest, and the effects of sexual intercourse on the child victim will undoubtedly exceed the effects of sexual interest. Also, the role that a child plays in cases of sexual intercourse is likely to be significantly different from the role a child plays in cases of sexual interest. Therefore, research conclusions are likely to be contradictory when different definitions of incest are used.

To complicate matters even further, some researchers do not even require that the sexual behavior occur between blood relatives before a case is labeled an incest case. They believe that in those cases in which a person has *served* as a family member, such as an adoptive, foster or stepparent; and in cases in which a person is considered to be *like* a family member, such as a very close family friend, sexual behavior between that person and a child may be considered incestuous in nature. Finally, some researchers have refused to even acknowledge the possibility (and the reality) of homosexual incest, and therefore do not include such cases in their studies.

Second, the methodologies used in conducting research on incest also vary. Most studies are clearly quasiexperimental in nature, since it is rare to find an incest study which utilizes a control group. These quasiexperimental studies rely primarily on the analysis of case histories, a methodology that is quite subjective in nature and may not render results which can be accurately generalized.

Researchers most often tend to concentrate their attentions on older incest victims who are asked to describe their earlier victimizations and only rarely on children who are at the time involved in the incest, or who are just emerging from their incest experiences. While one must respect the ethical responsibilities inherent in this type of research, it must also be recognized that such retrospective descriptions are subject to the weaknesses of long-term memory and to the perceptual and affectual distortions that are likely to have occurred over the years.

Most incest research concentrates on the victim. In fact, most of it uses the victims' accounts to draw conclusions about the incest offenders and about the nonparticipating members of incestuous families. In others words, a significant proportion of our knowledge about the incestuous family comes from the recollections, assessments and judgments of the victims, who are unlikely to be the most objective observers and reporters. Those studies which do concentrate on the incest offenders and the nonparticipating family members may reach conclusions about incest inconsistent with the conclusions drawn in those studies utilizing only the victims' accounts.

Third, the populations from which researchers draw their samples for study also vary widely. Incest victims, offenders and nonparticipating family members are obviously not likely to be found in any one setting, yet the setting in which a researcher finds his or her sample is likely to affect the conclusions of the research. Many incest studies, in fact most of them, create their samples from psychotherapy caseloads. While these are convenient sources of subjects for study, the outcome of the research is likely to be skewed since it can be convincingly argued that psychotherapy patients are either those who have been the most seriously traumatized by the incest or who have made the most healthy adjustments to the incest because of their very involvement in psychotherapy. Whatever the case, these subjects may not represent the "typical" incest victim, offender or nonparticipating family member.

A similar problem exists when subjects for incest studies are taken from court caseloads or from prison and jail roles. Since so few cases of incest are ever officially reported it can be argued that those cases which are, and are therefore found within the criminal justice system, do not fairly and adequately represent "typical" cases of incest. It is therefore apparent that the populations used in incest studies vary widely and that the source of each population may skew the research results.

Fourth, because incest conjures up so many contradictory feelings, from which even researchers are not immune, serious students of incest must be sensitive to any hidden emotional agendas in incest research. A researcher's own bias and prejudices certainly may infiltrate a study and since few researchers openly state their bias and claim their prejudices, the student of incest behavior is best warned to be sensitive to the possibility of these hidden emotional agendas.

THE CLINICAL SAMPLE

In this study incest is defined as sexual intercourse, attempted sexual intercourse, or sexual contact of either a heterosexual or a homosexual nature between people too closely related to legally marry. In order to study incest, a large clinical sample composed of incest victims, offenders, and nonparticipating family members was created.

The Victims

Eighty victims of incest are part of that large clinical sample. At the time of the study they ranged in age from four to 53 years, with a mean age at the time of the study of 23 years. Eight (10%) of those 80 victims are males. Obviously that wide age range means that some of the victims were just emerging from their incest experience at the time of the study while others were retrospectively describing their experiences.

It is interesting how this victim sample was created. Some of the victims were on the author's court caseload, having been convicted of felony offenses. The author serves on a part-time basis as a clinical consultant to the circuit court of a large metropolitan county. Most of the victims are or have been the author's students in a large community college, and many of these students encouraged friends and relatives who also had been incestuously victimized to contact the author. Finally, some of these victims are community people who contacted the author after an article she wrote on incest appeared in a local magazine.

It took three years to draw together this victim population. While it is certainly a test of patience to develop a sample in this manner, the wait was well worth it. With victims from such widely divergent groups the research results are less likely to be skewed in any one direction and therefore may be more generalizeable.

All 80 victims were interviewed by the author, most of them on more than one occasion. The interviews were structured so that certain data could be obtained yet at the same time were open enough so that the author could make clinical observations of the victims. The author preferred to take as truth all information which was shared unless there was an obvious reason to be suspicious; consequently, no concerted attempts were made to verify the information and experiences shared by the victims.

Some demographic data on these victims may be of some interest and can be found in Table 1.

TABLE 1. SELECTED DEMOGRAPHIC DATA ON 80 INCEST VICTIMS

Type of Victimization	No. of Cases
Paternal	66
Maternal	4
Sibling	5
Grandfather-Granddaughter	2
Uncle-Niece	3

Ethnicity	No. of Cases
White	75
Black	3
Hispanic	2
Other	0

Religious Preference	No. of Cases
Protestant	24
Catholic	34
Jewish	0
Other	1
None	21

The Incest Offenders

The clinical sample also contains a total of 69 incest offenders who ranged in age at the time of the study from 13 to 69 years, with a mean age at the time of the study of 35 years.

This part of the clinical sample was drawn largely from the author's court caseload of convicted felons. Most but not all of them had been convicted of sexual offenses against children. All of these offenders were fresh from their incest experiences at the time of the study and are not retrospectively describing their experiences. A few of these incest offenders had never been convicted or even arrested for that matter. They were referred to the author by therapists who were treating them.

Again, each offender was interviewed by the author with the particular goals of accumulating data as well as of forming diagnostic impressions. In court cases specific details of the incest shared by the offenders were checked for accuracy against official reports included in court files.

Selected demographic data on the incest offenders are in Table 2.

TABLE 2. SELECTED DEMOGRAPHIC DATA ON 69 INCEST OFFENDERS

Type of Victimization	No. of Cases
Paternal	55
Maternal	4
Sibling	5
Grandfather-Granddaughter	2
Uncle-Niece	3

Ethnicity	No. of Cases
White	64
Black	4
Hispanic	1
Other	0

Religious Preference	No. of Cases
Protestant	21
Catholic	22
Jewish	0
Other	0
None	26

Occupation Group	No. of Cases
Professional	3
Skilled	21
Unskilled	11
Unemployed	27
Other (retired, student)	7

Nonparticipating Family Members

If incest is a symptom of family pathology then the roles that nonparticipating members of incestuous families play are important to any study of incest. Recognizing that, the clinical sample also contains some family members who did not, themselves, directly participate in the incest.

The wives of eight of the incestuous fathers were interviewed as were four nonmolested siblings of paternal incest victims. Brief interviews were also conducted with the fathers of two boys who had been incestuously victimized by their mothers, and with the mothers of two boys who had been incestuously victimized by their fathers.

CHAPTER 2: THE INCEST TABOO

Isolated primitive societies as well as those of times long past have received a great deal of attention of late in the ongoing debate which centers around the universality of the incest taboo. Those who would argue that the taboo is not universal cite the Kalang Tribe of Java which views mother-son marriage as a harbinger of good fortune; the Bantus of East Africa who permit intrafamily marriages if the sons are too poor to buy wives (Maisch, 1972); and the sibling marriages of Egypt which were encouraged to retain family property and wealth (Middleton, 1962).

Advocates of the universality of the incest taboo warn us to be skeptical of these exceptions. Our own prejudices and ignorance may render us gullible to accounts of depraved practices and beliefs among different cultures. Also, it is argued, these accounts of incest taboo exceptions often do not hold true under scientific scrutiny (Murdock, 1949).

While both sides make significant points in advancing their respective positions, the truth may lie somewhere between. It does appear that there have been, historically speaking, and are now exceptions to the incest taboo. However, these exceptions are few and far between. For the most part, the taboo against nuclear family incest is not only largely universal, it is remarkably so.

The origin of this taboo is also vehemently debated with, at times, the same kind of professional jealousy which characterizes the debate over the taboo's universality. Surely there is great stock to be held in the argument that the incest taboo has its roots in biology. Segner and Collins (1967), for example, discovered that one-third of all of the recorded myths of primitive societies which have incest as a theme describe deformed offspring or infertility as a consequence of incest. Thus, it is alleged, primitive societies recognized that their biological survival is based upon nonincestuous sexual relationships. A very early study by Morgan (1877) proposed that incest was common among many cultures but was prohibited when the deleterious effects of such practices were noticed.

The effects of consanguineous marriages on the offspring is the most powerful argument for the biological origin of the incest taboo. Schull and Neel (1965) compared the children of married first cousins with the children of nonconsanguineous marriages. The former group tended to be somewhat smaller, more susceptible to infections, and less intelligent than the latter group of offspring. The children of cousins were also more likely to be born

6

with congenital defects. Adams and Neel (1967) studied 18 children born of incestuous relationships and compared them to a control group matched for age, race, weight, height, intelligence and socio-economic status. The children were examined at birth and again at six months of age. Seven of the children born of incestuous relationships tested normally at birth and again at six months. However, five others died in early infancy; two were severely retarded and seizure-disordered; three had borderline I.Q.'s; and one was born with a bilateral cleft palate. These defected children are notable not only for their defects but for the rate at which these defects occur in their group compared to that of the control population, in which 15 of the 18 infants were normal; one had congenital birth defects; and two were retained for further intelligence testing.

In one of the largest studies conducted on the children born of incestuous relationships similar dismal results were found. Seemanova (1971) studied 161 children born of incestuous relationships and compared them to 95 children who are their half-siblings. She found that 25% of the children born of incest were mentally retarded, compared to none of the controls; 20% had congenital defects while only 5% of the controls had such defects; 6% had multiple congenital malformations, while none of the controls suffered such malformations. Seemanova concludes that only 43% of the children born of incest were "normal" in any sense of that term.

While the biological argument for the origin of the incest taboo is powerful, it faces strong opposition from those who would insist that the origin of the taboo is psychosocial in nature. Malinowski (1927), an early proponent of this theory, believed that because incest means the "upsetting of age distinctions, the mixing up of generations, the disorganization of sentiments, and a violent exchange of roles" (p. 251), its widespread occurrence would certainly lead to the disintegration of the family system and of the society in which families interact. Parsons (1954) agrees that incest must be taboo so that individuals can develop those "transfamilial roles" which are vital to the continuation of society. Part of the survival of any society surely rests on its economic stability. Justice and Justice (1979) suggest that the incest taboo assured economic survival in that it forced families to pool their strengths and resources with other families. According to them, "sex between nonmarried members of a family would disrupt the division of labor and cooperative relationship necessary for the smooth functioning of the economic unit" (p. 36). This increased economic stability then leads to the increased exchange of things and ideas necessary for cultural evolution (White, 1948).

Westermark (1922) took a slightly different slant to this psychosocial theory of the origin of the incest taboo. He argues that there is a natural aversion to sex among members of a family so that the taboo originated in the family itself. Summit and Kryso (1978) counter that argument by insisting that "people who live together, who depend on each other for love and support, and who have intimate daily contact with each other will tend to develop sexual relationships with each other" (p. 239), therefore, the incest taboo must originate outside of the family.

Again, this debate like the one over the universality of the taboo, may present only the extreme positions and the truth may be a combination of the two positions. Murdock (1949) was the first to suggest a multidisciplinary perspective on the origin of the incest taboo, and while that at first may appear to be an academic compromise, it really may not be that. Murdock recognized that the taboo which assures the biological survival of the human race is inextricably bound to the taboo which assures the cultural survival of the society in which that race lives and with which it interacts. To insist that the incest taboo serves only one component and not the other is to be ignorant of the complex interaction of the two.

CHAPTER 3: PATERNAL INCEST — THE CHARACTERS

"Incest is a game the whole family can play!" is a common example of graffiti most often found on subway station and restroom walls. Its message is tasteless and disgusting but it also contains the smallest kernel of truth. Of course incest is not a "game" and families certainly do not "play" it, and the jocular, good-natured implication of this statement hardly reflects the real life experiences of incest participants. The truth of the statement is not contained in these elements; it is contained in the connotation that the "whole family" participates in the incest.

Incest is a product of family pathology and, except on the rarest occasions, all family members contribute in some way to the pathology that breeds the incest. This is a much more subtle and collusive process than perhaps this statement at first implies. Muldoon (1979) suggests the label "character disordered family" to describe the insidious role reversals, distortions of affectional patterns, and generational boundary blurrings so common in these families. Recognizing that the family, as a system, is in a delicate homeostatic balance and that this balance is maintained through the interdependence of all family members, then it is clear that any change in one part of the family system will have an effect on and will be accommodated by the rest of the system. Therefore, the "incestuous family" will be examined through the roles which the individual members in this family play.

THE INCESTUOUS FATHER

One of the outstanding characteristics of an incestuous family is that it is patriarchal in nature (Herman and Hirschman, 1977). The father exploits his authority and abuses his intrafamilial power. That abuse certainly involves the incest, but it also frequently involves the physical abuse which may concur with the incest or independently of it. This is a finding frequently overlooked in the literature; it makes so many of the dynamics of incest as well as the effects of incest on the victims so much more understandable.

In the clinical sample of 60 victims of paternal incest, 22 (37%) were also victims of repeated physical abuse perpetrated by their fathers or stepfathers. An additional 11 (18%) were victims of occasional physical abuse

9

within their families. Even those incest victims who were not physically battered often viewed physical abuse directed against their mothers or their
siblings by their fathers or stepfathers. De Young (1981a) states that there is an
aura of physical violence in most incestuous families which, even if not acted
upon, contributes to many of the dynamics and effects of incest.

Some would undoubtedly dismiss the recollections of the physical
abuse of incest victims in the clinical sample as questionable because of the
weaknesses of long-term memory and subjective nature of the definition of
physical abuse. However, the clinical sample also contains a total of 51 incestuous fathers and stepfathers and they were also surveyed as to their own
assessments of the amount of physical abuse they themselves perpetrated
within their own families. Incest victimization is difficult enough to admit,
and being asked to confess to physical abuse as well undoubtedly creates an
ideal opportunity to deny or distort the rate of its occurrence. Yet 12 (24%) of
the incestuous fathers and stepfathers admitted that they also frequently or
occasionally beat their children or their wives.

Perhaps one of the reasons for this high rate of physical abuse within
incestuous families lies in the character of the incestuous father. Sgroi (1979)
refers to this type of father as a "me-first" person who frequently has his entire
family revolving around him, meeting his needs. Why this is so reflects some
of the deprivations the incestuous father had experienced in his own
childhood.

Early Childhood

Incestuous fathers frequently have a history of deprivation during
their childhoods. In some cases that deprivation is economic in nature. Riemer
(1940), in one of the earlier studies of incestuous fathers, found that a majority
of his sample had grown up in poverty. This finding is most common in earlier
studies of incest since most latter studies underplay the role of economic
deprivation in the etiology of incest.

What is more likely to be found in the childhoods of incestuous fathers
is emotional or relationship deprivations. Gebhard et al. (1965) in their study
of incarcerated sex offenders, found that 59% of their sample of incestuous
fathers came from broken homes (p. 208). In the clinical sample, 12 (24%)
came from broken homes.

However a broken home is only one way through which emotional
deprivation may be experienced. What is more commonly found is a negative
or at best ambivalent relationship with the parents, particularly the father, as
the case of Mr. Anderson who had incestuously victimized his daughter illustrates:

> From the outside my family looked real good. We went to church, my dad
> worked and my mom kept the house clean. But there wasn't much love
> there. My mom was sick a lot and I was scared of my old man. He never
> beat me or nothing, but he was the king of the house. We all waited on him
> hand and foot. He hardly ever talked to us or took us anywheres. He figured
> if he put food in our bellies and a roof over our heads he was doing his
> job and being a good father.

Frequently the feelings toward the father are much more negative than this, and for good reason. Twenty-two (43%) of the incestuous fathers and stepfathers in the clinical sample had been physically abused as children by their own fathers. Since physical abuse is often transmitted from generation to generation, this finding in the clinical sample lends support to the theory that physical abuse occurs frequently within incestuous families. Had some of these fathers and stepfathers been sexually abused as children as well? This, again, is a particularly difficult experience for many men to admit, but the clinical sample did demonstrate either some personal victimization or some exposure to sexual victimization as Table 3 demonstrates.

TABLE 3. CHILDHOOD SEXUAL EXPERIENCES
OF 51 INCESTUOUS FATHERS AND STEPFATHERS

Type of Experience	No. of Reports	Average Age at First Occurrence
Victim of paternal incest	3	8.6 years
Victim of maternal incest	2	12.2 years
Participant in sibling incest	3	12.4 years
Nonparticipating member of an incestuous family	5	12.1 years
Molestation by adult male acquaintance	3	9.9 years
Molestation by adult female acquaintance	1	7.6 years
Molestation by adult male stranger	2	10.6 years

Again, there is some reason to believe that the personal victimization experiences and the exposure to sexual victimization may be underreported by the incestuous fathers and stepfathers. However, as Table 3 illustrates, 19 (or 37%) of the incestuous fathers and stepfathers in the clinical sample had been either sexual victimized as children or had been raised in a family in which incestuous victimization was taking place even though they, themselves, had not been victims.

The net effect of this early history of deprivation, abuse and victimization is that incestuous fathers and stepfathers are left without competent role models to emulate. Simply stated, they do not know how to father. Since that lack of ability can cause frustration and anxiety, they tend to overcompensate and to rely on their own early experiences by becoming abusive and patriarchal.

Marriage Relationship

When this type of person emerges from his childhood experiences he carries with him into his marriage relationship the emotional scars incurred during his childhood. Consequently, his marriage relationship is likely to be tense and unhappy.

Kroth (1979), in analyzing the referrals to the Child Sexual Abuse Treatment Program in California, found that 17% of the parents were emotionally alienated from each other and that 15% were sexually alienated (p.46). Frequently that emotional and sexual alienation, about which more will be said, motivates the incestuous father to become involved with another woman. In the clinical sample, 38 (75%) of them had had at least one extramarital affair. In an earlier study, Gebhard et al. (1965) found that figure to be 84% (p. 218). At least part of the motivation for seeking another woman is that same overcompensation that contributes to the patriarchal nature of the family and, eventually, to the incest. Mr. Baker, who had victimized his two daughters, exemplifies this finding:

> I'm a long-haul truck driver and I've got a woman in every city. I think it's O.K. for a man to be involved with a lot of different women. That's a man's nature. That's what makes him a real man.

It is that same sexual alienation which may lead to seeking a daughter as a source of sexual satisfaction. Weinberg (1955) refers to this type of father as an "endogamic type," which he defines as an 'ingrown personality type who confines his sexual objects to family members...because he does not cultivate and does not crave social or sexual contacts with women outside the family" (p. 94). Meiselman (1978) suggests that this type of incestuous father is more likely to commit incest with more than one of his daughters.

The sexual alienation of the wife from the incestuous father is more pronounced in the clinical sample than it was in Kroth's study. Twenty-two (43%) of the incestuous fathers and stepfathers reported sexual alienation and in each case that alienation preceded the incest. Again, this is a much more complicated dynamic than it may at first appear and will be examined more thoroughly when the role of the nonparticipating mother in the incestuous family is presented.

Rationalizations

A history of deprivation and marriage problems certainly can create difficulties in daily living, but they do not inevitably lead to incest. One thing which must occur before the incest is initiated is that the father or stepfather must convince himself that becoming sexually involved with his daughter is acceptable and even normal. He accomplishes this through the development of a complicated rationalization system. Each incestuous father and stepfather in the clinical sample was asked to name the one primary reason for the sexual victimization of his daughter. The reasons stated do not account for all of the rationalizations used by incestuous fathers, of course, but it is interesting that some of those rationalizations appear so frequently in the clinical sample as well as in the samples used by other research studies.

Sex Education Rationalization. Twenty-five (49%) of the incestuous fathers and stepfathers in the clinical sample stated that their primary reason for the incest was the sexual education of their daughters. Justice and Justice (1979) refer to this type of father as the "teacher" who "fully convinces himself that what he is doing to his daughter is for her own good" (p. 73).

It is interesting to note that this rationalization is so intimately related to other dynamics which are occuring in the incestuous family.

> Mr. Allen, 38, who had incestuously victimized his daughter states, "Her mom doesn't like sex, see. She says that she feels uncomfortable and that sometimes it even hurts her like there is something wrong physically, except that I know it's mental. I didn't want my daughter to have those same problems so I figured if I showed her what sex is all about she would not have those hang-ups when she grows up."

> Mr. Mason, 41, who had incestuously victimized his daughter explains his reason for doing so in the following way: "I was raped as a kid. Yeah, raped, by a coach at my junior high school. I was 12 at the time and I didn't know anything about sex, except for some things I heard out on the streets. I figure if I had known something about sex I wouldn't have been raped. Everybody knows that girls get raped more often than boys, so I figured I would teach my daughter something about sex so it wouldn't happen to her. So I went to bed with her a few times."

In the clinical sample, this rationalization was most commonly heard from those fathers and stepfathers who had incestuously victimized daughters who were just beginning to go through puberty. Many of the daughters had just started menstruating at the time of the initiation of the incest and were just developing secondary sex characteristics. The fathers and stepfathers obviously confused that physical development with sexuality and sexual desires.

Seduction Rationalization. Eighteen (35%) of the incestuous fathers and stepfathers in the clinical sample stated that their primary reason for the incest was that they had been seduced by their daughters. Even though this is a primary rationalization in slightly more than one-third of the cases, virtually every father and stepfather in the clinical sample voiced this rationalization at one time or another during the interview.

Unfortunately, there is a tendency to blame the victim in cases of incest. One can hardly forget Lukianowicz's (1972) conclusion that the victims in his sample were often "provocative seductresses" (p. 309) because this statement so often reflects the conclusions of other research studies. To this extent, the incestuous father or stepfather who uses this seduction rationalization has an ally in contemporary incest research.

What this rationalization really proves is not the culpability of the victim but the lack of impulse control of the incestuous father or stepfather. Researchers and practitioners often forget that the victim is a child, often very young such as in Lukianowicz's sample where the average age of the victims was only 8½ years old, and that the offending parent is an adult. The unfortunate tendency to be adultomorphic with children by attributing to them all kinds of mature feelings and attitudes makes this rationalization at least somewhat believable to so many people. When that tendency is eliminated and the age of the child is kept in mind, this rationalization appears much more flimsy and considerably less believable.

> Mr. Kent, 29, states that his 8 year old daughter seduced him. "She kept wanting me to give her a bath and then she wanted me to get in the tub with her. Once she even ran out of the bathroom with no clothes on and when I caught her she kissed me on the lips. I figured she was asking for something more. I know she's just a kid but she was acting like a whore."

> Mr. Nichols, 36, incestuously victimized his 12 year old stepdaughter. "She was always acting sexual around me, you know, like hugging and kissing me and offering to rub my back. I figure that kids these days know a lot more about sex than I ever did so I figured that she knew what she was doing. It was a real come-on, so I just took her up on it."

The alleged seductiveness of the incest victims is a complicated dynamic and reflects so many variables within the incestuous family. It will be examined in greater detail when the role of the victim is presented.

Alcohol Rationalization. Seven (14%) of the clinical sample of incestuous fathers and stepfathers gave as their primary rationalization for the incest their emotional state and controls weakened by alcohol. All seven of these fathers and stepfathers are confessed alcoholics.

Contrary to the stereotypical perception of the drunken father raping his daughter, alcoholism is infrequently reported by incestuous fathers. Kroth (1979) found 12% of his referrals were alcoholics (p. 56): Lukianowicz (1972) found a total of 15% in his sample (p. 310); Justice and Justice (1979) estimated that 10% to 15% of their sample were alcoholics; and Cavallin (1966) found that 33% of his sample of incestuous fathers were "drinkers" (p. 1134), although the exact definition of that term is not clear.

Mental Illness Rationalization. One (2%) father in the clinical sample rationalized that he would not have incestuously victimized his daughter if he had not been "crazy" at the time. The man in question is severely neurotic and was in a great deal of psychic pain at the time of the incest.

It is certainly more comfortable to believe that only a "crazy" father or stepfather would incestuously victimize his daughter, but mental illness is not frequently found in samples of incestuous fathers. Psychosis and neurosis are rarely present, although some character disorder features are frequently found. Weiner (1962) gave five incestuous fathers a battery of psychological tests including the Rorschach, the Bender-Gestalt and the Thematic Apperception Test. The results show a well integrated defense system, identity confusion and paranoid thinking, but no psychosis or neurosis.

There is also a great deal of evidence to support the conclusion that incestuous fathers are no more inclined to be intellectually impaired. Most studies indicate that they operate well within the normal range of intellectual functioning. In fact, some studies indicate that incestuous fathers and stepfathers are often intellectually superior (Cormier et al., 1962; Weiner, 1962; Gebhard et al., 1965).

Possession Rationalization. No one in the clinical sample stated this as a primary rationalization, but it was frequently heard from the men in the sample that their daughters are their possessions and therefore subject to their needs and desires. Rush (1980) states that from earliest history children have been considered the possessions of their fathers and that this attitude has been supported by both custom and law. With this rich tradition upon which an incestuous father or stepfather can rest his case, it is no wonder that this rationalization is heard so frequently.

At least part of the ability to see the child as a possession relies on the capacity of the incestuous father or stepfather to dehumanize his daughter. Of course, any time a person is perceived as an object or possession, dehumanization takes place. Weiner (1962), however, states this dehumanization also occurs when the fathers or stepfathers see their daughters in "segments or as caricatures or mythological figures" (p. 623).

> Mr. Nelson describes his 13 year old daughter whom he had incestuously victimized for two years as his "china doll." He states: She is just a perfect little doll with hair of spun gold and eyes like sapphires. Sometimes she does not even seem real to me because she is so beautiful."

> Mr. Olds sees his 15 year old daughter as a "typical teenager." What can I say about her? She's a typical kid. Describe any kid her age and you've described her. Throw her in with a bunch of kids and I'll have a hard time picking her out."

Sexual Liberation Rationalization. Another rationalization of incestuous fathers and stepfathers which did not appear in the clinical sample but has been reported on occasion in the literature is the sexual liberation theme. Justice and Justice (1979) describe this rationalization in the following manner: "The parent who has already convinced himself that having sex with friends and neighbors is simply a form of sexual liberation does not find it difficult to extent his freedom of expression to relatives" (p. 77). This type of father carries into his home the activities in which he engages outside of the home. He may rationalize that everyone, including his own children, needs to be liberated from archaic and repressive sexual attitudes.

Duty Rationalization. Finally, some incestuous fathers and stepfathers rationalize that it is their daughters' duty to have sexual relations with them. No father or stepfather in the clinical sample stated this as a primary motivation for victimizing his daughter, but it is a rationalization commonly found in the literature. Because of the incapacitation or absence of the mother, the daughter is looked upon by the father as an acceptable sexual partner. He may rationalize that it is preferable to victimize her than to have an affair or to seek a prostitute. The father or stepfather who uses this rationalization appears to be endogamic in type as described by Weinberg (1955).

INCESTUOUS STEPFATHERS

Children's fairy tales and fantasies are replete with images of cruel and conniving wicked stepparents. These images, according to Bettelheim (1977) serve the children well in that they act as an imaginary target onto which the children can project their anger and ambivalence which they occasionally experience in relation to their natural parents. In that way, they suggest how the children can manage contradictory and ambivalent feelings about their parents, feelings which would otherwise be too overwhelming to manage.

The image of the wicked stepparent is probably more myth than reality, but there is a particular problem with the introduction of a stepfather into a family; a problem which researchers often have mentioned but have rarely seriously considered. That problem is the increased vulnerability of the female stepchild to incestuous victimization by the stepfather.

This rather cavalier attitude of researchers is striking in its contrast to the demographics of modern American society, since the rate of divorce and remarriage in our culture has created constantly shifting family structures. It is estimated that 75% of all divorced women and 83% of all divorced men remarry, usually within the three years following their divorces (Glick, 1975:15). The net effect of that trend is that in 1975 alone, 15 million young-sters under the age of 18 were living in stepfamilies, and 25 million adults were stepparents (Vischer and Vischer, 1979:4).

This statistical trend in the increase in stepfamilies is reflected in the statistics regarding the incestuous victimization of children. De Francis (1969) found that 11% of his sample of incest victims had experienced that victimiza-tion by their stepfathers (p. 81). A decade later, Finkelhor (1979) discovered that 29% of the women victims he surveyed had been victims of stepfather in-cest (p. 87). In the clinical sample of 60 victims of paternal incest, 21 (35%) were victims of stepfather incest. Of the 51 incest offenders in the clinical sample, 20 (39%) are stepfathers.

The uncomfortable fact that begins to emerge is that the introduction of a stepfather into a family does increase the possibility that the stepdaughter will become a victim of incest. Finkelhor (1979) calculates that girls with stepfathers are actually 150% as likely to be the victims of incest than are girls living with their natural fathers (p. 122). Obviously, incest does not take place in all stepfamilies, but the fact that it happens in some should raise questions as to the dynamics which underlie its occurrence.

Weakened Incest Taboo

The incest taboo has generally served to protect both the families and the society in which they live and with whom they interact. Yet the taboo has not always held for stepparents and their stepchildren. As late as 1940, for example, 26 states permitted stepfather-stepdaughter marriages (Fast and Cain, 1966:489).

Burgess *et al.* (1978) have examined the consequences of this weakened taboo in stepfamilies: "The father-daughter incest taboo is so great in our society that professionals and lay people within the community tend to view child sexual assault by stepfathers with far less alarm and discomfort than when the natural father is the perpetrator" (p. 134). Although the community in general and the helping professions in particular regard incest between stepfather and stepdaughter with less alarm and discomfort, the incest victims of stepfathers rarely share that benevolent attitude.

Finkelhor (1979) asked the female victims of stepfather incest to rate the trauma of the experience on a scale from one to five, with one indicating a very positive experience and five representing a very negative experience. The mean trauma score for female victims of stepfather incest is 4.5 (p. 102). This clearly indicates that regardless of how relaxed the incest taboo is in the eyes of the community, the trauma the stepdaughter experiences is great, indeed. This is especially evident when that mean trauma score of 4.5 is compared to the mean trauma score of 4.8 for daughters who had been incestuously vic-timized by their natural fathers (p. 102).

Stirring of Sexual Feelings

Often stepparents have unrealistic expectations of instant family love and instant family feelings (Stinnett and Walters, 1977). If those expectations are not met, the stepfather may "court" his stepdaughter, buying her gifts and granting her special privileges to ease his transition into her family. Once he has entered the family, he and the child's mother may engage in openly affectionate behavior in the presence of the family (Vischer and Vischer, 1979). As normal and natural as this behavior may be, when it is coupled with the "courting" of the stepdaughter, it may stir sexual feelings in the stepdaughter and may lead to naive sexual imitation.

None of this is to imply that the stepdaughter is evoking or otherwise encouraging the incest behavior. That this behavior may be viewed by the stepfather as consciously seductive and as inviting of a sexual response on his part is an indication both of his poor impulse control and the absence or unwillingness of the mother to define that behavior in its proper context and to protect her daughter from sexual advances.

Lack of Developmental History

A stepfather often comes into his stepdaughter's life at a particular point in her development without a full appreciation of or participation in the experiences, situations, interactions and feelings that brought her to that point. Not having shared these with her, he is less likely to feel emotionally bonded to his stepdaughter. Therefore he is less likely to feel paternal, protective, tender or whatever other feelings a natural father is more likely to experience — feelings which then may act as deterrents to incest.

Unfortunately, stepdaughters have a higher rate of sexual victimization in general. In other words, the presence of a stepfather increases a girl's vulnerability to sexual assault by other, nonfamily persons (Finkelhor, 1979). This occurs because the stepfather brings with him into his new family a whole coterie of friends and acquaintances, none of whom is restrained by the incest taboo and all of whom lack that crucial sense of the developmental history of the child. These friends and acquaintances are likely to use as a model the stepfather's attitudes and behaviors toward his stepdaughter. If they sense in him a lack of paternal and protective feelings, they are likely to assume the same posture toward the child, and that increases the possibility that she will be sexually victimized by them.

Family Disorganization

It is entirely possible that some stepfamilies, perhaps because of the excessive and rapid changes to which they must accommodate in order to become reconstituted families, are simply more disorganized, however temporarily, than are other families (Justice and Justice, 1979). Disorganization in a family system is dysfunctional and adversely affects all family members.

According to Kent (1980), severely disorganized families cope with the dysfunction in one of two ways. They may become "centrifugal" in nature by projecting family difficulties on one another and by casting members into rigid, inflexible roles; or they may become "centripetal" in that they express their difficulties through social isolation.

Both the "centrifugal" and the "centripetal" families are incest-prone. In an examination of the family dynamics in cases of paternal incest, Warner (1980) discovered two consistent patterns: the chaotic, multiproblem family characterized by rigid, uncompromising roles and symptomatic acting out; and the secretive, enmeshed family which meets all of its needs, including sexual needs, within the family unit. The first pattern equates with the centrifugal family as described by Kent; the second with her description of the centripetal family. Both are, by virtue of their disorganization and ineffective coping skills, incest-prone families.

THE NONPARTICIPATING MOTHERS

If the family is a social system then any pathology of any individual family member must be accommodated by the other family members. Therefore, in an incestuous family, the roles of those family members who do not participate in the incest become critical to the understanding of the incest. The role that the mother plays in an incestuous family is especially critical because, as a parent, she has the opportunity to wield a great deal of intrafamilial power and it is that power which can prevent the incest or stop it from continuing. The fact that in incestuous families the incest has not been prevented and that it frequently continues uninterrupted for many years attests to what happens when that power is abridged.

In the clinical sample of 51 incestuous fathers and stepfathers, eight of their wives were also interviewed. These interviews will illustrate the dynamics that research has uncovered for nonparticipating mothers in incestuous families.

Early Childhood

Nonparticipating mothers in incestuous families frequently have had early childhoods characterized by feelings of insecurity. Part of these feelings originate in an unstable and unpredictable family life. Four of the eight mothers in the clinical sample came from broken homes; two had experienced the early death of one of their parents; and one of the women had been raised in an orphanage. The remaining mother, whose family had been intact, had spent months of each year living with relatives when child care responsibilities had become too overwhelming for her emotionally fragile mother.

This early childhood history of broken homes, institutionalization and death of a parent is frequently documented in the backgrounds of nonparticipating mothers in incestuous families (Eist and Mandel, 1968; Maisch, 1972; Meiselman, 1978). Like incest victims themselves, the mothers are rendered insecure and extremely dependent as a result of these experiences. They are also infused with a large dose of separation anxiety that is likely to be pervasive throughout their adult lives.

The seven mothers from the clinical sample who had mothers in their homes as children remember them with thinly disguised negative feelings. All of them see their own mothers as cold, rejecting and demanding. That they attempted to get their dependency needs met by this type of rejecting parent, and that they continued to do so throughout their adult lives, speaks of the desparation and the self-defeating quality of that relationship. Eist and Mandel (1968) describe an incident which occurred during the early part of their psychotherapeutic treatment of a mother of an incest victim (p. 219) which clearly illustrates this point:

> During the early part of the treatment a situation arose which exemplifies Mrs. T.'s frenzied attempts to obtain maternal approval. Mrs. T.'s mother wrote, mentioning that she would be coming into town for a visit... No specific time of arrival was provided, but it was clear that either bus or airplane would be the alternatives as far as her mother's choice of transportation was concerned. For several days, Mrs. T. darted back and forth between the air terminal and the bus station, meeting all the planes and buses arriving from her mother's place of residence. She did manage to meet her mother and was very disappointed that her mother had decided to go on rather than stay.

In the clinical sample of eight nonparticipating mothers, three had themselves been victims of paternal incest as children, and one had been the victim of sibling incest. Above anything else, this 50-percent figure attests to the intergenerational transmission of incest, in which the nonparticipating mothers recreate their own childhood experiences within their own homes and then model their own mothers' lack of protectiveness and intervention.

Marriage Relationship

Often eager to escape the unhappiness and insecurity of their own homes, nonparticipating mothers tend to marry early (Tormes, 1968). The average age at which the women in the clinical sample married was 18.6.

All too frequently the marriage relationship is far from ideal. The incestuous father already has been described as patriarchal and to accommodate, or complement, this behavior, the mother becomes passive and detached. Because the patriarchal father is also frequently abusive, she may become the target of his rage and frustration. Six of the eight women stated that they had been frequently or occasionally beaten by their husbands.

The nonparticipating mothers tend to develop certain coping strategies to deal with the abuse and with their unhappiness, and it is these strategies which may set, however inadvertently, the stage for paternal incest. Again, this is not to blame the mothers, since so many of these strategies are developed unconsciously and since placing blame is much too simplistic a measure to adequately address a complicated problem like incest. However, it is necessary to understand incest as a family dynamic, so these coping strategies are important to that dynamic.

Sexual Withdrawal. In many cases of paternal incest, the mother sexually withdraws from her husband before incest is actually initiated (Cormier *et al.*, 1962; Weiner, 1962; Lustig *et al.*, 1966; Molnar and Cameron, 1975). This sometimes subtle and sometimes outright denial of sex leaves the husband without a socially acceptable outlet for his sexual desires. Six of the mothers in the clinical sample had sexually withdrawn from their husbands prior to the initiation of the incest.

> Mrs. Gordon, whose husband had incestuously victimized their daughter, states that she sexually withdrew from her husband as a way of "getting back at him" for his frequently abusive tirades. "Sex is the only weapon I have." she explains. "I thought that if I withdrew from him it would force him to have an affair or get a prostitute. If he did and I found out about it, I'd have all the more reason to divorce him."

The mothers frequently convey their unhappiness about the sexual demands put upon them by their husbands to their daughters. In some cases, this disclosure may place an unusual burden on the daughter who may feel obliged to protect her mother from his sexual advances.

Another manner a mother can use to facilitate this withdrawal is by assuming the mother role in relation to her husband. By doing so, she essentially makes herself ineligible for sexual relations with her husband.

Physical and Emotional Incapacitation. Frequently the nonparticipating mother becomes physically and/or emotionally incapacitated, thereby withdrawing from her role responsibilities. That incapacitation may be real or it may be imagined; regardless, it is a coping strategy assumed to deal with her unhappy marriage and home life. It is interesting that all of the nonparticipating mothers in the clinical sample had used this strategy at least once, always with good results, as the following two cases illustrate:

> Mrs. May is an alcoholic whose drinking binges would leave her incapacitated for days at a time. She always drank at home which put the burden for dealing with her on her family. No one could put demands on her if she was drunk, and any demands put on her when she was sober would initiate a drinking binge that would last for days.

> Mrs. Farmer suffered from periodic bouts of incapacitating depression which would send her to her room for weeks at a time. During those periods she would have to be force fed and bathed by her family. When she recovered her family would be so concerned about her fragile mental state that they would put no demands on her. Yet the slightest pressure of any kind would trigger yet another depressive reaction.

Absence. At times the mother copes with her family problems by physically withdrawing from the home. She may do this by working or by being constantly involved in activities that necessitate her being absent from the home. In some cases that absence occurs because of hospitalization, incarceration or institutionalization.

Role Reversal with the Daughter. What is so frequently found in cases of paternal incest is that the withdrawal or incapacitation of the mother thrusts her daughter into the "little mother" role. Once that role reversal has occurred, in the eyes of the impulse-ridden father or stepfather, the daughter becomes a permissable alternative to his wife. This is a considerably more complicated dynamic than it may initially appear.

Just before the incest is initiated, there is an almost universal estrangement of the mother and daughter (Herman and Hirschman, 1977). The tension builds between the two of them as the daughter begins to mature and the mother withdraws. When the daughter is finally thrust into the "little mother" role, the mother has little else to do except to become dependent on her daughter, and it is that childlike dependency that resurrects those unhappy, insecure feelings the mother had experienced as a child in relation to her own mother. And all of the repressed anger and hostility, so difficult and dangerous to express as a child, now becomes mobilized by the adult mother and is focused on her daughter.

> Mrs. Burnett describes her daughter in the following way: "She's a tyrant, bossing around her little brothers and me like she owned the place. She makes me so angry, especially around dinner time. She reminds me of my mother, making me feel guilty for not liking the food she cooked and for not appreciating the way she straightened up the house." Mrs. Burnett's daughter, an incest victim for two years, is nine years old.

This role reversal is absolutely critical for it sets the final stage for the paternal incest to occur. Yet what makes this process so much more difficult and complicated than it sounds is that it is largely unconscious in nature. It occurs so subtly and insidiously that it is virtually impossible to detect until it has actually occurred. Once the overt incest begins, the mother's unconsciously collusive role is facilitated and strengthened by her use of the defense mechanism of denial.

This denial mechanism is invoked for a variety of reasons. First, the mother who knows or suspects that the incest is occurring has a great deal to lose if she exercises her intrafamilial power and intervenes in the victimization. Her unresolved dependency needs tie her to her husband, and her submissive and passive behavior do not give her the assertiveness necessary to intervene in the incest. Fearing the dissolution of her marriage, public humiliation, and the loss of financial support, she finds it more expedient to deny the incest than to confront it.

A second reason for the denial is "like the majority of people in our society, she probably believes that incest is a one-in-a-million event that is mainly limited to families of the Jukes and Kallikaks types" (Meiselman, 1978: 169). Aided and abetted in her denial by prevailing community attitudes which also only reluctantly acknowledge the reality of incest, the mother makes incest such a rare and bizarre occurrence that in her mind it cannot possibly be happening in her family.

> "Incest!" exclaimed Mrs. Heath when her daughter's victimization was disclosed. "Why, that kind of thing only happens in poor families from the wrong side of the tracks. It couldn't be happening in my family! We're a nice family. That's the kind of thing that only happens in sick families. We're a nice family!"

A third reason for the denial is that if she acknowledges the incest, she is responsible for doing something about it, and if she is responsible, then she must wield her intrafamilial power and relinquish her childlike, dependent role. That requires a strength and assertiveness that if the mother possessed or had access to in the first place, the incest might never have occurred.

This case for collusion can even be taken a step further. On rare occasions mothers will consciously set up their daughters to become victims of paternal incest. Only one woman in the clinical sample did so, deliberately scheming to bring her husband and daughter together, believing that if she did so, she would be left alone to live her own life.

> Mrs. Jones encouraged her husband and their only daughter to do things together, and would continually make sexual references to them. "I said to Bill, 'ain't she got nice tits, Bill? She's a looker, huh? I bet you'd like to get a piece of her, huh?' Then I'd say to her, 'Your dad thinks you got nice tits honey. He's real good in bed, believe you me!' I figure what harm could it do! They love each other so he ain't gonna rape her or nothing. I figure it will keep her out of the backseats of cars with boys and it'll keep him out of my hair for awhile."

Taking all of these things into consideration, it would come as no surprise that most of the nonparticipating mothers in incestuous families know about the incest or at least suspect that it is occurring, but choose to do nothing about it. Their collusion, in part, sets the stage for the incest in the first place and, in part, allows its continuation over time. In Meiselman's (1978) study, no mother acknowledged the incest and stopped it; in the clinical sample that same observation holds true.

There undoubtedly are some mothers who simply do not know about the incest and appear to not even suspect that anything unusual is happening despite the data from the clinical sample. It is unclear whether this type of mother has such a strong denial mechanism that her perception of her family is distorted or if the incest is so successfully hidden from her. Although no mothers from the clinical sample fall into this category, Kroth (1979) in his analysis of 103 nonparticipating mothers found that 20% of them had been totally unaware of the paternal incest (p. 53).

It is important to reemphasize that incest is much too complicated a family problem to expediently blame on one person. Research has tended on occasion to blame the nonparticipating mothers for the paternal incest, leading psychiatric social worker and feminist Florence Rush into an angry tirade about the "relentless tendency to blame women for male sexual transgression" (Rush, 1980:194). In the point that blaming one person for the incest does not contribute to our understanding of the problem, Ms. Rush is certainly correct. However, if the old adage, "If you're not part of the solution you're part of the problem" is invoked, then Ms. Rush's anger is a bit misfocused. Of course it is the offending father or stepfather in cases of paternal incest who must bear the ultimate responsibility and consequences for the sexual victimization of his daughter. However, because the family is a social system in a delicate homeostatic balance, the roles of the nonparticipating members of the family and that of the child victim herself must be critically examined.

THE CHILD VICTIM

The female victim of paternal incest plays a critical role in the family while incest is taking place. Unfortunately, her role is often shrouded in misinformation, naive interpretation, and even myth, much of it propagated by researchers.

The Choice of an Incest Victim

How a father or stepfather "chooses" a daughter to be a victim of his incestuous behavior is a subject of much speculation. The victim's cry of "Why me?" deserves to be answered.

Oldest Daughter. In the clinical sample of 60 victims of paternal incest, fifty (83%) are the oldest daughters and three (5%) are the only daughters. Most research indicates that the incestuous father is most likely to victimize his oldest daughter. It is she who goes through puberty first; it is she with whom the father gets to try out all kinds of behaviors and attitudes. The first child is typically the guinea pig upon whom all kinds of experimentations of parenthood are conducted. In certain families, being born first increases the vulnerability to sexual victimization.

"Special" Daughters. In an interesting study of admissions to the psychiatric inpatient unit of the Yale–New Haven Hospital, Davies (1979) compared the 22 incest victims admitted to the other children who were admitted but were not incest victims. He found that of the 22 victims, 17 had abnormal EEG's and six of those children had experienced seizures. That means that a full 77% of the incest victims had abnormal EEG's compared to only 20% of the other admissions and 5% to 30% of the general population. Davies then chronicles the other findings for the incest victims in his study: five were in the "dull normal" range of intelligence; seven had problems in perceptual motor tasks, concrete thinking and word finding; 18 engaged in "impulsive behaviors"; and 12 had "frequent feelings of depersonalization" (p. 244).

All of this leads Davies to conclude that such neuropsychiatric handicaps increase a child's vulnerability to incest since such handicaps "are frequently associated with disturbances in the limbic regions which may mediate identity formation and the sense of personal boundaries" (p. 245). Davies is careful to observe that such factors are not necessary or sufficient to cause the incest, but may "underlie and augment other family problems that contribute to the incest" (p. 245).

This "special daughter" theme is echoed by Browning and Boatman (1977) who take a slightly more social psychological approach to the definition of a "special child." In their sample of fourteen child victims of incest referred for psychiatric treatment, they found one who was hearing and speech impaired due to congenital rubella; one who had been disfigured by burns; one with a seizure disorder and minimal brain dysfunction; four who had been born out of wedlock; and one who had been abandoned by her mother. They conclude that what makes these children "special" also makes them vulnerable to incest and more likely to be "chosen" as victims.

Attractiveness. A rather romantic notion of paternal incest is that the father or stepfather chooses the most attractive daughter to be the victim of incest. Beauty is certainly in the eye of the beholder and much too subjective a concept to operationally define for the purposes of this study. Meiselman (1978) asked the therapists from whom she collected her sample of incest victims to rate the attractiveness of the victims. Appreciating the subjective nature of these evaluations, she nonetheless concludes that "attractiveness plays a rather unimportant role in predisposing the daughter to incest" (Meiselman, 1978:132).

Recognition Motivation. In 1923, Marcuse coined the term "recognition motivation" to describe the increased vulnerability of a daughter to paternal incest if she looks like her mother (Marcuse, 1923). The father's sexual feelings are then displaced unto her, a mechanism that is particularly easy to do if a role reversal between the mother and daughter has preceded the incest (Cavalin, 1966; Meiselman, 1978).

Seduction by the Daughter. An unfortunately popular theme in incest research is that the daughter seduces, encourages, or otherwise brings on the incestuous victimization. Henderson (1972), for example, in explaining the dynamics of paternal incest, states that the daughters play a collusive role in most incest relationships. In a later examination of the same subject, he clarified that assumption: "In father-daughter incest, the father is aided and abetted in his liaison by conscious or unconscious seduction by his daughter... The daughters collude in the incest relationship and play active and even initiating roles in establishing the pattern" (Henderson, 1975:1533). This conclusion was also reached by Lukianowicz (1972) in his examination of 26 victims of paternal incest: "[T]he children were far from being innocent victims; on the contrary, they were willing partners and often provocative seductresses" (p. 309).

Such conclusions which place at least some responsibility on the child for her own sexual victimization are dangerous assumptions in that they minimize the roles and responsibilities of the offending parent and the nonparticipating family members. They also serve to disparage the negative effects and consequences of incest on the victims. It is as if many believe that if the child encourages the incest the encounter itself cannot be harmful to the child. Yet these assumptions regarding the daughter's role in encouraging the incest are based on scientifically accumulated data, not on the whimsy of naive persons; and for that reason, this conclusion carries a great deal of weight. De Young (1982a) suggests that there are four sources of data which could be used to support this assumption of victim culpability: the passivity of the victim during the incest relationship; the incest offenders' rationalizations; the preincest promiscuity occasionally reported for victims; and the victims' behavior in a therapeutic context. Isolated, each of these observations could be used to support the assumption that the incest victim seduces or otherwise brings on the incest and is therefore at least partially responsible for her own victimization. However, when each of these observations are properly placed within their familial or therapeutic contexts, victim culpability begins to diminish.

In her study of 37 incestuously victimized girls, Gligor (1966) found that 67% of them were passive throughout the victimization. Maisch (1972) calculated a similar percentage for his sample of incest victims. By simply taking this data on the passivity of the victim during the incestuous relationship and by isolating it from its familial context, one could assume that the incest victims tolerated, enjoyed or even encouraged the incest. However, when the patriarchal and frequently abusive familial context of that behavior is recognized, then it is clear that passivity is a coping and survival mechanism and not at all a reflection of the victim's culpability.

Incest offenders' rationalizations can also be used to support the conclusion of victim culpability. In Gebhard's *et al.* (1965) study, a majority of the incarcerated incest offenders blamed their daughters for the incest, often stating that they had been actively seduced by them. Yet another study by Cormier *et al.* (1962) documented this same tendency for incestuous fathers to blame their daughters for the incest. Once again, if these data are used independently of any considerations of incest offender psychology or of the deviance disavowal techniques such as projection of responsibility used by incestuous fathers and stepfathers to preserve a normal and healthy self-image (McCaghy, 1968) then the conclusion of victim responsibility for the incest is inevitable.

Some studies have indicated that the preincest promiscuity of the daughter may be a possible cause of the incest itself (Weinberg, 1955; Gligor, 1966; Maisch, 1972). In other words, the daughter brings her sexually active, seductive behavior into the home and thereby encourages her father or stepfather to respond in kind. Meiselman (1978), however, puts this occasionally reported promiscuity into its familial context, describing it as part of a larger pattern of character-disordered behavior which tends to develop in the daughter as a result of the preincest family dynamics. Yet by taking this occasionally reported data and isolating it from its familial context, it would be easy to conclude that the incest is but another form of sexually promiscuous behavior in which these youngsters engage.

Finally, another source of the belief that the incest victim seduces or otherwise encourages her own sexual victimization is the observation of the victim's behavior in therapy. Krieger *et al.* (1980) relate a number of cases in which incestuously victimized children referred for therapy "initially presented provocative or seductive behavior" in the therapy setting. This behavior includes "coy allusions to the incest"; "seductive flattering" of the therapist; "teasing and taunting" comments; and even poorly disguised attempts to touch and fondle the therapist (pp. 82–83). Again, when these observations are isolated from both their familial and therapeutic contexts, it appears that the incestuously victimized child is engaging in the same seductive behavior with the therapist as she had engaged in with her father or stepfather. Krieger *et al.* did recognize the familial context of this behavior stating that "the sexual forum may have become the child's typical method of gaining attention and nurturance, a method [she] carries into the therapeutic situation" (p. 84). They also acknowledged the therapeutic context of this behavior: "[W]e hypothesize that the child's seductive behavior represents the child's testing of the therapist, perhaps asking, is this a safe place?" (p. 85).

When the larger context in which incest takes place is taken into consideration, the origins of the frequently observed "seductive" behavior of incest victims become more clear, and as they do, the culpability of the children diminishes. De Young (1982a) proposes six origins of the allegedly seductive behavior and explains each in terms of the familial context in which they occur.

First, since incestuous families tend to be patriarchal families which produce attention- and affection-starved children (Peters, 1976), if the father or stepfather is gentle in his sexual advances, and if he rewards his daughter or buys her silence and cooperation with gifts and special privileges, she may be motivated to encourage the incest relationship, not because she enjoys the incest, but because she knows of no other way to get the attention and affection she craves. This same observation holds true for children who are not "gently" victimized. Even a battered or raped daughter may perceive the abuse as preferable to being ignored. Remember that the child is not getting these needs met by her mother because of the estrangement between them, and, as will be discussed later, she is not getting these needs met by her siblings, either.

Second, another source of this "seductive" behavior is the role reversal which has occurred between the nonparticipating mother and the child victim. While taking on the "little mother" responsibilities, the daughter assumes a pseudomaturity commensurate with that role. This pseudomaturity is an adaptive response on the part of the daughter; it is also a response which, in the perception of an impulse-ridden father or stepfather, seems to invite a sexual reaction.

Third, a daughter may also invite the incest or encourage its continuation if she feels that by doing so her family will remain intact. Since members of incestuous families tend to have histories of abandonment, desertion, and incapacitation, a rather pervasive separation anxiety permeates the entire family. If the daughter is made to feel that by participating in the incest she will hold her family together, it takes no great effort at empathy to understand why the youngster may do everything possible to continue the incest, and may behave in a "seductive" fashion if she has learned that such behavior will be responded to sexually.

Fourth, at times a daughter will passively continue in the incest, or even actively encourage it by "seductive" behavior, if she believes herself to have been responsible for the incest in the first place. Since a young child is dependent on her parents for definitions of both morality and reality, she may enter into the incestuous relationship naively and when she later realizes that it is both illegal and morally repugnant to others, she already may have been inextricably bound to that relationship for years. The girl may then give herself a new identity of harlot or whore — an identity that may then be reinforced by the deviance disavowal techniques of her father or stepfather. A self-fulfilling prophecy then may ensue in which the child engages actively in the incest because it is commensurate with her new identity. In doing so, she reduces any cognitive dissonance which could produce overwhelming anxiety if her behavior were inconsistent with her self-image. By actively or even passively engaging in the incest, the daughter reinforces that new identity and, in her eyes, gets nothing more than she deserves.

Fifth, another source of this allegedly seductive behavior of an incest victim is her identification with the aggressor. In Freudian terminology, this process represents a "defense manuever based on the child's need to protect [herself] from severe anxiety experienced in relation to the object" (Freedman *et al.*, 1972:109). The incest victim, therefore, seeks to become allied with her incestuous father or stepfather in order to share his power rather than to be powerless before him. Therefore, if the father or stepfather is seductive and encouraging before and during the incest, the daughter may take on those same characteristics.

Finally, a last source of the girl's "seductive" behavior is her simple inability to say "no." The greatest source of this inability is the lack of a self-protective model with whom the child can identify and emulate. In most incestuous families, the mother "is a weak figure and finds it impossible to be assertive with her husband" (Meiselman, 1978:174). As such, she contributes to the potential of incestuous victimization by not modeling self-protective behavior; by not giving her daughter adequate sexual information; and by not competently supervising her. All of this renders the daughter passive, not seductive, an important distinction since many would assume that the terms are synonymous. The net result is a child who cannot say "no" and lacks the assertiveness necessary to resist her father's or stepfather's sexual advances (Dietz and Craft, 1980).

Although the child who is an incest vicim may play a pivotal role in the incestuous family, the role is always that of a victim. As such, incest is always a reflection of adult culpability.

THE SIBLINGS

When Kroth (1979) evaluated the Child Sexual Abuse Treatment Program in California he remarked that a clinical oversight of the program was that it ignored the effects of family incest dynamics on the nonmolested siblings of incest victims. That oversight has occurred in the professional literature as well. The brothers and sisters of incest victims live in the same family that encouraged the incest in the first place. Even if they are unaware that the incest is taking place, the siblings are likely to be affected by the role changes and collusions that are occuring within the family. Although they, themselves, may not be victimized, they very well may be victims of the pathology of the incestuous family.

Four nonmolested siblings of incest victims are part of the clinical sample. All four are now adults, looking back on their childhoods. Thus the investigator is afforded a retrospective interpretation of the effects of an incestuous family on nonmolested siblings.

Rivalry and Jealousy

As previously stated, coldly paternalistic families tend to create attention- and affection-starved children. When one child, in this case the incest victim, is singled out to receive special attention, even though the reasons may be unknown to her siblings, her brothers and sisters may develop feelings of envy and become rivals for that attention, as the case of Lyle illustrates (de Young, 1981b:6):

> Lyle stated that he became curious about what was occurring in his family when his abusive father began showering his oldest daughter and youngest son with gifts. Lyle soon discovered that his father was sexually involved with his siblings. Only six at the time, Lyle yearned for what he perceived was the attention and affection his siblings were receiving. He became overwhelmed with feelings of envy and resentment.

How a youngster acts out on those feelings of jealousy and resentment can contribute to an already disorganized family. The "compulsive masochistic reaction" characteristic of so many incest victims (Bigras *et al.*, 1966) is found in the childhoods of the four nonmolested siblings in the clinical sample. All four had histories of running away from home, truancy and other self-destructive acts, many of which could be considered bids for attention and affection.

> Will's only sister Connie was incestuously victimized by their father, a successful surgeon. "He was hardly ever home," Will recalls, "but when he was all of his attention went to Connie. He bought her all kinds of gifts and was always touching and hugging her. I was always jealous, so I got into a lot of trouble at school and even tried to commit suicide three or four times to get him to pay attention to me. God, I didn't know *why* Connie was getting all that attention. I never even looked at how she reacted to him. It just made me mad that she got it all and all I got was shit!"

Incest victims, due to the role reversal and the subsequent special role in the family may "exhibit a misleading facade of sophistication and maturity" (Muldoon, 1979:15). Competitive feelings on the part of the siblings may cause them to imitate this behavior. Because this seductive-like facade of the incest victim is rewarded with paternal attention and even affection, her siblings may imitate this behavior in the hopes of reaping what seems to them to be the same rewards. Lyle exemplifies this observation (de Young, 1981b:7):

> Lyle by age 9 had developed a flirtatious, pseudomature demeanor which he imitated from his victimized siblings. This behavior was noted in both the school and the church as well as in the home. The behavior was so persistent that his father's two younger sisters, both of them teenagers, attempted to sexually molest him, later explaining that Lyle had seduced them.

It is certainly true that four cases do not constitute a large enough sample upon which to make wide-sweeping generalizations about the effects of paternal incest on the nonmolested siblings of the victim, but one fact gleaned from this small sample is of particular interest. Like the paternal incest victim herself, the nonmolested siblings experience an unusually high incidence of sexual victimization by older people. In the clinical sample, three of the four siblings had been molested as children by someone other than the incestuous father or stepfather, as Table 4 illustrates.

What these data may demonstrate is that naive imitation of sexual or seductive behavior may bring about sexual victimization by older people. Also, the lack of protective skills so common of incest victims may also be true of their siblings as well. After all, they are exposed to the same family dynamics which encourage the incest in the first place and allow its continuation over time.

TABLE 4. SEXUAL VICTIMIZATION
OF SIBLINGS OF PATERNAL INCEST VICTIMS

Case	Type of Sexual Victimization	Age at Occurrence
Will	none	—
Lyle	attempted molestation by two aunts	9 years
	molestation by adult male acquaintance	14 years
Wendy	rape by adult male stranger	13 years
Penny	molestation by adult male acquaintance	11 years

Collusion

Frequently the siblings of incest victims realize that the incest is taking place and actually play unconsciously or even consciously collusive roles in setting up the victim. This is especially the case when the incest has been initiated by an act of rape and is kept secret by threats and violence. Then the siblings feel justifiably frightened that one of them will be the next victim.

> Wendy was aware that her alcoholic stepfather was engaging in incest with her older sister. She would see her sister, often bruised and battered, leave her stepfather's bed. When her stepfather would come home in the afternoon, drunk and angry, Wendy would beg him, "Go see Debbie, she's in her room. Debbie wants you to go to her room!" Later her stepfather would emerge from Debbie's room, still drunk, but calm and satisfied [de Young, 1981b:7].

Yet another reason why the brothers and sisters may play a collusive role in the incest affair is the same reason why the nonparticipating mother so often denies the incest. The separation anxiety which is likely to have permeated the entire family may motivate all of them to play collusive roles. By maintaining the incest, they maintain the family.

> Penny's mother was so depressed that she rarely left her bedroom. When Penny told her about her sister's incestuous victimization by their father, her mother responded, "Keep quiet. Do you want your father to go to jail? I'm too weak to support us. We need him, don't cause any problems!"

The net effect of the sibling's collusion is usually guilt which is especially overpowering if the incest is finally disclosed and legal or protective service authorities begin questioning the family as to their knowledge of the incest. In fact, these guilt feelings have persisted into adulthood for all four of the siblings in the clinical sample.

Premature Sexual Stimulation

Yet another negative effect which incest can have on the siblings of child victims is the premature arousal of sexual feelings. Since so many relationships, experiences and feelings may become sexualized in these families, the siblings may be adversely affected.

> Lyle became very sexually aroused knowing that the incest was occurring in his own home. This, coupled with his own molestation experience at age 9, increased his sexual curiosity. At age 11, again at age 12, and several more times during his adolescence, he was discovered engaging in sexually exploratory or sexually assaultive behavior with boys and girls his own age [de Young, 1981b:8].

Discipline Problems

The child incest victim, through the process of role reversal, often becomes the female authority of the household. This authority frequently involves child care responsibilities for her siblings; responsibilities which she is unlikely to be able to competently carry out because of her tender age and the lack of a competent role model to imitate.

The siblings are likely to respond to that authority with resentment and confusion. They "see the victim with power and privileges appropriate to a parent and yet they know she is the sibling" (Justice and Justice, 1979:168). Out of this confusion they see a poor model of how to parent, and this model, in turn, creates more discipline problems with the siblings which then contribute to family pathology and disorganization.

Rejection

An overwhelming feeling of rejection often overcomes the siblings. Although they certainly may not crave the sexual victimization, they often desire the attention and physical contact that accompanies it. That they were not "chosen" by the incestuous father or stepfather creates a powerful feeling of worthlessness.

On occasion that feeling is so powerful and persistent that it produces emotional problems in the siblings. Berry (1975), for example, examines two cases of "incest envy" in which the knowledge of the incestuous victimizations of their sisters caused two women to develop serious psychological disturbances many years later. Meiselman (1978) also reports a case of a 22-year-old woman who had an identical twin sister who had been the victim of paternal incest throughout her adolescence. The patient had residual feelings of guilt and anger and felt rejected by the stepfather. Meiselman concludes that the sister was actually more emotionally disturbed than the incest victim.

In the clinical sample of four nonmolested siblings, two had definite signs of emotional disturbance. However it is impossible to say whether the knowledge of their siblings' victimizations caused those disturbances or whether they are the products of the family pathologies which gave rise to the incest in the first place.

Chapter 4: Paternal Incest — The "Affair"

Over the decades gothic novels and B-movies have capitalized on and, in some instances perhaps, have created the public's perception of love and romance. The settings vary of course, from windswept beaches to cozy rooms filled with flickering candlelight and soft music, but the cast of characters remains strikingly constant: two attractive, willing people, destined to become passionate lovers. Although their affair may be stormy and fraught with difficulties to be gallantly overcome, the conclusion is clear: they were meant for each other. Love conquers all.

At times this scenario is so persistent in our minds that it affects our thinking about incest as well. To shield ourselves from the horror of incest, we redefine it and create an illusion of it; an illusion that frequently is reinforced by the popular culture. Take as an example this letter to the editor of a popular pornography magazine:

> My father is often mistaken for one of my boyfriends. We have a great deal of fun with this and it also amuses my mother. When we dance together, mom is always encouraging dad to touch me and to be intimate in ways fathers are just not usually with their young, beautiful daughters. One afternoon in the city I was with her and dad. She excused herself from the luncheon table... Pretty soon the waiters and managers were looking and dad grinned and said it was obvious that they thought he and I were married. "Let's really act it, dad," I said, suddenly feeling very passionate... "Touch my breasts," I whispered, cuddling closer to him. And when I felt his hand and then his fingers sliding over my breasts... I began to kiss my father's cheeks, then his lips. Pretty soon he was responding. I was innocently toying with my fingers on his thigh. I could feel the heat of his penis as it began to stiffen... My fingers brushed over his penis and then I felt his body sag and he let out a faint breath... P.S. I really like your magazine. So does dad and mom. We're now a lively family!

A "lively family." What a comforting illusion for a society which at times adamantly has refused to acknowledge the reality and consequences of incest; what a comforting illusion for those whose image of love is rooted in the romanticism of B-movies and gothic novels. Yet it is an illusion which betrays the real life experiences of countless incest victims, and in no other aspect is it more illusory than when the nature of the paternal incest "affair" is exposed.

In the clinical sample of 60 female paternal incest victims, the average

age at which the overt incest was initiated by the father or stepfather is 10.2 years. By merely taking this age into consideration, all possibilities of a willing, mutually satisfying sexual relationship are seen to be nonexistent. In the clinical sample, the average duration of the paternal incest "affair" is 2.7 years, and that is a considerable period of time during which a youngster may feel exploited, manipulated and used.

Most incestuous "affairs," for lack of a better term, run a fairly well defined course, from initiation, through a prolonged secrecy stage, to its disclosure or termination. What happens to a youngster and her family in each state will determine to a great extent the effects that the incestuous victimization will have on the daughter on both a short- and a long-term basis.

INITIATION INTO INCEST

The techniques used by an incestuous father or stepfather to initiate his daughter into incest are best understood when the nature of the incestuous family is kept in mind. Typically the family is patriarchal in nature and, as such, is characterized by a rigid, controlling father, and a submissive, depenent mother. Physical abuse directed against the mother and/or the children is common in these families, and even if that physical abuse never occurs, there is so often an aura of violence which reflects the patriarchal structure of the family.

It is also important to recognize that covertly incestuous behavior is likely to have preceded the onset of the overt incestuous act by many years. The clinical sample of 60 women averaged about 10 years old at the first act, yet many of them recognized tentative, covert incestuous approaches by their fathers or stepfathers preceding the overt act, in some cases by many years. How incest is overtly initiated, however, is a clue to the nature of the incestuous family as a social system.

Rape

Initiation into incest infrequently begins with an act of rape. In the clinical sample, five (8%) of the 60 victims were raped by their father or stepfather. In determining this particular figure, rape is defined as intercourse, attempted intercourse, or aggressive sexual contact against the will of the victim. Of course it can be convincingly argued that because incestuous acts are directed against children who, in the eyes of the law, cannot give or withhold consent, then incest is always initiated by an act of rape. There is a logic to this argument that cannot be overlooked; however, for the purposes of this study, rape will be specifically defined so that it may be differentiated from other initiation techniques.

Although rape is not always clearly defined in other research studies, similarly low incident rates have been documented. For example, Gebhard *et al.* (1965) find that only a little over 1% of the 147 incarcerated incest offenders they studied initiated incest by an act of rape (p. 220). Maisch (1972) finds that only 6% of his sample of victims had been raped (p. 16); and Kroth (1979), in his analysis of referrals to the Child Sexual Abuse Treatment Program in California, finds that 15% to 16% of the referrals had used physical force or coercion to initiate the incest (p. 48). The lone dissenter from this trend is Szabo (1962), who states that a full 42% of the 96 French victims he studied had been initiated into incest by an act of "violence" which one would assume means rape (p. 240).

Rape is, of course, an act of violence, and Finkelhor (1979) finds that the victims of this violence tend in later years to most vividly remember the violent content of the act rather than its sexual nature. This observation is certainly confirmed by the five victims in the clinical sample.

> Denise, now 41, had been incestuously victimized by her father for two years. When he raped her she was 12 years old. "So here I am, almost thirty years later. My father is dead, I haven't really spoken to my mother in years, but I still dream about that afternoon. You know, it's really incredible. In some ways I've forgotten the two years of incest that followed the rape that afternoon, but I'm sure I'll never forget that afternoon. I have never felt so helpless, vulnerable and frightened in my life."

On a short term basis, this initiation technique is likely to create a traumatic reaction in the child, similar to the rape trauma syndrome described by Burgess and Holmstrom (1974). This syndrome refers to the acute phase and the long-term reorganization process that occurs as a result of forcible rape or attempted forcible rape. It is this acute phase that is of the greater concern when incest is initiated by rape. It is during this phase that the child victim is likely to experience somatic reactions and emotional trauma. One of the five victims in the clinical sample who had been initiated into incest by an act of rape is 15-year-old Susan, who had been raped by her father the previous year. He then carried out a one-year incestuous relationship with her which ended when he was killed in an automobile accident. Because her rape experience was so recent, she best exemplifies the acute phase of the rape trauma syndrome.

> "He raped me one night when my mother and sister were shopping. I was in my room listening to a new album. He came in, slammed the door closed, and threw himself on me. At first I thought he was playing a trick on me. I told him he was hurting me, but he wouldn't stop. He practically ripped my clothes off and then he took off his pants. When he went inside me it really hurt, but it just didn't seem real, like it was a dream, a bad dream, or something. I thought I was going to die. I mean I was really surprised that I was still alive when he got off me and left. For days after I had a terrible stomachache and it even hurt when I went to the bathroom. I was so scared of him. Every time I saw him my heart would pound and I would get dizzy. I was so depressed and I cried all the time. I thought about suicide."

The father or stepfather who initiates his daughter into incest by an act of rape is typically one who is the most impulse-ridden and has the fewest and weakest ego controls. In the clinical sample of 51 incestuous fathers and stepfathers, three (6%) raped their daughters. It is interesting to note that all three of them are alcoholics, and all three were significantly intoxicated at the time the rape took place. Two of the three men also have criminal records; one for relatively minor property offenses; the other for assaults, none of them sexual in nature but all of them committed while he was intoxicated. The fact of these criminal records speaks to the men's poor impulse control, which is also reflected in other areas of their lives. For example, all three men had dropped out of high school; all three had poor employment histories; and two of them frequently beat their wives and children. The incest initiation technique of rape, then, is symptomatic of this poor impulse control. These three fathers, by the way, are no strangers to incest, themselves. Two had been the victims of paternal incest and one the victim of a coercive sibling incest relationship.

Of course a question which must be asked when incest is initiated in this manner is, where is the mother? In each of the rape-initiated incest cases in the clinical sample, the victimization of the daughter continued for years. Yet in no case did the mothers intervene in the incest.

In fact, in no case did the mothers acknowledge the incest despite the fact that their daughters all went through an acute phase and long-term reorganization phase as a result of the rape, and it is during these phases that symptoms of the trauma are likely to be profound and noticeable. The fact that these mothers neither acknowledged that rape nor intervened in the subsequent incestuous victimization speaks of both the strength of their denial systems and the degree of family pathology which created for the mother the necessity of developing passive, self-protective coping mechanisms. The net effect of this emotional abandonment on the child victim is likely to be profound.

> "After my father raped me, I was distraught for weeks," explains Denise. "I remember I felt terrified of him, I couldn't eat and I didn't dare sleep. I bled for several days, too, and every time I'd put my underpants into the hamper I'd think, 'Why doesn't mom notice there's blood on them?' Then I'd think, 'And why doesn't she notice I'm not eating and sleeping and that I practically jump out of my skin every time my dad walks into the room?' I always made excuses for her, but now I know that if I had a child, I'd surely know if she'd been raped!"

One manner of initiating a child into incest short of rape which still has an overwhelmingly negative effect on the child is with the use of threats and other forms of coercion. In strongly patriarchial families, as incestuous families most often tend to be, the power of this technique must never be underestimated. Because of the actual physical violence, or the aura of it, in many of these families a well spoken word has as much power as a slap.

Fifteen (29%) of the incestuous fathers and stepfathers used threats in the initiation of incest. The two most commonly heard threats were "I'll kill (or hurt) you if you resist" and "I'll do this to your sister (or brother or mother) if you don't cooperate." Again, threats like these are not to be taken lightly. The fathers and stepfathers who used these threats had themselves been the victims of physical violence as children and knew how to deliver these threats with the greatest possible effect.

Those fathers and stepfathers who used that technique were also more likely to be physically coercive with their daughters in their sexual activity. Five of the fathers had intercourse with their daughters; two attempted intercourse; one had anal intercourse; four penetrated their daughters with their fingers or some other object; and the remaining three had oral-genital sex with their daughters. Not content with fondling and masturbation, these fathers and stepfathers were very sexually coercive with their daughters and the coercion is even more notable when the young age of the victim is kept in mind.

Evolved Incest

A majority of incestuous fathers and stepfathers "rehearse" incest, for lack of a better term, with their daughters. This technique was used by sixteen (31%) of the incestuous fathers in the clinical sample. This type of parent begins with years of special attention to his daughter, caressing and hugging her and slowly encroaching on her personal life and free time, all the while continuing his tentative, covert sexual advances. Gradually he progresses to fondling, especially the buttocks, genitals and breasts. The actual overt incestuous behavior evolves slowly and the youngster may not perceive it as a logical consequence of the provisional sexual behavior that preceded it.

> Judith, 23, remembers her father's initiation of their two year incestuous relationship. "I was his special girl. He always told me that, and he told everybody else too. He always touched and hugged me. I was eight at the time and I loved the attention. When I was nine he started kissing me on the lips and touching my breasts. I remember that I wondered if daddy's were supposed to do that, but I didn't really care. It was nice and it felt good when he masturbated me. I just thought it was daddy's way of showing love. When I found out later it was wrong it stopped feeling good."

As Judith's case illustrates, youngsters initiated into incest in this manner often do not resist and may even physically enjoy the experience until they realize that it is both illegal and immoral in the eyes of many people, or until it feels so emotionally suffocating and possessive that it must be terminated. By this time, however, the incestuous "affair" may have been ongoing for years. They are then inextricably enmeshed in the "affair" and are likely to experience a lifetime of feelings of guilt and shame for their passive, or even on some occasions, willing participation in the incest.

Devious Behavior

Some youngsters are initiated into incest in an extremely devious manner. Their fathers or stepfathers sneak into bed with them and begin the overt sexual contact while they are asleep. Meiselman (1978) finds that 43% of the incest victims in her sample had been initiated into incest in this manner (p. 168). Of the 60 paternal incest victims in the clinical sample, 11 (18%) had been initiated into incest through this technique, and of the 51 incestuous fathers and stepfathers in the clinical sample, eight (16%) used this technique.

> Mr. Little, 41, who initiated his daughter into incest in this manner, explains his behavior in the following manner: "Sure, I wanted to have sex with her, but I knew it was wrong and I sure didn't want to hurt her. So I'd wait until she was sleeping. Then I'd sneak into her room and sit on the bed and rub her back, and then her buttocks and then between her legs. Then I'd masturbate myself. Once she woke up, but I just told her she had a bad

dream and I was concerned about her, that's why I was patting her back. she just went back to sleep. It made me feel good and she didn't even know. Is that so bad?"

Mr. Little's lament may be a bit misfocused, however. All of the eleven victims in the clinical sample who had been initiated into incest in this manner knew at the time what their fathers or stepfathers were doing, and all pretended to be asleep, hoping their fathers or stepfathers would go away. Because this initiation technique is so deceptive, all of the victims felt confused and frightened, but above anything else, they felt used.

> Inger's father used this approach for three years. "I sometimes think that I should be grateful that he didn't rape me or beat me. But God, this was awful. I was only a little kid but I kept thinking that what he was doing must be really horrible because he's sneaking around doing it. I remember feeling used as a kid; what an awful feeling for a kid to have."

These feelings of being used, frightened and confused deal a serious blow to trust, and each time trust is diminished, the next surreptitious incestuous act feels more coercive and frightening. When that happens, the youngster who is initiated into incest in that devious manner feels no differently than a youngster who has been initiated by rape or evolved incest.

> LouAnne experienced three years of incestuous victimization that never progressed beyond the devious behavior. "I felt like a piece of meat," she explains, "like a nonperson with no rights or feelings. He was so fucking sneaky! All I could think about was, 'Why didn't he ask me? Why didn't he discuss it with me?' Whatever trust existed between the two of us was destroyed. If I couldn't trust him with my own body, I couldn't trust him, period!"

Courting Behavior

Finally, a few incestuous fathers and stepfathers quite literally court their daughters, using gifts and special privileges to bribe them into participating in the incestuous "affair." Five (8%) of the incestuous fathers and stepfathers in the clinical sample used this technique.

Cormier et al. (1962) describe such a father in terms of a lovestruck adolescent making clumsy attempts at courtship behavior, giving his daughter gifts of money and clothing, guarding her jealously from outside people, yet continually invoking his status as an all-powerful father. In a patriarchal family that attention may be flattering to the daughter but it is also likely to alienate her from her mother and siblings. That alienation, in turn, binds her even more closely to her father.

> Mr. Nelson courted his daughter and in essence bribed her to take part in the incest. "I wanted to be her lover not the victimizer," he explains. "I wanted her to remember our affair as one of affection and warmth, not fear and pain."

One Time Only

Two of the paternal incest victims in the clinical sample had been incestuously victimized only once by their respective fathers. Both of the victims were very young; one 4 and the other, 7 years old. Both experienced a rape trauma type of reaction, especially characterized by somatic symptomatology. In neither case did the mother intervene to prevent further victimization; neither of the fathers was arrested. Yet, in both cases the victimization was never repeated. One father explained that he "felt bad" and did not repeat his behavior; the other father could offer no real explanation for why he did not continue in the incest.

Two of the fathers and stepfathers in the clinical sample also victimized their respective daughters only once. One had been drinking at the time of the incestuous assault and felt so remorseful afterwards that he committed himself to an alcohol detoxification program; the other confessed the act to a priest and was successfully persuaded to seek therapy. Obviously in both cases, the presence of a strong superego generated enough guilt and shame to act as a deterrent to further incestuous victimization.

SECRECY STAGE

What turns incest into an especially exploitative and harmful type of victimization is the secret-keeping techniques used by the incestuous father or stepfather. In the clinical sample, the average duration of the incestuous "affair" is 2.7 years. However, some of them continued for four, six and even eight years. That means that once the incest has been initiated, months or even years of pressure by the offending parent to keep the incest secret then follow. And it is during that secrecy stage that reality is distorted, morality is redefined, and the family role structure is altered.

Another point must be made before these secret-keeping techniques are examined and that is that incestuous fathers and stepfathers do not generally confine themselves to one, consistent technique throughout the incestuous "affair." The techniques are fluid in nature and are responsive to the reactions of the youngster to the incest and of the family to the victimization. This fluid nature makes it particularly difficult to calculate and predict the most predominant techniques used by the offenders in the clinical sample.

Force and Threats

In some cases the incestuous father or stepfather uses physical violence to impress upon his daughter the necessity of keeping their incestuous relationship a secret. Few incest victims are strangers to physical violence. In the clinical sample of 60 female victims of paternal incest, 22 (37%) were victims of repeated physical abuse within their families, and 11 (18%) more were victims of occasional physical abuse.

Many incest victims are persuaded to keep their incestuous relationship secret by the mere threat of physical violence. Although the father or stepfather may never raise a hand against his daughter, the patriarchal nature of most incestuous families creates an aura of physical violence that cannot be overlooked. A daughter who is "accustomed to obeying such a father is most likely to go along passively with his demands for sexual activity, for physical resistance is unthinkable to her" (Meiselman, 1978:149).

> Barbara, now in her thirties, clearly remembers her six year incestuous relationship with her father. "I knew it was wrong from the start, and although he never hit me once, I lived in fear he would. I once saw him try to run over our pet dog. Another time he hit my brother so hard that he broke his nose and he was always beating my mom. So when he'd get out of my bed at night and say, 'If you tell anyone about this, so help me God, I just don't know what I'd do to you,' I believed that he would hurt me or even kill me" [de Young, 1981a:64].

On some occasions, the incestuous father or stepfather makes third party threats against the youngster's siblings or her mother. The awesome burden of protecting the physical well-being of the family then falls on the shoulders of that child. That responsibility weighs heavily and usually convinces the child not to disclose the incest.

Perhaps the most profound threat an incestuous father or stepfather can use is the threat of abandonment or separation. Frequently the parents of these families had experienced loss and separation as children. As adults they frequently have nomadic lifestyles characterized by temporary separations. Also, the cast of characters in many incestuous families may often change, with boyfriends, girlfriends, stepparents, stepsiblings, and half-brothers and half-sisters entering and leaving the family. The net effect of all this is a pervasive separation anxiety which permeates the entire family and which may be capitalized upon by a father or stepfather who needs an effective threat to convince his daughter to keep the incest secret.

> Joan, now 37, remembers that her stepfather kept their incestuous relationship secret by subtle but extremely effective threats. "He told me that if I didn't keep doing what he wanted, he'd have my mother put me in an orphanage. Except for what was happening between the two of us, I loved my family. I couldn't conceive of living apart from them. I traded my security for two more years of sexual abuse" [de Young, 1980:30].

Forced to choose between the lesser of two evils, separation from the family or the secretive continuation of the incestuous relationship, most victims choose the latter. In the words of Meiselman (1978): "No great effort at empathy is required to imagine the child's perception of this situation and the possibility that the incestuous activities constitute a 'known evil' that is preferable to the unknown" (p. 168).

Promises and Gifts

Some incestuous fathers and stepfathers use a different tack in persuading their daughters to keep the incest secret. In essence, they bribe them to keep the secret. In fact, in many cases the father or stepfather behaves like a possessive lover, jealously guarding his daughter from outside relationships, angrily interfering in any that may develop, and showering her with gifts to protect the bond between them (Weinberg, 1955; Cormier et al., 1962).

> Mr. Marks used this technique to persuade his daughter to keep secret their incestuous relationship. "The last thing I wanted to do was hurt her. I was always gentle. So I bought her things to show her how grateful I was to her.

Sure, you could call it a bribe, in some ways it was. But it was also a way to show love and respect, and even more than that, it was a way to show her that she could trust me. I mean, a rapist doesn't send flowers to his victim, does he?"

Many times the gifts and special privileges given to the youngster actually may entice her to share the secret with others. Eager to show her friends or siblings her gifts or, if she is older, to flaunt her special privileges, the youngster may, perhaps inadvertently, tell the secret of the incest to others. One authority on childrearing explains why this may occur: "It is very difficult to keep children from blurting out confidences, for they know all too well that they can be sensational by saying precisely that which should be left unsaid" (Dreikurs, 1972:18).

Reinterpretation of Morality

A very common technique of incestuous fathers and stepfathers is to so seriously distort reality and morality that their daughters are led to believe that the incest is necessary, healthy, and normal. This father or stepfather then compounds the lie and builds a wall around himself and his daughter which isolates them from the outside world. He tells the daughter that not everyone agrees with his philosophy and practice so she must be careful to not share their secret with anyone, including members of their family.

Children naturally look to their parents for moral education and leadership. If that education and leadership are consistent with the morality of the world outside of the family the youngster will experience little anxiety. The incestuous father or stepfather knows the outside world will not support his interpretation of morality so, in order to prevent his daughter from experiencing any dissonance that may motivate her to check reality by telling someone about the incest, he isolates her as much as possible from the outside world. He and his daughter become self-sufficient, getting all of their needs met, including sexual needs, within the family.

Realization of Guilt

Because of their young ages, most children enter into incestuous relationships naively. If the father or stepfather is gentle the sexual contact may at first feel physically and emotionally like an expression of love. As the father or stepfather begins to coerce her to keep the relationship secret, the incestuous "affair" begins to feel increasingly intimidating and frightening. Finally, when she comes to realize that their sexual relationship is wrong in many different connotations of the term, she already may have been sexually involved with him for some time. All he need do, then, is remind her of her lack of resistance to the relationship in the past to trigger guilt, and it is the guilt which then serves as a deterrent to the disclosure of the incest secret.

Reminders from the father or stepfather that "no one will believe you," or that "people will think it's your fault, not mine," reinforce the guilt and ensure the silence. Hesitant attempts to test the reactions of others to the incest relationship will more than likely substantiate her father's or stepfather's claim. The youngster is then "inextricably bound into a secret sexual relation-ship by her own feelings of guilt, reinforced by her father (or stepfather) who needs their relationship to be secret, and by a society which often is unwilling to listen and intervene (de Young, 1981a:69).

The Issue of Passivity

In the clinical sample of 60 victims of paternal incest, 51 (85%) characterized their own behavior during the incestuous "affair" as "passive" most of the time. The issue of victim passivity causes a great deal of conster-nation for many researchers. Brunold (1964), for example, wonders why two-thirds of the children in his sample offered no or little resistance to their father's or stepfather's incestuous advances. Henderson (1972), wondering about that same thing, could only conclude that the victim's passivity during the incest "affair" was a technique used to "avoid guilt feelings" (p. 308).

For all intents and purposes, it appears that the victims' most common reaction to the incest is passivity. However, the passivity issue is not nearly as mysterious as many researchers believe. First of all, remember that incest vic-tims are usually children, and their child status is characterized not only by a tender age but also a lack of alternatives for handling family problems and a lack of sophisticated and mature coping mechanisms. Therefore, passivity during the incest is not only the most self-protective coping mechanism the child victim has in her naive repertoire, it is the *only* coping mechanism. As such it does not reflect the culpability of the child and should never be used as a basis of an assumption that the youngster encourages, seduces, or otherwise brings on the incest (de Young, 1982a). The following reasons for a passive response were heard from the victims in the clinical sample.

Fear. Of the 51 victims in the clinical sample who stated that passivity was their predominate response to the incest victimization, 29 (57%) said they were passive primarily out of fear. This should come as no surprise, given the patriarchal nature of the incestuous family and the high rate of physical abuse that has been documented in the families of the victims in the clinical sample.

Pleasure. Six (12%) of the victims in the clinical sample state that their predominant reason for remaining passive throughout the incest "affair" was because the incest was pleasurable to them. This is a difficult thing for many incest victims to say especially in the light of so many people's tendency to use that admission as a springboard for accusations of seduction and willingness to participate in the victimization. However, incest victims who say that are not implying that the victimization, per se, was pleasurable, but that the atten-tion and affection which accompanied it were.

Lack of Assertiveness. Ten (20%) of those victims who had remained passive state that they had done so because they simply lacked the ability to say "no" and to resist the offending parent's advances. Again, this is not sur-prising. Children in strongly paternalistic families become accustomed to obeying their parents, and when their mothers fail to model self-protective, assertive skills, the youngster has no basis upon which to initiate this behavior in relation to her father or stepfather (Dietz and Craft, 1980).

Confusion. The remaining six (12%) victims say they remained passive because they were too confused about what was happening to them to know if it was right or wrong; sick or healthy. An incestuous father or stepfather who reinterprets both morality and reality for his daughter creates a tremendous confusion in that youngster's mind. Also, the dependency needs of the child tie her to her father or stepfather, and to risk having those needs be unmet is too frightening and does not allow the child to transcend her confusion and resist her parent.

The Impact of the Secret

The impact on the victim of the pressure to keep the incest secret must never be discounted. Once the incest has been initiated the secrecy stage usually lasts for years and during that period of time, the youngster is continually exposed to lies, threats, and bribes while around her reality is distorted and morality is reinterpreted.

To demonstrate the impact of that pressure on the child, Saffer *et al.* (1979) relate a case of a 15-year-old girl who was diagnosed as having a schizoid personality disorder with depressive features. She had been very withdrawn, had refused to go to school, and had stopped socializing with her friends. In between her daydreams and fantasies, she cried continually and even heard voices speaking to her out of magazines and books. When psychological tests failed to confirm the diagnosis, intensive psychotherapy revealed that she had been the victim of repeated incestuous advances from her father. Saffer *et al.* conclude that these psychotic symptoms were due to the pressure of keeping the family secret, and are symbolic cries for help to relieve that pressure.

The pressure to keep that secret does not inevitably produce psychotic symptoms but it certainly can cause a wide range of symptomatic acting out and self-destructive behavior. That fact puts a special burden on helping professionals who may interact with these youngsters to not be content to treat only the obvious symptomatology but to delve into its origin.

THE DISCLOSURE OF INCEST

Once the incest has been initiated it is likely to continue for years. What happens to bring about the termination or the disclosure of incest is a subject which must be carefully examined.

Terminated Incest

In many cases the incest is never disclosed to anyone. The "affair" literally runs its course and eventually terminates without any outside interference. In the clinical sample of 60 female victims, the incest eventually terminated of its own accord for 47 (78%) of them. Most of these victims to this day have told few people about the incest.

Fran, now 50, disclosed the incestuous experience she had forty years earlier for the first time a year ago. "You talk about secrets," she exclaims. "My stepfather used to threaten to kill me when I was a kid if anyone found out about the incest. Well I've kept that secret for forty years. I don't think about the incest every day, of course, but I do think about it, and I do think it's hurt me in many ways I still feel today."

What Fran and so many victims like her are saying is that they often carry the burden of the secret with them for years after the incest has terminated. That means years of feelings that can interfere with daily living.

In most of the cases in which the incest terminated without outside interference, that termination occurs when the victim matures. It is normal for a youngster to move emotionally from her family as she gets older. The age-old adolescent struggle for independence occurs in incestuous families too, in fact it may be an even more desperate struggle in those families because of their patriarchal nature. At this age, the girl has more of an opportunity to avoid her family and more safety if she decides to break the rules of the family. An incestuous father or stepfather will begin to let go at this point, realizing that his daughter's increased independence also affords her increased opportunities to disclose the secret. The victim's and the offender's interpretations of this critical issue are provided by Marva and Mr. Crandall.

"I was under my dad's thumb for four years, from the time I was ten," Marva explains. "Four years I let him screw around with me. But I'm telling you, when I got to be a teenager I was never home. I ate with friends at their house; I was in the band so I had to stay at school and practice; and I was on just about every sports team. I wasn't around enough for him to get his hands on me, and when he did try, I talked him out of it, and a couple of times I even threatened him."

"I could control my daughter when she was young," states Mr. Crandall. "She never made decisions, they were always mine. And because I never let her out of my sight I knew where she was and I knew she couldn't tell anyone about the incest. I couldn't guarantee that when she got older. She wouldn't obey me and she made her own decisions. God, I was scared! What if she told someone? So I just stopped having sex with her."

Disclosure

Obviously some victims disclose the incest and do not wait for it to terminate on its own accord. Thirteen (22%) of the victims in the clinical sample disclosed the incest.

Most of the victims symbolically disclosed the incest first. That is, they put themselves into a position to be questioned about their behavior and their family life. This was usually accomplished by running away from home, school problems, and other types of self-destructive acting-out behavior which would force some adult authority to pay attention to them. Even if questioned the youngster may then deny any incestuous victimization because of the guilt, confusion and fear which bind her to that relationship. These youngsters should not be judged harshly. They have a sense of what the disclosure of incest can do to the whole family and they are understandably reticent to disrupt or even destroy their families.

A breakdown of whom each of these 13 victims told is provided in Table 5. In each case, the person told is the person who by some means or another brought about the termination of the incest.

TABLE 5. PERSONS TO WHOM THE INCEST WAS DISCLOSED

Person	Number
Friend/Friend's Parent	5
Counselor	2
Teacher	2
Medical Doctor	1
Extended Family Member	1
Minister	1
Neighbor	1

When reviewing Table 5 it becomes clear that the youngsters' increased independence put them in contact with more people who could serve as their advocates when the incest was disclosed. Table 5 also shows that one person obviously not trusted with the disclosure or not willing to serve as an advocate is the youngster's mother.

The estrangement of the daughter from her mother does not facilitate a trusting relationship in which the incest can be disclosed, and the collusion and role reversal often does not leave the mother strong enough to serve as her daughter's advocate. The mother's denial system also effectively blocks even the awareness of the incest, as a recorded dialog between a mother and her victimized daughter reveals (Machota *et al.*, 1967:106-107):

DAUGHTER: You don't see how we could have done it...

MOTHER: No, un-unh. No.

DAUGHTER: We went into the dump. We went into the sticks. Right out there in the cow pasture. Okay, you went away. Everybody was away from the house. We had it in your bed. We've had it on the bathroom floor.

MOTHER: (Utters loud moan).

DAUGHTER: We've had it in the basement, in the bedroom down there, and also in the furnace room.

MOTHER: I can't believe it, I just can't, just can't!

DAUGHTER: Mom...

MOTHER: Just can't see how anything like this could possibly happen and how you could treat me like this.

DAUGHTER: Because...

MOTHER: After all I've done for you! I've tried to be a mother to you. I've tried to be respectable, and you accuse your father of something that is so horrible that...

DAUGHTER: Mother, it's true! You've got to believe it!

MOTHER: She's my daughter and I love her, but I cannot believe this!

Nonparticipating mothers of incestuous families, although tenaciously strong in their denial, may not be the only adults who refuse to acknowledge the incestuous victimization of their daughters. Many adults refuse to believe a child's disclosure of incest, and their refusal to do so, probably unknowably to them, reflects what Rush (1980) calls the "Freudian gaslight."

Sigmund Freud, "the father of psychoanalysis," developed the first comprehensive framework for the study of human behavior and personality. His contributions to psychiatry and psychotherapy are legendary, but he did little service to the victims of incest.

In his 19th century psychoanalytic practice Freud treated many women suffering from hysteria, a uniquely female malady, he believed, characterized by symptomatology which was often sexual in nature. Hearing these patients' accounts of childhood incest victimization, Freud logically drew a causal connection between early incest experiences and later hysterical neurosis, in which the patient symbolically acted out the repressed memory of her victimization. Freud published his theory in 1896 and was clearly chagrined at the ambivalent response it received from his peers. But something else worried him even more. He was acquainted with the fathers of some of his patients and he could not rectify their daughters' accounts of their behavior with his perception of them as fine, Victorian gentlemen. At the same time he was trying to resolve this conflict, he began to see hysterically neurotic symptoms in his own siblings. Did that mean that his own revered father had incestuously victimized his own children? No, Freud reasoned, that was no more possible than it was for the fathers of his patients to have incestuously victimized them. In exonerating his father from the role of victimizer, Freud exonerated all fathers.

So, from where did these accounts of childhood sexual victimization come? Freud reasoned they came from the *fantasies* of the patients who had developed what he called a "defensive fiction" in order to passively express hostility toward their fathers.

By relegating these accounts of incest to the fertile imaginings of children, Freud began a tradition which is in practice to this very day. It is a tradition in which many adults side with the parents, in essence, by denying the reality of the children's disclosure of incest; and in denying that reality, refuse to serve as advocates for the victimized children.

Impact of the Disclosure

Of course the believed and acted upon disclosure of incest has the potential to destroy the delicate homeostatic balance of the family unit. The youngster herself is likely to feel guilt, embarrassment and fear. The incestuous father or stepfather will also experience fear and anger and also may go through a grief syndrome if a significant degree of attachment was present in his relationship with his daughter (Meiselman, 1978). The mother and siblings will also go through some trauma, all of which attests to the necessity of a family treatment modality after the incest is disclosed.

Postscript

There may be more cases than are realized in which incest is terminated through an act of violence. No research has been done on this subject and no cases of it occurred in the clinical sample. Yet every day adolescents with lifetimes ahead of them take their own lives and every year there are several news accounts of children who kill their parents. How many of these young people are incest victims?

CHAPTER 5: PATERNAL INCEST — EFFECTS ON THE VICTIMS

On the rear of a well-traveled stationwagon was a bright orange bump-ersticker that proclaimed to fellow motorists: "Incest Is Best!" It produced a few embarrassed snickers from those who read it, but most people found its suggestion tasteless and disgusting. However, when such assertions are shrouded in academic robes they are more likely to be seriously considered.

Take for example the 1978 meeting of the American Psychiatric Association's Institute on Hospital and Community Psychiatry in which Joan A. Nelson presented her master's thesis proposing that "some incest experiences appear to be positive and even beneficial" (De Mott, 1980:11). Ms. Nelson, herself a participant (she does not consider herself a victim) in a long-term incestuous affair with her father, described that childhood relationship as "the happiest period in my life," during which she states she experienced "a healthy self-actualization." A year later, West Virginia University social work professor Warren Farrell announced in a conference on child abuse that incest in many cases "may be either a positive, healthy experience or, at worst, neutral and dull" (De Mott, 1980:11). No less an authority than the Sex Information and Education Council of the United States (SIECUS) recently stated that not only are children inaccurate reporters of incest who sometimes initiate or willingly participate in the affair, but also that most incidents of incest are only "minimally harmful" in their effects on the children.

These "proincest" researchers are not to be dismissed as academic crackpots; their conclusions are based upon a rich scientific tradition which has historically undermined the negative effects of incest on the child. This tradition most likely began with a 1937 article published by Lauretta Bender and Abraham Blau in which they stated that: "the experiences of the child in its sexual relationship with adults does not seem always to have a traumatic effect.... [T]he experience seems to satisfy instinctual drives.... [T]he experience offers an opportunity for the child to test in reality an infantile fantasy.... The emotional balance is thus in favor of contentment" (Bender and Blau, 1937:516).

A careful reading of the Bender and Blau article shows that of the 16 youngsters they studied, only four were incest victims while the remaining children had been molested by adults who were not family members. Yet this piece of research is often used to substantiate the conclusion that incest is relatively or even completely harmless. For example, Sloane and Karpinsky (1942) echoing the conclusion of Bender and Blau, state that incest may not be harmful to this child because the child "often unconsciously desires the sexual activity" (p. 666).

Rascovsky and Rascovsky (1950), after examining only one case of paternal incest, conclude: "[T]he actual consummation of the incest relationship ... diminishes the subject's chance of psychosis and allows better adjustment to the external world" (p. 45). Continuing in this positive vein, Brunold (1964) states, perhaps correctly, that researchers have a tendency to generalize from psychically damaged incest victims and then give little or no thought to the possibility that there may be children who are able to assimilate such early sexual experiences in such a healthy manner that their lives are essentially unaffected by the incest. While it is a well deserved criticism that some researchers make broad-brushed generalizations based on a small sample of cases, Brunold did not heed his own warning. In his own study of 62 cases, fewer than 20 of which were of paternal incest victims, he concludes, "It may be said in general that lasting psychological injury as a result of sexual assaults ... is not very common" (p. 65).

Henderson (1975) not only believes that incest is generally not harmful but that it actually may be beneficial. He states: "The father-daughter liaison satisfies instinctual drives in a setting where mutual alliance with an omnipotent adult condones the transgression. Moreover, the act offers an opportunity to test in reality an infantile fantasy whose consequences are found to be gratifying and pleasurable" (p. 1537). Henderson then refers to the Rascovskys' study and further concludes that "it has even been suggested that the ego's capacity for sublimation is favored by the pleasure afforded by incest and that such incest activity diminishes the subject's chance of psychosis and allows a better adjustment to the external world" (p. 1537).

In making such positive statements about incest, it is occasionally necessary for the investigators to distort or even deny the context in which these observations are made. Yorukaglu and Kemph (1966), in an article optimistically titled, "Children Not Severely Damaged by Incest with a Parent," recount the cases of Jim and Jean: the former a 13½-year-old victim of mother-son incest; the latter a 17-year-old victim of paternal incest. Both were patients at the University of Michigan's Children's Psychiatric Hospital at the time of the study. Jim had been admitted there after 18 months of involvement in various detention and child care facilities in which he was placed after his mother's incarceration. During this time, he stole, set fires, ran away and destroyed property. He exhibited himself to fellow boy detainees, homosexually assaulted another boy and engaged in obviously suicidal behavior. Jean was hospitalized after her several years long incestuous relationship with her father was disclosed. She had experienced severe anxiety attacks, psychosomatic complaints, and escapist fantasies during and after her victimization. She was also so overwhelmed with guilt feelings about her involvement in the incest and her father's subsequent commitment to a mental hospital that she sought psychiatric treatment.

Yet with these youngsters' symptoms of suicidal tendencies, anxiety attacks, psychosomatic complaints and destructive acting out before them in a psychiatric hospital setting, Yorukaglu and Kemph conclude that "the reason these children *were not severely affected* is that they had developed adequate ego functioning including defensive functions along with the resolution of early conflicts and adequate psychosexual development prior to their having incestual relations" (p. 124; italics added). One may justifiably wonder whether Jim and Jean shared the authors' conclusion that they had not been seriously affected by the incest.

Schultz (1980), while reluctant to conclude that incest is relatively or completely harmless, nonetheless attacks the "verbal overkill" which he finds is characteristic of studies of incest. For example, he states that suggesting that incest victims may suffer "trauma" implies a life-threatening injury and requires only hearsay justification for its use. He also has a problem with references to incest "victims," a word which he insists "artificially creates a new generation of victims in a self-fulfilling charade" (p. 94). Schultz concludes that most of the research which supports the conclusion that incest has harmful effects on the victim is "rhetorically manipulative and abounding in cliches and myths" (p. 95). Acknowledging that to believe so is to "invite abuse and disbelief," Schultz nonetheless states that the literature does not support a causal relationship between incest and any single piece of pre- or postincest behavior.

Schultz is correct; that *causal* link is virtually impossible to prove. However, the quest should not yet be abandoned for two important reasons. First, the vast majority of research demonstrates a clear correlation between incest victimization and both short- and long-term behavioral and psychological negative effects. This correlation may be short of the highly valued causal link but to dismiss it because it cannot demonstrate cause and effect is to ignore a great deal of credible research which clearly transcends Schultz's concern about cliches and myth-ridden data. Second, the kinds of disordered, pathological family structures which are conducive to incest in the first place can, in and of themselves, produce noticeable developmental difficulties in children even if the incest never occurs (Meiselman, 1978; Muldoon, 1979). And if the incest *does* occur, it brings about critical role changes within the family that are likely to have long-range effects of their own.

EFFECTS DURING AND IMMEDIATELY
AFTER THE INCEST VICTIMIZATION

Once again, a clinical sample will be used to illustrate the effect of incest on the victim both as a child and as an adult. Out of a total of 80 victims in the clinical sample, 60 were victims of paternal incest. They ranged in age from 4 to 53. Twelve of those 60 victims were just emerging from the incest experience at the time of this study, and they will be used to illustrate the effects of the incest experienced during and immediately after the victimization. The remaining 48 women are adults and will illustrate the long-term effects of paternal incest.

Isolation in the Family

When a daughter in a family is chosen by a father or stepfather to be involved in a sexual experience with him, that daughter takes on a unique role in that family. When the incest is then kept secret through the father's or stepfather's techniques of bribery, threats, and reinterpretations of morality and reality, the continuing unique role of the daughter frequently isolates her from the rest of the family (de Young, 1981a).

That isolation, in fact, actually may have preceded the overt incest. Herman and Hirschman (1977) in their study of 15 cases of paternal incest, found that an "almost universal estrangement of the mother and daughter" (p. 737) preceded the actual incest by some time. In their words, the mothers transmit a very clear message to their daughters: "Your father first, you second. It is dangerous to fight back, for if I lose him, I lose everything. For my own survival, I must leave you to your own devices. I cannot defend you, and if necessary, I will sacrifice you to your father" (p. 740).

Once the incest begins, the chosen daughter may be estranged from her siblings as well (de Young, 1981b). Therefore, left without the advocacy of her siblings and the protection of her mother, the daughter is rendered vulnerable and helpless. The net effect of that isolation in the family is the creation of anxiety in the daughter (Kaufman *et al.*, 1954.) Yet this isolation also creates feelings of worthlessness which may be very pronounced and which may underlie other pathological reactions to the incest.

> Carla, 18, had been incestuously victimized by her father for two years. "I still struggle with these feelings of worthlessness. They're not hard to come by. My mom wouldn't protect me from my dad; my sister wouldn't have anything to do with me because he was bribing me with gifts so I'd keep the incest a secret and she was jealous because he never bought her anything. So it's not hard to figure out when you're a little kid that the reason that no one comes to your aid is because you just don't deserve it. It didn't take long before I started treating myself like I didn't deserve anything good."

Power

Isolated though she may be, the daughter who is an incest victim also wields an unusual amount of power in the family. Part of that power comes from the role reversal she is likely to have experienced with her mother. Given the responsibilities for cooking, cleaning, child care and sexual intimacy with her father or stepfather, the daughter plays a pivotal role in the family power structure. Lustig *et al.* (1966), in their study of six cases of paternal incest, observed that all of the daughters in their sample "had become the female authority in the households by the age of eight. Their advice was sought by the mothers on topics from groceries to sex" (p. 34).

Obviously this is a kind of power which the daughter is unlikely to be able to administer effectively because of her young age and the lack of a competent role model to imitate, as the case of Debby illustrates (de Young, 1981a:9):

> Debbie had full responsibility for the household at age 12, and until she ran away at 15, she ran the house like a tyrant, capriciously setting rules and regulations and enforcing all of them with a passion. In addition, she did most of the cooking, all of the shopping and cleaning and paid most of the bills.

The siblings are likely to respond to this authority with resentment and confusion, thereby increasing the isolation of the daughter in the family. The mother as well may be envious, perhaps because she consciously or even unconsciously recognizes that she has set up her daughter to receive the sexual contacts from her husband which she herself may desire but is reticent, for whatever reason, to receive. Again, this puts the daughter in an isolated but powerful position within the family.

Another source of that power the daughter has in incestuous families is her power to destroy the family by the disclosure of the incest (Herman and Hirschman, 1977). That power brings with it an awesome responsibility: if she has the power to destroy the family, she has the same power to hold it together. Since separation anxiety is such a prevalent feature of incestuous families, that power weighs heavily on the daughter.

Guilt

It is not a long jump from feelings of worthlessness, vulnerability yet power, to feelings of guilt. The worthlessness and vulnerability are easily connected to the guilt. The feeling that somehow she deserves what she gets and is therefore also to blame for the incest is a very recognizable feature of incest victims. Yet even the feeling of power can create feelings of guilt. When a daughter has assumed household responsibilities as well as the awesome responsibility for keeping the family together, any failure to live up to these responsibilities can create feelings of guilt.

> "When my stepfather got arrested for drunk driving," Debbie recalls, "I felt responsible. After all, I was cooking for him, cleaning and doing laundry for him. I was practically raising his kids and I was sleeping with him. When he spent the night in jail, I felt guilty, like maybe I wasn't doing enough to keep him from drinking."

Adults may scoff at that logic, correctly analyzing that people are ultimately responsible for their own behaviors and it can hardly be the child's fault if a parent fails in some way or if the family does not stay together. Yet, that is adult logic, and by definition, is based upon more wisdom, intelligence and life experiences than is the naive, unsophisticated paralogic of a child. Children feel responsible for the failures of their families, and in a society that has a tendency to blame the incest victim for her family pathology as well as for her own victimization, guilt is a very predictable feeling in incest victims.

Acting Out

What does an incest victim do with these feelings of worthlessness, guilt and power? Several researchers have demonstrated an unusual degree of acting-out behavior, often self-destructive in nature, in incest victims.

Bigras *et al.* (1966) refer to this behavior as constituting a "compulsive masochistic reaction," implying that such acts as running away, drug use and suicide attempts are essentially self-destructive in nature. That conclusion is inescapable but these acts may also represent the child's maladaptive attempts to cope with the family pathology. Children in general have few healthy, functional coping mechanisms and strategies available to them; their personal and environmental resources are limited simply because they are children. So they cope with the family pathology in the best way they are able and with the most expedient strategies available: they run away from home, take drugs, skip school, even attempt suicide. If all of that is true for youngsters in general, it is particularly true of incest victims.

> Leigh explains this in the following manner. "O.K., here I am, 12 years old and my dad's screwing me practically every night. If I tell someone he goes to jail, my brothers and sister won't speak to me, and my mom'll have a heart attack or something. But if I let him keep screwing me I'll go nuts. So what do I do? Tell my folks I need a weekend alone at the Holiday Inn to think things over; or tell them I'm going to the corner bar to have a few drinks and discuss it with my pals? No, I pack up my clothes, rob my piggy bank, stick out my thumb and split. And I keep on splitting every time the cops catch me and bring me home."

Reich and Gutierres (1979) refer to that behavior as "escape behavior." In their study of 747 juvenile crimes in Maricopa County, Arizona, they discovered that 55% of the youngsters who had engaged in the "escape behavior" of running away from home, truancy or becoming missing persons were incest victims. That figure is over three times higher than the rate of runaway or truancy in children who had not been incestuously victimized (p. 241). They also found that incest victims were no more likely to engage in aggressive acts such as disturbing the peace, assault or robbery than are youngsters who are not incest victims, giving support to the theory that "escape behavior" may be a coping mechanism.

These acts also may be cries for help (Spencer, 1978). Because they are not really criminal in nature, the commission of these acts of escape is more likely to expose the child to the rehabilitative than the punitive function of the juvenile justice system. In contact there with helping professionals who are trained in listening and intervention skills, the paternal incest victim has an excellent opportunity to disclose her incestuous victimization to someone who can effectively intervene and protect her. All of this is theoretical, of course, since even at this point her disclosure of the incest may be dependent on many different factors.

> "The first time I ran away," Leigh explains, "the cops caught me. I thought to myself that this was a great chance to tell them about the incest. But they never asked why I ran, and they never asked me any of the other times I ran either. So one day they put me in a juvenile detention center and I had to talk to this lady shrink. We talked about all kinds of family problems, but she never even asked about the big one — incest. You see, I couldn't just tell her because I had this kind of magical thing — if someone would say the word I'd talk about it, but I couldn't bring the subject up. You see, if I did, and my dad went to jail, it would be my fault. But if someone else brought it up and I talked about it, it would be their fault!"

This kind of magical thinking discussed by Leigh is very typical of young incest victims. It represents their efforts to control and make some kind of sense out of what is happening to them. Frequently these efforts take on a desparate, compulsive quality:

> Debbie believed as a youngster that if she said the rosary twice a day, prayed for one hour every day and did one good deed each day, her step-father would stop sexually abusing her. When he did not stop, she increased the duration of her prayer to ninety minutes and performed two good deeds each day. She then gave him six months to stop and when he did not, she stopped saying the rosary and started reading the Bible for one half hour every day. This bargaining and magical thinking continued for the entire four years of her incestuous victimization.

Despite the fact that this "escape behavior" represents attempts to cope with a pathological family, girls who behave in this manner risk being caught and punished. James (1977) estimates that 12% of the girls incapacitated in a residential treatment center were incest victims, while Halleck (1962) finds that 15% of all of the girls in training schools throughout the country were incest victims. Conventional wisdom would suggest that those estimates are low.

It is obvious that these coping mechanisms are often self-destructive. Regarding suicide attempts: In the clinical sample of 60 female victims of paternal incest, 41 (68%) have attempted suicide at least once. In each case, the first suicide attempt occurred either during the incestuous victimization or within the two years following its termination. Of the 41 victims who had attempted suicide, 27 (66%) attempted suicide more than once; and with the exception of four very young victims, every female in the clinical sample had seriously entertained suicidal thoughts during at least one time in her life.

Other types of self-injurious behavior in the clinical sample were also noted. Over 50% of the victims had engaged in such acts as cutting and slashing, bruising, scratching and burning themselves, deliberate attempts to break bones, and self-poisoning during or immediately after a period of incest victimization. Virtually every area of the body was injured, including the breasts and genital area.

What would cause a youngster to engage in such self-injurious and obviously painful behavior? A number of hypotheses have been posited by de Young (1982c). First, self-injurious behavior can be but another example of the magical thinking in which incest victims engage. Overwhelmed by the emotional entrapment of an incestuous family and the physical oppression of the incest itself, the victim resorts to self-injurious behavior as a strategy to prevent what is happening to her.

> Leslie had repeatedly cut and bruised her face throughout the years of her victimization. "I kept wanting to make myself ugly," she explains, "because every time my stepfather would have sex with me he'd tell me he was doing it because I was so pretty. I thought that if I made myself ugly he'd stop."

Most of the self-injuring victims said that at least part of their motivation for injuring themselves was as punishment. That need to punish appears to have stemmed from one of two sources. One source is the child's introjection of the parents' hostility and abuse. Encouraged to assume responsibility for the incest by the reality-distorting techniques of her father or stepfather and by the denial techniques of her mother, the youngster may create for herself a self-image of whore. And since that is a reprehensible identity that most surely will elicit punishment from others, she engages in behavior congruent with that expectation. The other possible reason for self-punishment may lie in the child's perception that her body has betrayed her. The child may be able to control her feelings about the incest, but will not be able to control her body's involuntary response to the sexual stimulation. And if the body responds with feelings of pleasure, the child may be even more likely to loathe herself and to perceive herself as deserving of punishment.

Finally, self-injuring behavior may be a symptom of the ego's attempt to reintegrate. Incest abuse can develop a punitive conscience in a child which, under stress, can overwhelm the child's delicate ego defenses and thereby trigger the self-injury. The self-injurious act is then followed by a feeling of psychic calm and relief as well as decreased tension, all of which indicate that the defenses have reintegrated.

> Debby had repeatedly cut her breasts and genitals with razor blades during his incest victimization. "I used to stand naked in front of a mirror and do it," she explains. "I would do it after things got out of control, and I was really frightened and confused. I swear that I'd go into a trance or something, and I never felt any pain, even though I cut deep. When I saw the blood, I'd come out of the trance, and I'd laugh and my whole body would shiver. Then I'd put a bandage on the cut and go to school or out to play."

The sight of the injury frees the child from the intense feelings that led to the act, and restores the defenses that enable her to tolerate the continuing incest.

Sexual Acting Out

A child who becomes prematurely sexually stimulated within the family environment and who learns that the sexual forum is an appropriate expression for all kinds of feelings, may sexually act out during and immediately after her incestuous victimization. Of the 60 victims of paternal incest in the clinical sample, 17 (28%) reported behaviors that could be indicative of sexual acting out. Most of these behaviors were basically promiscuous in nature in that they involved the indiscriminate acting out of impulses in a sexual manner. This is not an unusual finding. Researchers have rather consistently found that promiscuity is often a symptom of incest victimization (Kaufman *et al.*, 1954; Kubo, 1959; Lukianowicz, 1972). Maisch (1972) found that 13% of his court-collected sample of paternal incest victims showed symptoms of sexual acting out, the origin of which usually coincided with other antisocial activities such as stealing and lying. He believes that all of these symptoms result from the family pathology that gives rise to the incest in the first place.

Meiselman (1978) studied 11 girls either during their incest victimization or within one year of its termination. She found that three of these girls had molested other children during or shortly after their own incest experiences. She states that this molestation, which she defines as going "much further in their initiation of sex play than was the norm in their neighborhoods" was a product of the "spilling over" into peer interactions the sexual stimulation received at home (p. 192).

Two such cases were found in the clinical sample. One involved a 5-year-old girl who was so preoccupied with sexual words and activities that her kindergarten teacher notified juvenile authorities. The investigation later revealed that the little girl had engaged in masturbation and fellatio with her stepfather during the previous year. The second case involved a 13-year-old who had been incestuously victimized by her father for one year. She had coerced her younger sister into engaging in mutual masturbation and had attempted to do the same with a young female playmate.

Sexual Victimization by Others

If the female incest victim occasionally sexually acts out, she is more often likely to be sexually victimized by other people. Researchers have rarely recognized this possibility. Twenty-three (38%) of the 60 incest victims in the clinical sample were also victims of someone other than the father or stepfather either during their incest victimization or within two years after its termination.

Summit and Kryso (1978) offer an explanation of this startling finding: "A bizarre spin-off of the labeling process is the fascination the girl presents to others. She may be regarded by relatives as dangerously attractive.... Publicly deflowered as she is, she is regarded as no longer deserving of respect or protection" (p. 244). They found four cases in which male relatives attempted seduction after the girls had disclosed their involvements with their fathers.

This "dangerously attractive" little victim may even be sexually victimized by more than one other person. The analysis in Table 6 of the 23 cases of multiple sexual victimization from the clinical sample clearly demonstrates that fact: All 23 of these victims were also victims of at least one person other than the father or stepfather. All were additionally victimized either while the incest was occurring or within two years of its termination. By definition, any additional victimization is nonconsensual in nature.

It is true that many of these reports of additional sexual victimization are retrospective in nature and therefore subject to the weaknesses of long-term memory, but even if this figure were not as high as that reported in this sample, it is obvious that an alarming number of paternal incest victims will be additionally sexually victimized. That begs the question, why?

Finkelhor (1979) believes that when mothers fail to present a model of self-protective behavior (a characteristic commonly found in nonparticipating mothers in incestuous families), do not provide their daughters with accurate sexual information, and do not adequately supervise them, the likelihood of additional sexual victimization increases drastically. He notes that "when mothers themselves are victims, when they are not equal parents, they apparently cannot transmit effective coping and self-protective skills to their daughters" (p. 126). Dietz and Craft (1980) support that conclusion. It is their belief that daughters from incestuous families learn to tolerate abuse from the examples set by their mothers and that they emulate the passivity and submissiveness of their mothers. In other words, they lack both the coping skills and the assertiveness necessary to resist additional sexual assaults.

TABLE 6. ADDITIONAL SEXUAL VICTIMIZATION OF FEMALE
PATERNAL INCEST VICTIMS

Case	Victimizer
Annie	older brother
Arlene	older brother
Beth	uncle; cousin
Bonnie	neighbor boy
Dara	brother; adult male stranger
Debbie	adult male stranger
Dyan	uncle
Effie	step-brother
Hilda	adult male acquaintance
Jacklyn	stepbrother
Jenny	half-brother
Jody	stepbrother; uncle
Karen	adult male stranger
Kendra	stepbrother
Kyle	half-brother
Leigh	adult male acquaintance
Lois	adult male acquaintance
Melinda	older brother
Peggy	stepbrother; uncle
René	cousin
Ruth	adult male stranger
Shirley	two step-brothers
Tonya	stepbrother; cousin

Another possible explanation for this phenomenon is offered by de
Young (1982a). She states that the child incest victim may give herself a new
identity of harlot or whore, an identity that may be reinforced by the unfortunate tendency of some people to blame her for her victimization. By
engaging, willingly or unwillingly, in other sexually victimizing experiences,
she creates a self-fulfilling prophecy which reduces any cognitive dissonance
she would experience if her behavior was not commensurate with her self-
identity.

Regardless of the source of this phenomenon, the reality remains the
same: an incest victim has an alarmingly high chance of being further sexually
victimized by someone other than her father or stepfather. That victimization
is most likely to occur during her own incest experience or within two years of
its termination.

Psychological Disturbance

In the clinical sample of 60 victims of paternal incest, 12 were just
emerging from the incest experience at the time of the study. All 12 demonstrate a whole range of neurotic, psychosomatic and behavioral symptoms, all
of which have been documented to at least some extent by various researchers
over the years.

Kaufman *et al.* (1954) studied 11 victims of paternal incest who had
been referred to the Judge Baker Guidance Center in Boston. They found that

all of the girls were depressed and many had suicidal thoughts. Psychosomatic complaints were common and learning disorders were documented for three of the girls. Rorschach findings showed depression, anxiety, sexual identity confusion, fear of sex, and both oral deprivation and oral sadism. Lukianowicz (1972) states that almost half of the sample of incest victims he studied had character disorders and approximately 15% demonstrated neurotic symptomatology (p. 309). In an interesting side note, Lukianowicz observed that 23% of his sample showed "no apparent ill effects from the incest" (p. 310). This observation is particularly curious since his entire sample of 26 cases was drawn from residential treatment centers for delinquent girls, psychiatric hospitals and outpatient clinics.

Molnar and Cameron (1975) also noted depression in their sample of ten incest victims who were psychiatric hospital inpatients at the time of their study. This depression was accompanied by suicidal thoughts and was so recognizable as a symptom cluster that they suggested that it be referred to as the "incest syndrome." Maisch (1972) states that fully 70% of his sample of paternal incest victims had some kind of personality disturbance. Approximately 28% were depressed, 33% had made at least one suicide attempt, 25% demonstrated antisocial characteristics, 12% showed traumatic neurosis with anxiety, compulsions and phobias, and 17% had psychosomatic complaints.

Meiselman (1978), in her study of 11 victims who were just emerging from the incest experience, found three were psychotic, three had character disorders, two were severely neurotic, and three presented mixed pictures of anxiety, antisocial tendencies and depression (p. 190). In the clinical sample of 12 recent victims, none was psychotic but traumatic neurotic symptoms were noted in seven of the girls; two were suicidally depressed; and the remaining three showed definite antisocial characteristics. Most of the girls also had physical complaints that were undoubtedly psychosomatic in nature.

Did incest cause all of this? Those with liberal or proincest sentiments would undoubtedly answer that a cause and effect relationship between paternal incest and these psychological symptoms cannot be proven. Again, that relationship may be more correlative than causal, but it would be absurd to deny that some relationship between the two does not exist. In an effort to address this difficult problem, Maisch (1972), whose study of postincest symptomatology is probably the most meticulous of all of the studies, concludes that the incest caused personality disturbances in 35% of his sample, exacerbated preexisting symptoms in 27% of the cases, and had no traceable relation to personality problems in the remaining 38% of the cases. If these figures hold true for other samples as well, a true relationship between paternal incest and a majority of postincest psychological disturbances begins to emerge.

Physical Complaints

The psychosomatic complaints so frequently documented with paternal incest victims may be symptomatic of internalized rage and guilt. However, a preteen or teenage incest victim has more of an opportunity to act out on these repressed feelings than does a younger victim.

When infants, toddlers, preschoolers, and young children are incest victims, their symptomatology is most likely to be physical in nature. Slager-Jorne (1978) finds eating and sleeping problems, vomiting, restlessness, and a failure-to-thrive syndrome in these young victims. Brant and Tisza (1977) conclude that since these youngsters have difficulty in expressing feelings in words, their symptoms are likely to be physical in nature and may include genital irritation, stomachaches, painful discharge of urine, altered sleeping patterns, enuresis, encopresis, and hyperactivity.

Both Brant and Tisza and Thomas (1980) caution medical professionals in particular to look for venereal disease in all sexually victimized children, including the infants and toddlers. Thomas states that sexually abused children have a 10% to 30% chance of contracting gonorrhea, a figure, incidentally, which Sgroi (1978) calls conservative.

LONG-RANGE EFFECTS OF INCEST

Years after the termination of the incest the effects of the sexual experience may linger and interfere with the normal, healthy functioning of the victim as an adult. Of course, the longer the time elapsed between the incest and these symptoms the more difficult it is to posit a causal relationship, but once again, the correlation between early sexual experiences and disruptions of normal adult living is clearly evident.

Family Disturbances

Incest is a product of a character-disordered family (Muldoon, 1979) in which relationships are strained, roles are changed and affectional patterns are distorted. Consequently, it would come as no surprise to learn that the relationships the incest victim as an adult has with others may be disturbed as well.

Incest victims as adults frequently have relationship problems with their husbands. Part of this may be due to the findings of various researchers which suggest that incest victims often seek "father figures" in adult heterosexual relationships (Tompkins, 1940; Rascovsky and Rascovsky, 1950; Rhinehart, 1961; Herman and Hirschman, 1977). Since their own relationships with their fathers were poor and abusive, their heterosexual relationships are likely to take on the same quality. In the clinical sample of 60 victims of paternal incest, 48 of whom are adults, only two women stated that this "father figure" dynamic was characteristic of their relationships with men.

> "It's a comfortable pattern, I guess," states Tonya. "Well, maybe not comfortable, but more like predictable. I've been married twice. Both were drinkers like my stepfather, and I was terrified of both of them just like I was of my stepfather. I'm 42 years old, and I've spent my whole life feeling helpless, scared and hating myself. I'm not sure I could feel any other way. And I'm still not sure I deserve to be treated any better than this."

Two women seeking a father-figure in a sample of 60 victims is a very small figure, expecially in light of the research which insists that this is a commonly found dynamic. Meiselman (1978) found no examples of this dynamic in her therapy sample of 57 victims. She explains this in the following manner: "[A] self-destructive search for a father figure in an adult sexual partner or husband is a relatively rare outcome even in a sample of psychologically disturbed women, and it was much more frequently observed that the adult daughter was trying to escape from men and sexuality rather than making unconscious attempts to recreate the incest situation" (p. 211).

Meiselman (1978) did find that incest victims as adults often said they were "used" by men, a complaint often voiced by the clinical sample as well. She states that since this type of complaint is usually accompanied by a degree of self-righteousness the women may have obtained some degree of satisfaction from their roles as victims. The clinical sample certainly substantiates that the victim role is one that is frequently played by incest victims as adults in many of their relationships. Perhaps this reflects the earlier stated finding that the dynamics and roles in incestuous families deprive a child of coping and assertiveness skills which would allow her, as an adult, to overcome her victim role.

Meiselman (1978) also generated some interesting data regarding the attitudes of adult female incest victims toward their parents. She found that 40% of them were clearly hostile towards their fathers or stepfathers and that the remainder, 60%, had "forgiven" them (p. 219).

In the clinical sample of 48 incest victims as adults, 25 (52%) were still very hostile towards their fathers or stepfathers, and seven (15%) forgave them. The remaining 16 (33%) of the victims as adults felt so ambivalent about their fathers or stepfathers that their attitudes about them changed daily, and in some cases, by the moment. The response of Dyan when asked about her feelings about her father is similar to reactions heard from other incest victims as adults:

> "Sometimes I feel so sorry for him my heart could break. He must have been really sick to do what he did to me. He really needed some kind of professional help. Other times I could kill the son-of-a-bitch. I hate him so much. But you know, other times I just plain don't feel anything. I just feel numb."

If the attitudes of the incest victims as adults toward their father or stepfathers cover a whole range of feelings, their attitudes about their mothers are almost uniformly negative. Thirty-eight (79%) of the victims as adults in the clinical sample had predominately hostile feelings toward their mothers, none of whom had overtly participated in the incest. Six (13%) women in the clinical sample had ambivalent feelings, and the remaining four (9%) had essentially positive feelings toward their mothers.

The origin of these commonly noted negative feelings toward the mothers is in the recognition that the mothers, above anyone else, had the power to stop the incest from continuing or to prevent it from occurring in the first place. Most of the mothers of the victim in the clinical sample chose not to exercise that power. Therefore, feelings of anger toward the offending father or stepfather ("How could he do this to me?") are easily transferred to the non-participating mother ("How could she *let* him do this to me?").

Although the incest victim as an adult usually has a strained relationship with one or both of her parents, she also has strong dependency needs, unresolved in childhood, which cause her to continually strive to maintain whatever threads of the relationship still exist. Sometimes that quest takes on a desperate and even self-defeating quality.

> Bonnie, now 37, would run to her mother whenever a decision was to be made or a problem had to be resolved. "And she never helped. She never supported me; she never seemed to care. I'd always leave her feeling more depressed and hating myself for going to her in the first place. But the next time something came up, I'd be back on her doorstep again."

> Leslie, 38, has spent her entire adult life trying to heal the relationship with her stepfather. "When I was a kid he raped me and beat me continually. I really hated him then and I guess I still do. But I want a dad — someone to love me and care for me. I keep trying to make him into that person. I'm only now beginning to understand that he'll never be that kind of father no matter how much I want him to be."

Psychological Disturbances

Fleck *et al.* (1959) suggest that paternal incest may be more of an etiological factor in schizophrenia than has been previously recognized. This suggestion is supported by Barry (1965) who adds that the incestuous family's tendency to distort both reality and morality for the child victim may impair the reality-testing skills and the psychological development of the victim. There is a logic to this argument; however only three cases of psychosis were discovered in the clinical sample.

Heims and Kaufman (1963) suggest that character disorders are found more frequently in incest victims as adults. In the clinical sample, 18 women clearly demonstrated character disorder symptomatology the type of which most often suggests diagnosis of a histrionic character disorder. Six women showed neurotic symptomatology of either an anxiety or hysterical nature, but the remaining 21 women, a full 65% of the adult clinical sample, showed no evidence of any diagnosable psychological disturbance. Obvious adjustment problems as adults are noted, however, although these symptoms fall short of mental illness. Problems with self-image, trust, control, assertiveness and guilt were universally found, to one degree or another, in the clinical sample. Although these problems alone may not lead to a diagnosis of mental illness, they certainly have the capacity to disrupt the daily living and interpersonal interaction skills of the incest victims as adults.

Yet many women in the clinical sample, 37 (77%) to be exact, had been or were in therapy at the time of this study. Their motivations for engaging in therapy are discussed in Table 7.

Table 7 only discusses the one primary motivation for seeking therapy for each woman. Meiselman (1978) found that therapy patients with histories of incest seem to have more complaints than a control group of therapy patients who do not have histories of incest. In fact, Meiselman found that the incest patients averaged 3.4 complaints (called "presenting problems") while the other patients averaged 2.5 presenting problems (p. 192).

TABLE 7. PRIMARY MOTIVATION FOR SEEKING THERAPY

Primary Motivation	Number of Adult Victims
Marital problems	17
Sexual problems	12
Depression	4
Alcohol/Drug Use	2
Anxiety	2

It may be wise to refrain from assuming that incest causes psychological disturbances in later years. Meiselman (1978) discusses the reason why: "It seems that incest is a serious source of stress that usually occurs in association with many other unfavorable background factors. As such, it tends to predispose the daughter to become psychologically disturbed, but the precise nature of that disturbance — character disorder, neurosis, or psychosis — is not conditioned by the incest but by a host of other genetic and environmental factors that are only tangentially connected with the incest" (p. 204). This is certainly not to suggest that incest cannot have a harmful effect on the psychological functioning of the adult, but that its source of serious psychological disturbances in adult life cannot be proven.

Sexual Problems

Sexual problems are more commonly reported by incest victims as adults than are psychological problems. These reported sexual problems vary as to type and chronicity.

Frigidity. Frigidity is a very difficult problem to define even when the term is divested of its moral and personal connotations. For the purposes of this study, frigidity is defined as a lack of sexual response or feeling, ranging from complete anesthesia to incomplete climax. Using this definition, forty (83%) of the incest victims as adults reported complete or selective frigidity in their sexual relationships.

Yet frigidity is rarely reported as a long-range effect of incest by other researchers. There is no reason to believe that there is anything unique about the clinical sample that would produce such a high figure, but there is at least a suspicion that other researchers, for whatever reasons, did not inquire about this sexual dysfunction in their sample populations. Meiselman (1978) adds an interesting observation to that assumption which may underly the problem: "Most women who are sexually non-responsive present no problems to the community and can easily appear well-adjusted if their sexual functioning is not considered to be important, and this lack of conspicuously antisocial behavior may have misled some early researchers who concluded that incest seldom has unfortunate aftereffects" (p. 241). Keeping that in mind, Meiselman found that 74% of her sample of adult women who had been incest victims had experienced some degree of frigidity (p. 234).

Promiscuity. Promiscuity is another difficult term to objectively define. For the purpose of this study, however, it is defined as indiscriminate sexual acting out motivated primarily by nonsexual needs. Using this definition, seven (15%) of the adult women in the clinical sample characterized their own sexual behavior as promiscuous in nature. One of the underlying factors in promiscuity is the confusion of affection with sex. Because the sexual forum was often the only means that a child incest victim could use to obtain nurturing, caring and affectionate responses, when she matures she may continue to use that sexual behavior to get these needs met.

> Shirley, 28, characterizes her sexual behavior as promiscuous in nature. "I love 'em and leave 'em," she laughs. "And as long as I'm in bed with them I feel loved. As soon as they leave, or I do, I feel empty again. So I find myself another guy to have sex with."

Using a similar definition of promiscuity, Meiselman (1978) found that 19% of her sample of incest victims as adults were promiscuous (p. 227). In the cases she discovered, the promiscuous behavior was compulsive and self-destructive, an observation confirmed by the seven women in the clinical sample. Quite a few of the women in her sample and in the clinical sample had outgrown, for lack of a better term, their promiscuity, usually while they were in their twenties.

Earlier studies have reported a much higher rate of promiscuity than the 19% from Meiselman's study and the 15% from the clinical sample. That observation requires some analysis. Part of the reason that Lukianowicz (1972), for example, found 42% of his sample to be promiscuous was a sampling bias. Lukianowicz drew his sample from psychiatric hospitals, outpatient psychiatric clinics and residential treatment centers for delinquent girls; all facilities in which promiscuity alone or in combination with other symptoms is likely to be discovered in a large percentage of the patients. Another reason why earlier researchers documented so much promiscuity in incest victims as adults is because most of the researchers never define promiscuity, leaving it to the personal interpretation of each woman involved.

The psychodynamics of promiscuity are not really understood. Gordon (1955) and Howard (1959) suggest that postincest promiscuity may be motivated by hostility against the parents. They tend to see this promiscuity as a form of revenge against the parents, perhaps an attempt to embarrass them since promiscuity, by definition, connotes a violation of the sexual norms of the culture. Kaufman *et al.* (1954) see postincest promiscuity in a more psychoanalytic light, as a kind of repetition compulsion used defensively by the women to both relive the incest experience and to work through their anxiety. Regardless of its psychodynamics, postincest promiscuity may in fact be less common than previously assumed.

Flashbacks. Twenty-three (48%) of the clinical sample of incest victims as adults have experienced "flashbacks" to their incestuous victimizations immediately before, during, or immediately after relations with their partners.

> Lois, 31, describes the flashback in the following manner: "I'm always anxious during a sexual relationship, but I'm in control unless the man I'm with fondles my breasts. Then I get really anxious and have to fight for that control. That doesn't make sexual intercourse too pleasurable for me. A couple of times I couldn't get that control back. Then I felt like a kid again and the man who's fondling my breasts becomes my father in my mind. Then it's not sex — it's pain and terror."

Jenny, 27, is married and enjoys a fulfilling sexual relationship with her husband of five years. "But he understands there is one thing he can *never* do. He can never get into our bed with liquor on his breath. That's what my father did for three years when I was a kid. The few times my husband did that, like after a party or something, I freaked out. I started crying and begging him not to hurt me. This may not make much sense, but I knew intellectually he was my husband, but emotionally I felt he was my father."

Tsai and Wagner (1978) also document these flashbacks in the participants of their therapy groups for women with a history of sexual victimization during childhood. In a later piece of research, Tsai *et al.* (1979) explained this phenomenon in the following manner (p. 415):

The pairing of the negative emotional response with the stimulus array constituting the molestation experience may produce a conditioned emotional response that is subjectively quite negative for the child. Then, through the process of stimulus generalization, these conditioned negative responses may later be elicited by sexual activities carried out even in a non-molestation situation and/or by other men with whom the women are intimately involved in their adult lives. Negative emotional reactions in these later situations, in turn, are likely to constitute or create, psychosexual problems.

Sexual Victimization

Like the recently incestuously victimized child, the incest victim as an adult has an increased chance of being sexually victimized by someone else. In the clinical sample of 48 victims as adults, 14 (29%) had also been sexually victimized as adults. Remember that in addition to the incest, many of these women had also been victimized as children by some person other than the offending father or stepfather. As adults, their vulnerability to sexual victimization obviously has not decreased. Table 8 shows the type of victimizations the 14 women had experienced.

These startling data illustrate the earlier assumption that child incest victims rarely have the opportunity to model self-protective and coping skills. In many ways, most notably sexual, they may be eternal victims. This observation was underscored by Miller *et al.* (1978) who analyzed a collection of two and a half years of data from the sexual assault team of the University of New Mexico Medical School. They found that 82 of the 341 rape victims counseled by the team had been raped more than once, and that 18% of those recidivists also had been victims of incest as children (p. 1104).

Three of the women in the clinical sample had experienced victimization at the hands of their therapists. Dara was sexually victimized by her psychologist; Shirley and Lois by their psychiatrists. In examining their cases, de Young (1982b) notes that the lack of self-protective skills of the women, coupled with the tendency of incest victims to sexualize the transference process, makes incest victims especially vulnerable to sexual exploitation during the therapy process. Also, the tendency of the therapist who is untrained in the dynamics of incest to see the patient as a "sexual being" or in a more dehumanized fashion as "spoiled goods" no longer deserving of care and protection, can lead to sexual exploitation.

TABLE 8. TYPES OF SEXUAL VICTIMIZATIONS EXPERIENCES

Case	Age; Occurrence	Additional Male Childhood Victimizers
Dara	25; sexual exploitation by her psychologist	brother; adult stranger
Debbie	23; acquaintance rape	adult stranger
Denise	24; raped by a stranger	none
Fran	22; raped by a stranger	none
Gail	25; acquaintance rape	none
Gloria	30; acquaintance rape	none
Leigh	19; acquaintance rape	adult acquaintance
Leslie	20; raped by a stranger	none
Lois	31; sexual exploitation by her psychiatrist	adult acquaintance
Melinda	19; acquaintance rape	none
Ruth	20; acquaintance rape	adult stranger
Shirley	28; sexual exploitation by her psychiatrist	two stepbrothers
Tonya	18; acquaintance rape	stepbrother; cousin
Yvonne	20; acquaintance rape	none

The little research that has been conducted on the dynamics and effects of therapist-patient sexual encounters have uniformly emphasized the negative effects that such encounters can have on the patient (Taylor and Wagner, 1976; Stone, 1976; Kirstein, 1979). Barnhouse (1978) states that this is due to the fact that such sexual encounters are "symbolically incestuous" because the patient tends to see, through the process of transference, the therapist as a father figure. If that statement is true for therapy patients in general, then sexual encounters between therapists and patients who were incest victims may well be, in the eyes of the patients, literally incestuous as well. That conclusion is certainly supported by de Young (1982b) who found that the impact of these encounters was devastating for the three women in her study, and that whatever therapeutic progress they had achieved prior to the exploitation was significantly reduced or even destroyed as a result of the encounter.

Lesbianism

Some incest victims as adults are so traumatized by their incest experiences that they reject a heterosexual role. Five (10.4%) of the clinical sample of adult incest victims are lesbians and all five feel that they had made conscious choices about their sexual preference and life style, and had come to the lesbian alternative because of their incest experiences as children.

Various research studies over the years have noted a variety of rates of lesbianism among paternal incest victims as adults. Sloane and Karpinsky (1942) could find no lesbians in their sample of five victims, Kaufman *et al.* (1954) found that a "few" of their sample of 11 cases were lesbians, and Medlicott (1967) found that 29% of his small sample of incest victims were lesbians. Meiselman (1978), who studied the largest sample, found that 30% were lesbians. Curiously, some of the largest and most comprehensive studies on incest victims never even examined the sexual preferences of their samples (Weinberg, 1955; Gligor, 1966; Maisch, 1972).

Gundlach and Riess (1967) surveyed 217 adult lesbians and compared them to 231 heterosexual adult women and found that lesbians had a significantly higher incident rate of coercive sexual experiences as children than did the heterosexual women. In a later study, Gundlach (1977) found that of the 17 women who had reported incest experience in his study of hundreds of women, 16 later became lesbians (p. 377). Rosen (1974) concludes that the factor that seems to have the most etiological weight in the development of adult lesbianism is the "importance of the first sexual experience and whether it is pleasurable and positive" (p. 70). The fact that the first sexual experience is neither pleasurable nor positive for most incest victims may be that etiological factor in the development of the "lesbian solution," in the words of Meiselman (1978), for some of those victims.

Prostitution

Four (8%) of the paternal incest victims as adults had actively engaged in prostitution during their adult years. This is not a large figure, but its size may reflect sampling bias more than it does reality. Most of the victims in the clinical sample are college and university students or therapy patients. When street prostitutes are studied — and they are not likely to be found in college classrooms or therapist's offices — that figure is very different.

James and Meyerding (1978) studied the early sexual histories of street prostitutes and concluded that there is a much higher incidence of incest in their childhoods than is found in the backgrounds of a control group. Greenwald (1958) studied 20 call girls, or "high class prostitutes," and found a similar incidence of early sexual victimization in their childhoods.

Once again, many major studies of postincest behavior have not examined the possibility of a prostitute lifestyle for incest victims. Those few which have offered varying rates do not lend themselves to any major conclusions about the etiology of this phenomenon.

Other Effects

Two other long-range effects of paternal incest must be reviewed. Malmquist et al. (1966) found that in their sample of 20 women with histories of repeated illegitimate pregnancies four had been victims of paternal incest.

Spivak (1980) found that 11 of the 41 women who were voluntarily seeking counseling for alcoholism had been victims of paternal incest. She also discovered that those incest victims took their first drink at an earlier age (13.7 years) than did the alcoholic women who were not incest victims (16.7 years).

CHAPTER 6: THE SEXUAL VICTIMIZATION OF SONS

The boxing match of the decade may have been between the fictional character, Bobby Fallon, and the real life head of the National Federation for Decency, the Rev. Donald Wildmon. Fallon, the protagonist of the televised version of Pete Hamill's novel, *Flesh and Blood*, is the sole support, financially, emotionally and sexually, of his libidinous mother, and it is that sexual support to which Wildmon and his group most vigorously object.

The televised version of *Flesh and Blood* makes allusions to a highly romanticized, noncoercive incestuous encounter between the teenager, Bobby, and his mother. CBS vice president Donn O'Brien vigorously supported the incest scenes and references in the television movie, claiming that "TV can deal with any sensitive subject if it does so tastefully." Wildmon angrily countered with a letter writing campaign and prayer-in that inundated CBS with more than 10,000 letters of protest before the movie ever appeared on television (*Newsweek*, Oct. 8, 1979:101–102).

In a sense, the match between Wildmon and Fallon was a draw. The portrayal of incest in *Flesh and Blood* is so cliché-ridden and over-romanticized that it barely if at all approximates the real life experiences of those sons who have been incestuously victimized by their mothers. Yet Wildmon's point that an incest theme does not belong on television because it is "gratuituos and excessive" also diminishes the experiences of male incest victims by implying that they are not victims but active participants in a mutually satisfying, excessively libidinous sexual relationship. Before there can be a rematch, media representatives must understand that when "good taste" is used as a standard for the portrayal of the incestuous victimization of children the final product will never reflect reality; and the Rev. Wildmon must accept the reality of incest and recognize that the media can be powerful vehicles for bringing this taboo subject into the consciousness of viewers.

Boys certainly can be and are incest victims — victims in the truest sense of the term. Finkelhor (1979), in his study of college and university students, found that 17% of the 266 males surveyed had been incestuously victimized as children (p. 60) and, contrary to media portrayals, 54% of those young men stated that the victimizers had used some force to gain their participation (p. 64).

In the clinical sample, only eight male victims are examined; six of

65

them victims of paternal incest while the remaining two are victims of maternal incest. This small number of victims in the clinical sample should not be used to reach the conclusion that boys are rarely victimized; it would be better used as support for the theory that boys are less inclined to reveal their victimizations, therefore they are less commonly found as patients of therapists, members of incest support groups, or as victims in court-referred cases, all of which are sources for the creation of a clinical sample.

MATERNAL INCEST

Only two boys in the clinical sample had been incestuously victimized by their mothers. Their mothers were also interviewed for the purposes of this study, thus affording at least a small opportunity to examine the family dynamics in each case.

The Incestuous Mother

Despite the Freudian emphasis on the erotic attachment between mother and son which must be resolved during the Oedipal stage of personality development, overtly incestuous mothers appear infrequently in research samples. Curiously, though, quite a great deal of research has been done on incestuous mothers. Perhaps the rarity of this type of victimization has stimulated interest in the subject.

Mental Illness. It bothers some people a great deal that incestuous mothers are frequently labeled mentally ill while incestuous fathers are rarely given that label. What may at first appear to be an overtly sexist practice may appear to be less so upon further analysis.

Meiselman (1978) states that "the unique dependent relationship that usually exists between a mother and her child seems to be antithetical to overt sexual behavior between them" (p. 298). In addition to that unique relationship, other role responsibilities most typically assumed by women as mothers may deter them from incestuous contacts with their children. For example, Finkelhor (1979) suggests that a mother's involvement with the genital and excretory functions of young children, and her presumed greater than a father's comfort in dealing with those functions, actually may defuse some of the sexual tension between her and her child. Also, because a mother has more direct care and supervisory experiences with children she may be more inclined to identify with the child's sense of well being, consequently she may have more empathy for the traumatic effect that sexual victimization may have on a child. Justice and Justice (1979) state that women are also less likely to substitute sexual intimacy for other forms of physical closeness; therefore, in her role as mother, her physical closeness needs are likely to be almost continually met by her children. Finkelhor adds that for women there is a greater emphasis on mutuality as a foundation for sexual involvement, and mutuality certainly cannot be found in any adult-child sexual relationships.

In summary, the "socially conditioned channels of sexual attraction draw women away from children" (Finkelhor, 1979:77). Consequently, when a woman violates this prescribed behavior, she is more likely to take on a deviant identity in the eyes of other people. One such label which reflects that deviant identity is "mentally ill."

Finch (1973) states that severe character disorders and occasionally borderline or even overt psychosis are commonly discovered in incestuous mothers. Frances and Frances (1976) insist that psychosis is almost always present in incestuous mothers, a conclusion that Meiselman (1978) mirrors in her observation that in cases of mother initiated incest, the mother is invariably mentally ill.

Both cases of mother-son incest in the clinical sample had been initiated by the mothers, and both mothers are psychologically disturbed. One is suffering from a severely decompensated hysterical neurosis; the other is schizophrenic and had been institutionalized on three separate occasions.

Promiscuity. Another commonly found feature of incestuous mothers is promiscuous acting out (Finch, 1973). In fact, Meiselman (1978) suggests that the blatant promiscuity of these mothers both antagonizes and tempts their sons.

If the mothers are not promiscuous they are almost certain to be quite seductive, with much of that behavior directed toward their sons.

> Mrs. Brent, 39, behaved very seductively around her 13 year old son, Simon. Her language was always sexually suggestive and if her son could not appreciate the risque nature of each double entendre, she always carefully explained. Mrs. Brent would model underwear and lingerie for her son and would seek his approval. She frequently walked naked through the house and encouraged her son to do the same.

Other Features. Finch (1973) suggests that incestuous mothers are likely to be alcoholics, but Wahl (1960) believes that the incest may take place during periods of alcohol intoxication, although the mother herself may not be an alcoholic. Neither of the women in the clinical sample is an alcoholic nor are they drug abusers.

Finch (1973) also suggest that a low self-esteem is common in incestuous mothers. This is confirmed by the small clinical sample but in terms of its severity, it is not a remarkable finding.

Early Childhood. The instability of the childhoods of incestuous mothers is often documented through case studies. For example, Yorukaglu and Kemph (1966) describe a case of a mother who had incestuously victimized her son and daughter over a two year period of time. She was the seventh of nine children of a fundamentalist preacher who had ruled his family with an iron hand. She had been raped at age 12 by her brother-in-law and had been punished for her alleged consenting role in that act by her father who had forced her to read the Bible and renounce all heterosexual activities as atonement for her sin. She escaped that oppressive home environment by marrying an alcoholic, abusive man from whom she separated 43 times in five years. After her eventual divorce from him, she married two more times.

The two incestuous mothers in the clinical sample come from similarly disorganized family backgrounds. Both of them also had been incestuously victimized.

Mrs. Brent had been incestuously victimized by her stepfather over a three year period of time. When she complained to her mother, she was dismissed as a "liar" and a "whore." Her mother rationalized their frequent beatings by her husband as "for our own good." Mrs. Brent was also raped when she was 15 by her stepfather's best friend. Again, she was blamed by her mother for seducing him and the friend continued to be welcome in their home.

Mrs. Underwood had been incestuously victimized by her mother, a frequently institutionalized paranoid schizophrenic who had conducted each separate incident of victimization in a ritualistic fashion. Prayers were chanted first and then the child was placed in scalding hot water for a "purifying bath." Clothespins were placed on the nipples of her breasts and various objects were then placed in her rectum and vagina. This ritual occurred twice a week for two years until her mother was once again institutionalized.

Both women were asked how traumatic their own early incest experiences had been and both replied that they had been extremely traumatic. Yet neither woman believes her son was or would be, in the long range sense, traumatized by the incest. Mrs. Brent rationalized that the incest was an act of love, and should be especially considered so because it was not accompanied by physical violence like her own victimization had been. Mrs. Underwood reasons that only girls can be incest victims; boys cannot because boys are "born knowing more about sex than girls are." That convoluted piece of logic must be recognized as a product of Mrs. Underwood's psychopathology and it does not appear to reflect the typical rationalizations used by incestuous mothers.

In addition to the incestuous victimization, both incestuous mothers in the clinical sample had experienced extremely disorganized family backgrounds, both characterized by economic deprivation, frequent uprootings of the families, and multiple marriages of their mothers. Both escaped the family disorganization by early marriages which, in both cases, only led to a replication of their early family experiences. Again, it is ill-advised to make sweeping generalizations based on such a small sample but case histories of incestuous mothers documented by other researchers over the years basically confirm the findings of family disorganization and early incest experiences.

The Nonparticipating Father

Like the nonparticipating mother in cases of paternal incest, the nonparticipating father in cases of maternal incest fails to act as a restraining agent by exercising his intrafamilial power. This may be true simply because he has a weak and ineffective personality. However, it is more likely to be true because he is not present enough or at all in the home to exercise a restraining influence.

If the clinical sample truly represents the dynamics of other cases of maternal incest, then it appears that the nonparticipating fathers are less likely to utilize the defense mechanism of denial than are the nonparticipating mothers in cases of paternal incest. Instead, they assume a kind of studied indifference to the victimizations of their sons.

Mr. Brent, who is separated from his wife, knew their son was being incestuously victimized by her because she told him about it. When asked how he felt about that disclosure, he responded, "It don't surprise me. She's been screwing anybody with pants on." Asked if he thought that this incestuous victimization could harm his son in any way, he replied, "It's not likely." Mr. Brent denied having been an incest victim himself but did state that "some old man in the neighborhood tried to get in my pants when I was seven or eight."

Mr. Underwood, a farmer, works his farm twelve to sixteen hours each day. He knew his wife was victimizing their son but perceived that victimization only as a symptom of her mental illness. He also does not believe that this incest experience can harm his son in any sense of the word. "Boys have got to learn about sex sometimes," he explains. "Better with his mother than with some diseased whore." Mr. Underwood also states that he had never experienced any type of sexual victimization as a child.

The Son

The same role reversal process that occurs with girl incest victims and their mothers occurs with boy incest victims and their fathers. These sons assume a "little father" role in the household. It is difficult to determine whether that role reversal is the product of the same kind of collusion that thrusts a girl into the "little mother" role in cases of paternal incest or if the incestuous mother's dependency needs draw her son into that role. Regardless, Forward and Buck (1978) state that by "stepping into his father's shoes the son symbolically becomes at the same time both the father and his father's rival." (p. 75).

Simon Brent appears to have been drawn into the "little father role" by his mother. Since his own father was absent from the home, he assumed many of his responsibilities, most notably as an advisor and companion to his mother. Since his mother is extremely passive and helpless in her relationships with men, she assumed the same behavior with him. That put a great deal of pressure on him to behave maturely and strongly; and the more mature and strong he became, the more dependent his mother became on him.

Noah Underwood was placed in the "little father" role by his own father who finds it almost impossible to deal with his psychotic wife. Noah's apparent ability to do so put him into the position of assuming many responsibilities for her care which his father had assumed early in their marriage.

When that role reversal takes place, the mother becomes extraordinarily dependent on her son. It does appear that an incestuous mother has strong dependency needs anyway (Forward and Buck, 1978; Justice and Justice, 1979), most likely because of the insecurities she had experienced during her own childhood. Consequently, the bond between her and her son is exceptionally strong.

Simon states, "I felt sorry for my mom. She needs a man, but my dad and her are separated and he doesn't come around here much. When he left she told me I would have to be the man of the house and help her in a lot of different ways because she is just a woman and not very strong." This is a responsibility that Simon did not take lightly, so when she asked him to go to bed with her, he did not hesitate. "She told me a woman needs a man to love her and I love my mother."

Noah recognizes that his mother is emotionally disturbed and he is proud that he can control her psychotic rages and episodes. He believes that it is his job to keep his mother out of a mental hospital and this responsibility weighs heavily on him. When his mother told him that God told her to go to bed with him, he did not hesitate. He believed their sexual relationship would keep her out of an institution.

Son Initiated Incest. In some cases the son is responsible for the initiation of the incest. This did not occur in the small clinical sample, but has been reported in the literature. Meiselman (1978) states that "in the great majority of reported cases in which the son initiates the incest, the son is schizophrenic or severely disturbed in some other way" (p. 300).

The case studies reported in the literature certainly seem to substantiate this conclusion. Brown (1963) reports a case of an adopted son who had seduced his mother on several different occasions during his adolescent years. The young man was a "borderline mental defective" with a predominantly homosexual orientation. He murdered his mother when their incestuous relationship was later discovered. Kubo (1959) reports a case of a brain damaged, violent and hypersexual son who initiated an incestuous relationship with his mother who acquiesced in the hopes that their sexual relationship would keep him from sexually acting out against other people. Medlicott (1967) discovered a case of mother-son incest which was initiated by the son who was in the early stages of paranoid schizophrenia, and who had initiated the incest at the command of voices. Shelton (1975) relates a case of a young man who had suffered a schizophrenic breakdown at age 21 after his father's death. He entered his mother's bedroom one evening and had intercourse with her. Not wanting to exacerbate his mental illness, she did not resist.

Other cases of son initiated incest appear to occur after the son and mother are reunited after a long period of separation. Undoubtedly that period of separation weakens the incest taboo and may sexualize the mother-son bond. Bender and Grugett (1952) report a case of a 6-year-old boy who repeatedly tried to have sex with his mother from whom he had been separated the first four years of his life. Weinberg (1955) recounts a case of a teenaged son who raped his mother when he returned to live with her after having spent several years living with relatives.

The Mother-Son Incest "Affair"

So much has been written about the course of the father-daughter incest "affair" from its initiation through its secrecy phase, to its disclosure or termination. Yet, virtually nothing is known about the course of the mother-son incest "affair."

A review of the literature would suggest that when the son initiates the incest, he frequently does so violently, by an act of rape. This violence may reflect the psychopathology of the son. In the clinical sample in which the two mothers initiated the incest, there was no violence. Mrs. Brent's case typifies "evolved incest" in which years of covert, tentative sexual contacts eventually evolved into overt incest. In Mrs. Underwood's case, her mental illness drew her son into the incest.

What is really remarkable in these two cases from the clinical sample is the lack of secret-keeping techniques used by the mothers to convince their sons to keep the incest secret. Both families were so socially isolated that the chances of outside intervention into the incest were minimal. Because both fathers knew about the incest while it was occurring and had a vested interest in its continuation, there was no pressure from the mothers to keep the incest from them.

> Asked why they did not tell anyone about the incest, Noah responded that to disclose the incest was to disclose in effect his mother's mental illness. Protective feelings for his mother precluded any desire to tell someone about the incest. Simon responded in a similar fashion, stating that the relationship he had with his mother was "special" and "private." He did not want to tell anyone about the incest. When asked if their mothers had pressured them in any way to keep the incest secret, they both responded that they had not.

In both cases, however, the incest was disclosed. Noah's victimization was disclosed by his mother during one of her therapy sessions after she had been institutionalized for the fourth time. Simon's victimization was disclosed to the police by his father who was carrying out a blackmail threat against his estranged wife. The average length of the "affair" for these two sons is 1.6 years.

Nasjleti (1980) suggests that boys are much less likely to disclose the incest than are girls. The culturally endorsed male role in society, a role in which the male is sexually aggressive, physically strong and nonnurturing may be antithetical to his incest experience with his mother. This incongruence between role expectation and behavior may create anxiety and shame as well as a need to keep the incest secret. What short- or long-term effects this repression of feeling is likely to have on the sons has yet to be determined.

EFFECTS OF MATERNAL INCEST ON THE SONS

In 1979 a New Jersey Superior Court ruled that no woman could be prosecuted for "carnally abusing" a boy under the age of 16. The explanation given for this ruling is that "young girls can become pregnant; young boys cannot. Young girls can suffer physical damage from intercourse or attempted intercourse; young boys cannot." The Court went on to note that a young girl who suffers physical injury can also suffer an emotional or psychological trauma that might adversely affect her outlook on sexuality throughout her life; presumably boys are immune from that trauma.

Some researchers have given credence to this ruling by insisting that maternal incest has few, if any, deleterious effects on the sons. Finch (1973), citing no cases or statistics to substantiate his claim, states that the sons "may emerge unharmed" from the incest experience (p. 191). Nobile (1977) states that maternal incest with sons comprises ten percent of all incest victimizations and is "70% positive" (p. 62).

Both Finch's and Nobile's conclusions are suspect since neither cite data to support their opinions. However, Finkelhor (1979) in his retrospective study of the victimization experiences of 796 college and university students concludes after a careful analysis of data that despite the similarities of experiences of male and female victims, "they do not all elicit the same kind of reaction from the children, and this is the key difference. Women provoked much less fear in the child they approached than the men did. The males are more likely to be interested in the experience and they also reported fewer negative feelings about it in retrospect" (p. 79). This conclusion did not separate maternal incest from other types of female-initiated sexual contacts with male children, however, and that may have affected the data, since some negative effects of maternal incest for the sons who are victims have been reported in the literature.

Mental Illness

There is no outstanding psychopathology noted in the two male victims of maternal incest in the clinical sample. Both were just emerging from the incest experiences at the time of this study so no opportunity for a longitudinal assessment existed. Both boys appeared quite withdrawn and were certainly reluctant to talk about their experiences and both were very protective of their mothers. The recency of their experiences and the confusion that was created when law enforcement officials were called in may have contributed more to that withdrawal.

There are no data which suggest a causal or even correlative relationship between maternal incest and mental illness. Some cases of psychopathology in adult males who have been victims of maternal incest have been reported but Meiselman (1978) concludes that the incest is not a causal factor in psychosis. In fact, she believes that the sons' psychosis "causes" the incest, not vice versa.

There may be a couple of reasons why this lack of psychological disturbance is noted. First, mothers who incestuously victimize their sons may not so seriously distort reality and morality and may be less inclined to use physical violence and threats to buy their sons' silence. If that is consistently true in cases of mother-son incest, then the son may not have to use pathological coping mechanisms with which to deal with the incest. Second, researchers and practitioners simply may not have taken the victimization of sons as seriously as they have taken the victimization of daughters and therefore they may be less inclined to attribute emotional or adjustment problems of the sons to the incest.

Sexual Problems

Sexual problems have been documented for male incest victims as adults. Masters and Johnson (1970) report three cases of adult males with histories of maternal incest who received therapy for primary impotence. Meiselman (1978) and Justice and Justice (1979) also suggest that sexual problems may occur for these sons. Meiselman relates two cases of male victims as adults who had a "warped kind of heterosexual expression that they themselves attributed in part to the incestuous relationship" (p. 311).

Nasjleti (1980) suggests that those sexual problems for sons who had been victims of maternal incest may be aggressive in nature. She states that maternal incest is found in the childhoods of many rapists, incestuous fathers, homosexuals and child molesters. The data she uses to support this conclusion are insufficient to utilize in the creation of theories designed to assess the impact of maternal incest on the sons' sexual behavior as adults, but her inference is well taken. Any child who is exposed to early, coercive forms of sexual experiences runs a greater risk of disturbances in adult sexual behavior and attitudes.

It is tempting to use the existing data on the effects of maternal incest on sons to draw the conclusion that this type of incest has few if any negative effects. However, it must be continually kept in mind that comprehensive longitudinal studies of male incest victims have yet to be performed. Until they are completed, all existing data must be considered tentative and speculative

PATERNAL INCEST

Father-son incest is also a tragically understudied type of sexual victimization. The literature boasts a large number of cases studied but virtually no theory construction and little consideration of the effects of this type of incest on the victims.

There are four fathers who have incestuously victimized their sons in the clinical sample, as well as six victims of paternal incest. These sons range in age from seven to 25; obviously the older sons can provide a longitudinal perspective on the victimization.

The Incestuous Father

All four incestuous fathers in the clinical sample are the natural fathers of the sons they had victimized. Each father had victimized only his son; in other words, cases of multiple incest are not part of this segment of the study.

Homosexuality. "Incest" is a horrible word, filled with all kinds of connotations that make people shudder; but "homosexual incest" carries a double stigma that makes this behavior even more difficult for most people to understand. Yet the alleged homosexuality of the incestuous father in cases of father-son incest is still a debatable issue despite the nature of the incest, itself.

Dixon *et al.* (1978) studied six cases of father-son incest and determined that none of the incestuous fathers had a history of homosexual involvement as an adult. Awad (1976) argues that many of these incestuous fathers struggle with latent homosexuality, but may never be inclined to act on these impulses. Meiselman (1978) substantiates that observation by stating that these fathers have "strong homosexual desires since early childhood but [have] married and presented a heterosexual facade to the community" (p. 318).

This "heterosexual facade" is certainly noted for the four fathers in the clinical sample. Each is married to his first wife and each has children. When asked to comment on their consensual homosexual history, two of the fathers stated that they had "some" homosexual contacts before their marriage, but not during it; one stated he had "some" homosexual contacts during his marriage; and the remaining father stated he had never had a homosexual contact at any time in his life. None of the four fathers would accept the identity of homosexual; curiously, none of them perceived his incestuous victimization of his son as homosexual in nature.

> "It's different when the kid's your son," Mr. Logan explains. "I mean to say if I molested a boy in the neighborhood or a boy that's a stranger, then I'd be a homosexual. But that kid's my flesh and blood, so it's different."
> "I'm sure outsiders would call it homosexual," offers Mr. Harris, "but I don't. What I did with my son was an expression of love. It may not have been the best expression, that's true, but it is love. And when that occurs between a father and a son, one could hardly correctly call that homosexual."

Perhaps one of the reasons why these fathers did not see this incest victimization as homosexual in nature is because of the stereotyped perceptions they all have of homosexuality. Granted, these perceptions may be defensive in nature, thereby protecting the fathers from this label. However, all four fathers see homosexuals as weak-wristed, lisping, effeminate individuals, possessing an unusual amount of libidinous energy which is directed against any male, young or old, indiscriminately. Because their behavior does not approximate this stereotype, in their perceptions, they cannot be homosexuals and their incestuous victimizations of their sons cannot be homosexual in nature.

All four fathers in the clinical sample had experienced sexual victimization themselves as children. Each was reluctant to admit the victimization and even more reluctant to discuss the details. The types of victimizations and the ages at first occurrence are presented in Table 9.

TABLE 9. CHILDHOOD SEXUAL VICTIMIZATION EXPERIENCES
OF FOUR INCESTUOUS FATHERS

Father	Type of Victimization	Age at first Occurrence
Adams	Paternal incest	10
Harris	Molestation by adult male acquaintance	9
Carpenter	Molestation by adult male acquaintance	12
Logan	Sibling incest	7

Once again, it becomes clear that the sexual victimization of children is an intergenerationally transmitted phenomenon. When each incestuous father was interviewed he was asked if, in his opinion, his early victimization experience is in any way a causal factor in his incestuous victimization of his son. Two of the fathers immediately answered yes; the remaining two fathers were clearly intrigued by the suggestion but had never given it serious thought before the question was posed.

Mental Illness. Dixon *et al.* (1978) found a history of sociopathic character-disordered behavior in several of the fathers they studied. This disorder is characterized by a lack of guilt, poor impulse control and emotional shallowness. Meiselman (1978), however, contends that most fathers who incestuously victimize their sons do not have a history of any psychological disturbance prior to the incest relationship.

That latter finding is supported by the cases in the clinical sample. One father is clearly obsessive-compulsive in his personality structure and one is slightly sociopathic. The remaining two demonstrate no noticeable psychopathology.

Alcoholism. Several case studies of incestuous fathers note a history of alcoholism (Langsley *et al.*, 1968; Awad, 1976; Dixon *et al.*, 1978). While it is certainly logical that alcohol can weaken whatever ego controls the father has which would deter him from incest, no alcoholics were found in the clinical sample.

The Nonparticipating Mother

As in any type of incestuous family, the nonparticipating parent may play a pivotal role, however unconsciously, in the initiation and the continuation of the incest. The nonparticipating mothers in families characterized by father-son incest rarely have been examined in the literature. Only two of the wives were available for this study and will be used to illustrate the tentative findings from the literature.

Denial. On the basis of the observations of the wives in the clinical sample, the denial process which is so characteristic of mothers whose daughters are victimized is considerably less for those mothers whose sons had been victimized. Both knew about the victimizations of their sons; neither intervened.

Their denial was more subtle than the denial examined in the cases of the other nonparticipating mothers, and focused on the alleged homosexuality of the incest, not on the incest, itself.

> "I'm still not sure this was incest," states Mrs. Logan. "It was done for very good reasons, out of love, not hate or sickness. That's not like real incest, is it?"

> Mrs. Carpenter believes that the incestuous victimization of her son was not homosexual in nature. "I don't care what people say, it can't be homosexual. Not when it's between a father and son. They love each other. What can it hurt?"

Despite their rather indifferent attitudes about the victimizations of their sons, both women had a vested interest in the continuation of the incest. Mrs. Carpenter had experienced marriage problems for many years and was relieved to have some of the sexual pressure taken from her when her husband turned his attention to their son. Mrs. Logan had long recognized her husband's homosexual tendencies and was relieved that he was acting out sexually with their son rather than in public where his behavior could bring shame to the whole family.

Beyond these few similarities that can be gleaned from scattered cases

reported in the literature, no other remarkable features of the nonparticipating mothers can be ascertained. It is tempting to side with Langsley *et al.*
(1968), who stated: "The stimulus for the incest is not found in the family as
much as it is in the father's own background" (p. 226). However, many more
comprehensive studies of father-son incest will have to be undertaken before
that conclusion can be substantiated.

The Father-Son Incest "Affair"

The average length of the incest "affair" for the six victimized sons in
the clinical sample is eight months. This is considerably less than the 2.7 year
average calculated for the daughters who had been victimized by their
fathers. At least a partial explanation why that is so may be found in the
nature of the father-son incest "affair."

Initiation. In all of the cases in the clinical sample, the incest "affair"
was initiated by the fathers. In no case did that initiation occur as an act of
violence; in fact violence and threats are remarkably absent in all of the cases
in the clinical sample. Instead, the incest in each case appeared to have
evolved slowly and tentatively over time.

> "We always touched and hugged a lot," explains Hal who was incestuously
> victimized by his father. "When I was 8 he and I went skinny-dipping in the
> pond. We started horsing around, diving under and pulling each other by
> the legs, stuff like that. He touched my penis when we were doing that, so I
> touched his. We did that for awhile, and when we laid on the grass after
> swimming, he put his mouth on my penis."

> "My dad was laying on his bed naked. I think he just took a shower," ex-
> plains Andy. "He asked me to come here, so I did. He says he'll show me
> something that feels good. He started playing with my cock and told me to
> play with his. We'd do that a couple of times each week."

The sons all seemed to react with curiosity to that initiation. Few admit to having been frightened. One reason for that may be that if the clinical
sample is a true representation of other cases of father-son incest, there is considerably less violence in these families than what has been documented for
other incestuous families in which the daughters have been victimized.
Another reason may be that because of the culturally sanctioned male role in
our society, it is harder for males to admit feeling frightened and helpless in
sexual situations.

Secrecy Phase. Because the father-son incest "affair" is typically short
in duration, secret-keeping techniques are difficult to determine. Again,
threats and coercion are rare in the clinical sample, at least, and it does not
appear that reality and morality are grossly distorted for the son. Rather, the
fathers in the clinical sample used their special father-son bond as a reason to
keep the incest secret.

> Sean, now 15, who had been victimized by his father three years earlier ex-
> plains how his father convinced him to keep the incest secret. "I really love
> my pop, and I still love to spend time with him. When we'd have sex, he'd
> say, 'This is special between us son. Don't tell no one.' I felt kind of impor-
> tant."

Disclosure. In most cases, the father-son incest "affair" terminates without outside intervention. Usually that termination occurs when the son refuses to participate further. Because there appears to be less dehumanization and less of an attitude that a son is a possession of the father than occurs in father-daughter incest, the wishes of the son are respected. In no case in the clinical sample did a father continue with the incest after his son verbally or physically resisted.

The son may have a vested interest in not disclosing the incest to anyone. He may have fears that other people will call him a homosexual or a "sissy" because he could not or would not protect himself from that victimization. Once again, the culturally endorsed male sexual role may work to silence the son who has been sexually victimized by his father, while it encourages him to cope with the victimization with acting-out behavior.

EFFECTS OF PATERNAL INCEST ON THE SONS

Despite the sketchy nature of the data accumulated on the nature and process of the father-son incest "affair," a great deal of data have been accumulated on the effects of paternal incest on the sons. The data overwhelmingly support Finkelhor's (1979) conclusion that incestuous "experiences with [victimizing] males [are] consistently more negative than experiences with females, whatever the sex of the child" (p. 103).

Self-Destructive Acting Out

The "compulsive masochistic reaction" documented for female victims of incest by Bigras *et al.* (1966) appears to occur with male victims as well. Dixon *et al.* (1978) report a case of a 5-year-old boy who was referred for therapy because of aggressiveness, hyperactivity, encopresis and poor peer relations. He had been incestuously victimized by his father for the year preceding the referral. They also report a case of an 11-year-old boy who was victimized by his stepfather. The boy was very accident prone: he had two near drownings, several serious falls, and was hit by a car during that two year period of victimization.

In the younger sons in the clinical sample, self-destructive acting out is also observed and reported in a retrospective sense by the older sons as well. These acts include running away, truancy and drug use, yet, if the value judgment is permitted, the extent and severity of these behaviors are less for the boy victims than for the girl victims.

Rhinehart (1961) also reports a case of an 18-year-old victim of paternal incest who was extremely suicidal. Of the six victimized sons in the clinical sample, one had attempted suicide and another reported suicidal thoughts.

Homicidal Ideation

Perhaps it is more culturally acceptable for boys to turn their angry and aggressive feelings outward while girls are expected to turn theirs inward.

This could account for the few reports of suicide attempts and suicide thoughts for boy victims of paternal incest. Dixon *et al.* (1978) report a case of homicidal ideation in a male incest victim. No son in the clinical sample demonstrated such thoughts however.

Mental Illness

Raybin (1969) reports a case of a prominent professor of theatre, himself a victim of paternal incest, who had initiated incest with his son. As a result of that incest relationship, the son suffered a psychotic episode and had to be institutionalized. Langsley *et al.* (1968) also document a case of a 20-year-old son who had been victimized by his father. The son had a phobia about homosexuality and suffered a psychotic episode after taking LSD. Medlicott (1967) studied three cases of father-son incest. Two of the sons were chronically neurotic as adults and the other had a psychotic episode during which he killed himself.

These cases would suggest that there is a strong relationship between incest and the son's later mental illness, but in the absence of comprehensive studies of large samples of sons that conclusion may be premature. None of the sons in the clinical sample is psychotic; in fact, outstanding psychopathology is not noted for any of them. Of course, only two sons in the clinical sample are adults so there is not enough of a longitudinal perspective to make any generalizations.

Sexual Problems

All six of the sons in the clinical sample have fears, some only occasional in frequency, that they are or will become homosexuals. None has had homosexual contacts outside of the father-son incest except for some exploratory sex play with peers that is certainly not abnormal for young boys.

> Marty, now 23, had been incestuously victimized by his father over ten years ago. "I play football with some guys every Sunday. Whenever anybody makes a good play, the guys pat them on the rear end. I never do. I'm scared I might get to like it, you know, and become a fag. What my old man did to me left me real scared about that."

Even the younger sons, many of them visualizing only the most stereotypical picture of a homosexual, have some fears that they may be or may become homosexual. Often these fears developed after the incest had been terminated or disclosed, when adults put the victimization into perspective.

Justice and Justice (1979) estimate that a large percentage of boy prostitutes in their hometown of Houston had been victims of paternal incest. Allen (1980) in his study of young male prostitutes may substantiate that perception. He found that 66% of the male prostitutes had their first sexual experience at the average age of 13.5 years with an older male (p. 411). Presumably some of those males are the fathers or stepfathers of the boys, but Allen does not separate out that statistic.

CHAPTER 7: SIBLING INCEST

When Victoria Pittorino learned she had been adopted, she yearned to discover her roots and make contact with her natural family. Told by her adoptive parents that she had a younger brother who also had been adopted, she spent four years searching for him by tediously examining adoption and birth records. In Lawrence, Massachusetts, the place of her birth, a clerk finally revealed the names of her natural mother and her brother, ending her search.

In April of 1978, Victoria met her brother, David Goddu. Raised as an only child in Holyoke, Massachusetts, David was a brooding, troubled young man who was a high school dropout and who had been shot by the police the previous year during a high speed chase with a stolen car. David, too, knew he had been adopted as an infant and although he seemed not to have been obsessed with contacting his natural family, he was at least curious about his sister.

What began as curiosity developed rapidly over the next several days into love — not sibling love, but romantic love. "We saw each other as a boy and a girl," explained Victoria. When David asked her to marry him several weeks after their first meeting, she quickly consented. "We discussed the morality of the marriage," Victoria commented, "but we could see nothing wrong." They were married within days of David's proposal.

Although Victoria and David could see nothing wrong with their marriage, their enthusiasm was hardly shared by others. In a flurry of legal activity, both sets of adoptive parents and the natural mother of the young couple sought to terminate the marriage. Invoking a Massachusetts law dating back to 1695, they signed a complaint alleging incest, a conviction upon which could bring a maximum sentence of 20 years in prison, although attorneys insisted that the couple would not be imprisoned if they agreed to undergo psychiatric counseling. Victoria and David considered the offer while they were vacationing in Florida, guests of the *National Enquirer*, who had purchased the exclusive right to their story.

The Pittorino-Goddu story is a modern version of the historically frequent phenomenon of sibling incest, the only difference being that ancient civilizations tolerated and, at times, even encouraged it. Sibling incest was frequent, for example, in royal families during the Pharaonic and Ptolemic periods in ancient Egypt. Brother-sister marriages were valued as a means of preserving the family wealth and the royal line. Such privileges were later ex-

79

tended to the wealthy so that property and estates could be protected by the family (Middleton, 1962).

Although the advent of Christianity brought moral prohibitions against sibling sexual relationships and marriages, being religious hardly prevented those things from occurring. Pope John XII, deposed in 963, was accused of having maintained an incestuous relationship with both his sister and his mother, and Pope John XIII was also relieved of his papal duties when his incestuous relationship with his sister was disclosed (Justice and Justice, 1979).

As incest became increasingly more proscribed, social support for that behavior diminished. Yet cases of sibling incest have not been difficult to find. The English poet William Wordsworth had a long-term incestuous affair with his sister, and Lord Byron had been sexually involved with his half-sister (*Newsweek*, July 2, 1979). The English novelist and critic Virginia Woolf had been molested at age 6 by her 19-year-old half-brother, George Duckworth, who continued to make secretive sexual advances until the writer was well into her teens (Brownmiller, 1975).

Sibling incest, made more illegal and morally reprehensible as time passed, infiltrated the popular culture. In music, the three operas of composer Richard Wagner have become an enduring testimony to the passion and tragedy of incest. In *Die Walküre*, the story is told of a twin brother and sister whose love produces a child who becomes a warrior hero. In *Sigfried*, the heroic offspring of this incestuous relationship rescues his goddess aunt and falls in love with her. In the final opera of the trilogy, *Die Götterdämmerung*, Siegfried forsakes his wife/aunt, who then provides conspiratorial assistance to his enemies who later take his life (Justice and Justice, 1979).

Humor becomes yet another way through which this forbidden behavior permeates the popular culture. Weeks (1976) states that in Virginia, a definition of a virgin is a "fourteen year old girl who does not have a brother" (p. 848). Masters (1963) gives the Ozark definition of a virgin as a "five year old girl who can outrun her pappy and her brothers" (p. 47). He also quoted an old Indian saying: "For a girl to still be a virgin at ten years old, she must have neither brothers, nor cousins, nor father" (p. 47).

EXTENT OF SIBLING INCEST

Despite the cultural and biological taboos against sibling incest, it does occur with some frequency in contemporary society. In fact, it actually may occur more often than any other type of incest. Both Lindzey (1967) and Lester (1972) estimate that sibling incest is five times more common than paternal incest. These estimates are speculative, but the data accumulated by Finkelhor (1980) in his retrospective study of 796 college undergraduates may support any prediction of increased occurrence. Finkelhor surveyed these young men and women as to their childhood sexual experiences, defining that term as "an invitation to do something sexual; the showing of sex organs; attempted or simulated intercourse; or sexual intercourse" (p. 173).

Finkelhor discovered that 13% of his sample had had sexual experiences as children with their siblings (p. 174). This figure, according to Finkelhor, is most certainly an underestimate since some of the respondents had no doubt concealed this activity, whether out of embarrassment or shame, while others had more than likely forgotten the experience. Also, many of these experiences occurred before the children were sophisticated enough to label these experiences as "sexual" in nature. Even if Finkelhor's figure were conservative, it would indicate more sibling incest than paternal incest within his sample.

Only five cases of sibling incest were documented in the clinical sample of 80 incest victims. This low figure may be due more to the tendency to underreport this type of incest than to its actual occurrence.

FAMILY ROLES IN SIBLING INCEST

As in all cases of incest, the familial context of sibling incest must be carefully examined.

The Parents

The fathers in families characterized by sibling incest typically fail to serve as "restraining agents" in that they do not exercise their intrafamilial power in preventing incest (Weinberg, 1955). They may also be absent from the home at the time that the incest is initiated or perhaps are incapacitated by physical or mental illness. Those fathers who are present in the home typically have weak personalities and lack the assertiveness necessary to prevent the incest. Meiselman (1978) found that 50% of the fathers in her psychotherapy sample were dead or weakened by alcoholism or psychosis (p. 264), attesting to the importance of the father as a restraining agent.

In the clinical sample, one of the five fathers was dead; one separated from his family; and one clearly incapacitated by mental illness. The remaining two fathers, although physically present in the home, are best characterized as emotionally absent, as the following case illustrates:

> Terry and Carol are the two youngest siblings in a family of nine children. Their mother is a quiet, religious woman who has devoted her entire life to what she refers to as the "wifely duties" of bearing and raising children. Their father is a stolid man who believes that children "should be seen and not heard." Terry and Carol remember never having played or even seriously conversed with their father. They also both insist that he has never hugged or kissed them. Consequently, they literally regard him as a "non-being" and entertain only the most rudimentary feelings of affection for him.

In some cases of sibling incest, the mother is also perceived as a nonbeing—a woman so passive and ineffectual that she lacks the assertiveness necessary to supervise her children. In other cases, she may be physically absent from the home, or may be so overwhelmed with responsibilities that she does not have the time nor the energy to adequately supervise her children. That issue of the lack of supervision must not be taken too lightly since it is a common precursor of sibling incest.

Yet an even more common characteristic of the mothers in cases of sibling incest is their rigid, puritanical attitudes toward sex. Because of these attitudes, the sexual education of the children within the home is not likely to have occurred. Ian McEwan, (1978), in his novel, *The Cement Garden*, a tale of sibling incest and other family secrets, describes the mother's effort at "sex education" when she catches her teenage son masturbating (p. 30):

> You can't get up in the mornings, you're tired all day, you're moody, you don't wash yourself or change your clothes, you're rude to your sisters and to me....Every time you do that, it takes two pints of blood to replace it!

Such puritanical and uncompromising attitudes about sex on the parts of these mothers may actually have a paradoxic effect in that they may stimulate the children's curiosity about this strongly forbidden behavior. That fact, coupled with the absence of parental supervision, may lead to experimental sexual behavior on the parts of the children.

The Brothers

When the father is absent from the home or is incapacitated for some reason, the boy in the family is frequently cast into the "little father" role (Kubo, 1959). Given household responsibilities far beyond his age, he attempts to carry them out with the limited talent he has. However, his lack of ability in this area forces him to rely on such age-specific skills as arguing, demanding and exercising power. It is little wonder, then, that Meiselman (1978) concludes that "to the extent that the brothers were described at all, the sisters pictured them as 'bullies' who teased them and liked to demonstrate their superior strength" (p. 295).

In this regard, it is interesting to note that two of the brothers in the clinical sample used the incest as "punishment" for their sisters' misbehaviors. Given responsibilities for correcting their siblings' misbehaviors because their parents were absent or incapacitated, these two boys used sex in the most coercive sense, as a tool of discipline. They also had plenty of opportunities to do so, since the lack of parental supervision within their home environments created unruly, undisciplined siblings.

> In explaining his motivation for his incestuous relationship with his sister, Jim stated that sex was the only thing "that could really hurt her." Jim had fatherly duties in the household and tried to discipline his nine year old sister with all of the techniques a socially deprived fifteen year old has available to him. When yelling, spanking and depriving her of privileges did not work, he threatened to rape her, and carried out that threat on several occasions in response to her misbehavior.

In all five cases, the brother, who was older in each case, initiated the incest. This is a finding supported by both Meiselman (1978) and Finkelhor (1980). However, the incest itself may be consummated through mutual consent which suggests that the sisters may not always be opposed to the behavior.

In an unusual finding in two cases in the clinical sample, the brothers had also molested some other nonfamily child, in both cases, neighbor girls close in age to their sisters. This is a rather high figure in an admittedly small sample, but one that should be treated cautiously. Both boys molested these girls in an unusually violent manner, given the young ages of the boys, suggesting perhaps displaced aggression with an origin in the family environment. Both boys stated that the molested girls "reminded" them, in behavior or in looks, of their sisters, an observation which may further support the displaced aggression hypothesis. In one case the molestation was relatively spontaneous in nature and appeared not to have reflected any prior planning. In the second case, that of 15-year-old Jim who already has been observed as a young man who used sexual assault as a tool of discipline, the molestation of the neighbor girl occurred when Jim was babysitting her and also occurred in response to her misbehavior that evening, a situation which exactly parallels the motivation for the sexual assaults of his sister.

The Sisters

Weinberg (1955) found that a majority of the sisters had lower than average intelligence, a finding not supported by the clinical sample in which only one sister was found to be in the dull normal range of intelligence. The sisters in the clinical sample presented no remarkable similarities, except that they were all younger than their brothers. All did evidence behavioral problems to some extent, but it is unclear as to whether these problems were pre- or postincest in origin.

A curious finding in Meiselman's (1978) psychotherapy sample was that four out of the eight sibling incest victims had been victims of rape by strangers or acquaintances after the initial incest had occurred. Meiselman hypothesized that "some of the sisters were perceived as 'bad girls' deserving to be raped after they began to have casual sex relations. Another causal link was their rebelliousness and willingness to take risks such as hitchhiking and leaving bars with strangers" (p. 283).

The clinical sample does not lend itself to this analysis since Meiselman deals with adults looking back on their sibling incest experiences, therefore affording her a longitudinal perspective, while the clinical sample is of youngsters just emerging from their incest experiences. It is interesting to note, however, that two of the five young girls in the clinical sample had been sexually molested, one by a stranger and the other by a neighbor, subsequent to their first incest experiences with their brothers. Rather than assuming that rebelliousness and risk taking are causal links in this phenomenon, it would no doubt be more appropriate to surmise that these young girls saw themselves, and were seen by others, as "spoiled goods" and were behaving and were treated in return, in a fashion commensurate with that identity. Since both of these young girls come from homes in which the mother is a particularly weak figure, it can also be assumed that these girls simply lacked the assertiveness to say "no" to an adult with sexual intentions, since that self-protective skill was never modeled nor taught by their mothers (Finkelhor, 1979; Dietz and Craft, 1980).

THE SIBLING INCEST "AFFAIR"

Like most incestuous relationships, the sibling incest "affair" runs a fairly well defined course, although the sexual contact itself may be intermittent in nature (Weinberg, 1955). The course of the sibling incest "affair" in Finkelhor's (1980) sample was over a year for 29% of the students surveyed. In fact, in his sample two people told about sibling incest experiences which lasted as long as ten years. Finkelhor also found that in 33% of the cases, the sibling sexual experience occurred only once (p. 177).

In the small clinical sample, the average duration of the incestuous contact was ten months. In only one case out of the five did the contact occur only once.

Initiation

The initiation of sibling incest, usually the responsibility of the brother, occurs in a variety of fashions.

Play. Meiselman (1978) states that a great deal of sibling incest begins with mutual interest and participation and may evolve slowly from sibling play activities. This contention was supported by Fox (1962) who believed that mutual stimulation during play activities could lead to heightened sexual stimulation which, in turn, could evolve into incest. McEwan (1978) describes one type of sibling play between a brother and two sisters in his novel (p. 6):

> Sue lay on the bed giggling with her knuckles in her mouth as Julie pushed a chair against the door. Together we rapidly stripped Sue of her clothes.... The game was that Julie and I were scientists examining a specimen from outer space. We spoke in clipped Germanic voices as we faced each other across the naked body.

In two of the five cases from the clinical sample, the sibling incest clearly evolved from play activities. In one case, the brother and sister, 12 and 11 respectively, became sexually stimulated while wrestling playfully on the bed. This activity eventually evolved into fondling and kissing. In the other case, the brother, aged 15, initiated a highly ritualized "game" with his 10-year-old sister. This "game" included placing objects such as pencils and hairpins into her vagina and rectum as part of "medical experiments" he performed on her in his role as a "famous doctor."

Finkelhor (1980) cautions, however, that sibling sex should not be regarded solely as sex play. He makes that distinction primarily on the observation that the brothers and sisters are developmentally too advanced to engage in play activities. In his sample, 73% of the sibling sex experiences occurred when at least one of the partners was older than 8 years, and 35% occurred when one was older than 12 years (p. 175).

Imitation. On some occasions, sibling incest may be an imitation of sexual behavior viewed by the children within the home environment. This apparently is most likely to occur within one of two specific familial environments. The first is a home characterized by a "loose sex culture" in which obscenities, nudity, overt sexual behavior and perhaps pornography are pervasive. Children within such an environment may become prematurely sexually stimulated at which point, in the absence of firm parental supervision, the stimulation can lead to sexual imitation (Marcuse, 1923; Weinberg, 1955; de Young, 1981b).

The second familial environment is one in which some other type of incest, usually paternal, has preceded the sibling incest (Eist and Mandel, 1968; Magal and Winnick, 1968). In two of the five cases in the clinical sample paternal incest had preceded sibling incest, suggesting again that imitation may have taken place, since both brothers knew about the sexual relationship between their fathers and their sisters. However, this figure also suggests that the sister, because of her incestuous victimization by her father, has taken on a new identity in the eyes of her brother. Now seeing her as "spoiled goods" the brother may see her as unworthy of his care and protection (Summit and Kryso, 1978).

Exploitation. Occasionally, sibling incest may be initiated in a coercive, exploitative fashion. Meiselman (1978) finds that many brothers initiate the incest through threats and bribes. Finkelhor (1980) states as a reminder that violence among siblings, although often overlooked or even ignored, is the most common form of family violence, reported in 82% of all families in a given year (p. 177). Therefore, extrapolation from that figure would suggest that some degree of coercion is likely to be present in many cases of sibling incest. Although his survey does not distinguish physical force from the threat of physical force, Finkelhor found that force entered into 25% of all of his cases of sibling incest (p. 177).

Sibling incest experiences can also be exploitative when there is a significantly large age difference between participants, even when no physical force is used. Older siblings can exploit younger siblings by misusing their authority and maturity, by manipulating punishments and rewards and by reinterpreting morality.

Secrecy

Sibling incest is likely to be an intermittent phenomenon over any given period of time, but the siblings in most cases pressure each other to keep the activity secret. Occasionally, the pressure to keep the secret is facilitated by threats and even physical violence. More often, however, the pressure is through mutual collusion between the siblings, as the case of Terry and Carol illustrates:

> Terry states that his mother told them that "sex is dirty and that we would go to Hell if we ever had sex with anyone before we got married." Terry assumes that his father feels the same way about sex because he "never hugs or kisses my mother." When Terry and Carol began engaging in mutual fondling and masturbation, they would always end the encounter by reminding each other to not tell anyone what they were doing because if other people would find out "we would burn in Hell forever."

Disclosure

It is certainly possible that a great deal of sibling incest, in fact perhaps most of it, is never disclosed to anyone or is disclosed only after many years. Finkelhor's (1980) study discovered that only 12% of his sample had ever told anyone about their sibling sexual experiences (p. 180).

If the incest is disclosed, the disclosure process itself is likely to be significantly less traumatic for both children than is the disclosure of paternal incest, for example (Meiselman, 1978). In three of the five sibling incest cases in the clinical sample, the sisters disclosed the incest. All three betrayed the secret in an attempt to get back at their brothers for a whole host of real and imagined wrongs. However, none of these three girls revealed the incest to her parents, an unfortunate testimony to the alienated parent-child relationship likely to be a feature of these families. In the other two cases, the sibling incest was discovered by an adult — in one case a neighbor and in the other a baby-sitter.

If the sibling incest is disclosed or revealed, most people have a tendency to dismiss it as "play" or "mischief" by the children and not to take it very seriously. Weinberg (1955) found that 72% of the people he surveyed viewed sibling incest as considerably less serious than paternal incest. While it is certainly true that sibling incest, for the most part, tends to be less serious in its impact than paternal incest, the mindset which dismisses it as harmless may represent a premature conclusion.

TYPES OF SIBLING INCEST BEHAVIOR

Sibling incest behavior appears to run the gamut in seriousness and its nature is dependent upon the age of the participants, as this breakdown of Finkelhor's (1980) sample demonstrates (p. 175).

TABLE 10. AGE AT THE TIME
OF SIBLING SEX EXPERIENCE

Age	Number of Persons
3	1
4	5
5	17
6	17
7	23
8	25
9	18
10	23
11	22
12	22
13	11
14	10
15	8
16	10
17	6
18	2
19 +	6

Age

Finkelhor (1980) found that 40% of his sample of sibling incest participants were under 8 years old when the incest occurred. The age breakdown of the sample is of some interest because it demonstrates not only the wide age range of the participants, but also the fact that the majority of those experiences occurred when the participants were between the ages of 8 and 11, or during the so-called "latency stage" when sexual interest is supposed to be minimal, according to Freud. The average age of Finkelhor's sample was 10.2 years; the average age of the clinical sample was 10.9 years. Finkelhor (p. 175) broke down the participants' ages as shown in Table 10.

Types of Sibling Incest Behavior

Finkelhor (1980:176) found that incest activities with siblings are largely age-specific activities as the breakdown in Table 11 suggests.

TABLE 11. TYPE OF SIBLING SEXUAL ACTIVITY
BY AGE OF RESPONDENT AT TIME OF ACTIVITY

Type of Activity	Age 0–8 (N = 45)	9–12 (N = 50)	13 + (N = 17)
Genital Exhibition	40%	24%	5%
Fondling and Touching of Genitals	53	60	64
Intercourse and Attempted Intercourse	5	15	18
Other	—	2	13

Activities tend to be age-specific. Younger children engage more often in genital exhibition, while adolescents are more likely to attempt or complete intercourse. Although touching and fondling occur frequently in all age groups, children may be more motivated by curiosity and experimentation with the forbidden, while adolescents may be more motivated by achieving sexual satisfaction.

EFFECTS OF SIBLING INCEST

Despite the fact that people tend to view sibling incest as less serious than other types of incest, some short- and long-term effects of sibling incest on the participants have been documented.

Short-Term Effects

During the course of the sibling incest "affair" and immediately after, some effects of the incest have been examined.

Pleasure. Quite a few of the sibling incest participants report that the sexual experience is pleasurable. This assessment reflects the mutuality of most of these types of sexual encounters. In fact, Meiselman (1978) concludes that there "seems to be a close relationship between the experience of incest pleasure and the voluntary participation of the sister" (p. 271).

Finkelhor (1980) reports that 30% of his sample described the sibling incest experience as "positive" and a full 40% felt so ambivalently about it that they could not describe the experience as positive or negative (p. 178). In the small clinical sample, two of the youngsters described the experience as positive, and one described it as neither positive nor negative.

The pleasurable aspect of sibling incest may be, however, a double-edged sword. On the one hand, it decreases the negative and at times traumatic impact on the youngster that is so often reported with other types of incest; on the other hand, it has the potential of increasing the guilt and shame of the participants who experienced pleasure in an act often condemned.

Negative Impression. Finkelhor (1980) found that 30% of his sample had a negative impression of the sibling sexual experience (p. 178). However, that reaction becomes even more vocal when those youngsters who had experienced coercion, exploitation or force are isolated from the larger sample. When that special population is taken into consideration, the reporting of negative impressions increases four times.

Finkelhor also found that the greater the age difference between the participants, the greater the negative impact the sibling incest had on the younger participants. This reflects his earlier assumption that sibling incest can be exploitative even if force is not used because of the authority, maturity and sophistication of the older participant.

Two youngsters in the clinical sample evaluated the experience as negative. Both of these youngsters had been treated aggressively by their brothers as well and that, coupled with the fact that they both came from particularly disorganized families, may have left them feeling vulnerable and overwhelmed.

Another negative short-term effect of sibling incest is an increase in the parent-child alienation when the incest is disclosed or revealed. All of the parents in the clinical sample acted extremely negatively toward the children when the incest was disclosed. One frequently heard reaction was "I'll never trust those kids again!" While the parent may be forgiven an angry reaction to the incest, no parent in the sample was willing to admit to any unconsciously or consciously collusive behaviors or attitudes on their parts which could have contributed to the incest.

In a flurry of activity and rationalizations to displace blame and excuse the behavior, strains in the sibling relationships are observed as well. Since the siblings in the clinical sample are just emerging from the incest relationship at the time the data was collected, not enough time has passed to observe when these rifts in the relationships will be mended.

Long-Term Effects

Few longitudinal studies have been done on sibling incest participants, and although it is admittedly difficult to prove a cause-and-effect relationship between the incest and any other adult behavior, some adult behaviors are at the very least correlated with early sexual experiences with siblings.

Promiscuity. Several researchers have indicated that sibling incest is highly correlated with promiscuity in adult women (Sloane and Karpinsky, 1942; Kubo, 1959; Spainer, 1973). In fact, Meiselman (1978) reported that a full 71% of her sample of adult women who had had sibling sexual experiences had gone through periods of sexual promiscuity (p. 281), suggesting that this early sexual behavior coupled with the poor family dynamics may have set a pattern for later adult sexual experiences.

Aversion to Sex. Other sexual problem behavior has also been reported as a long-range consequence of sibling incest. Aversion to sex has been reported in the sisters who had engaged in sibling incest as children (Greenland, 1958; Magal and Winnick, 1968).

Meiselman (1978) hypothesizes that this may be due to the masochism commonly reported in these women. She discovered that 71% of her sample could be described as masochistic (p. 281). She explains, however, that the incest may be only one factor in the creation of masochism, especially given the frequency of abusive, religiously conservative, poorly supervised home environments of sibling incest participants.

Increased Sexual Self-Esteem. In contrast to the data on sexual problems in adult women who had histories of sibling sexual experiences, Finkelhor (1980) discovered that young women coming out of that experience tend to have a higher sense of sexual self-esteem. He states that a "crucial developmental task in adolescence and early adulthood is learning to combine friendship and sex" (p. 187), so sibling incest may give these women a head start in completing that task.

Finkelhor does not suggest that this increase in sexual self-esteem will be found in young men as well. Since males tend to be initiators of sexual activity, in those cases in which sibling incest is a symptom of sexual maladjustment and conflict, this pathology is more likely to reside in the male and is consequently more likely to result in a decreased sexual self-esteem as an adult.

Relationship Problems. Meiselman (1978) found that relationships with the parents are not likely to be strained when the participants of sibling incest become adults. This holds true for the relationship between the brother and the sister as well. These observations are contradictory to the short-term relationship problems already discussed and may suggest a healing process in the relationship.

However, Meiselman also found that the sisters, as adults, are likely to have extreme difficulty in relating to their own sons, suggesting the sisters are displacing onto their sons their feelings about their brothers, as illustrated by two of her cases (pp. 278-279):

> Laura felt that she had been a victim of her older brothers. She attributed her difficulty in relating to men in general to her childhood experiences and freely told her therapist that she cried bitterly when she discovered that her first baby was a boy. When her son was 8, she beat him on the slightest excuse and regularly threatened to kill him.

Karen had loved having sexual relationships with her brother and freely admitted that she had initiated the activity. When seen in therapy with her 18 year old son, she was overtly seductive to him, and he became so uncomfortable that he withdrew from her.

Meiselman concludes that "having a young son reactivates the conflicts originally associated with sibling incest and that the sister's manner of relating to her son tends to recapitulate some aspects of her relationship with her brother, possibly even molding her son into her brother's image" (p. 279).

Mental Illness. Meiselman (1978) found that 38% of her sample of adult women with histories of sibling incest were severely mentally ill and that some of them had been institutionalized (p. 275). She does caution, however, not to generalize from this data because the statistics are based on a sample of only eight women who were already therapy patients. The few other studies conducted on the long-term effects of sibling incest do not mention mental illness.

No Negative Effects. Finally, some researchers have hypothesized that sibling incest rarely produces negative long-term effects on the participants (Weinberg, 1955; Lukianowicz, 1972). Finkelhor (1980) also concludes that "on the whole, the evidence weighs against an extremely alarmist view of sibling sex" (p. 191), although he cautions that this conclusion should not be construed as a proincest statement.

OTHER TYPES OF SIBLING INCEST

Most of the data on sibling incest has been accumulated on those cases in which the brother is the initiator and the sister is the victim. However, other types of sibling incest exist as well, although considerably less is known about them.

Finkelhor (1980) found that a total of 26% of his sample who had had sibling sexual experiences had them with a same-sex sibling (p. 174). He concludes, however, that "homosexual" experiences like these appear not to increase the trauma or the negative effects associated with the incest.

Incest between step-siblings or half-siblings is an area that deserves considerably more research. The incest taboo may not hold as strongly in reconstituted families and feelings of protection, care and love may be more difficult to form for children who have had to accommodate the introduction of a new sibling into the family. None of the cases in the clinical sample was of step-sibling or half-sibling incest, but that may reflect a fluke in reporting rather than data on actual occurrence.

Chapter 8: Other Types of Incest

Types of incest other than paternal and sibling are quite rare and have not been seriously studied. The clinical sample does contain some of these unusual types, however, only the small number of these cases does not lend itself to any widesweeping generalizations. In the clinical sample there are two cases of mother-daughter incest, three uncle-niece cases and two grandfather-granddaughter cases. Fortunately in all of these cases both the offending adult and the victimized child were interviewed, thus affording at least a small opportunity to study the family dynamics in each case.

MOTHER-DAUGHTER INCEST

There are two cases of mother-daughter incest in the clinical sample, neither of which came to the attention of law enforcement or protective service agencies. In both cases the victimized daughters, now in their twenties, sought therapeutic assistance for a variety of coping and emotional problems which they believed were not related to their earlier victimizations. Each of the mothers consented to be interviewed but were unwilling to participate in any long-term therapeutic process.

The Mothers

The two incestuous mothers each consented to an unfortunately brief interview. They both also were more willing to share the details of their childhoods than they were of their victimization of their daughters. While that creates some problems in gaining a familial perspective on the incest, the fact remains that their own respective case histories give some strong clues to the victimization that followed.

Mrs. Webber was born illegitimately to a fourteen year old. Her own grandparents assumed most of the responsibility for raising her. They were a poverty stricken family, socially and geographically isolated from the mainstream of society. When she was eight, Mrs. Webber was raped by her uncle; four years later he raped her again. She was married at sixteen and had her first child, Claudine, at seventeen. Her husband left her shortly after their daughter's birth. She then remarried and had five more children, all sons.

Mrs. Ramsey was born to religiously conservative, physically abusive parents. She was beaten severely for the most minor infraction and was expected to spend hours each day in prayer and scripture reading. Much of the punishment directed against her by her parents was sexual in nature. For example, they would vigorously wash her genitals with hot water and harsh soap, and later bound her developing breasts with a tight wrapping. She got pregnant at 15, ran away from home, and raised her daughter Marcy by herself. She never married nor did she have other children.

Both of these women clearly come from deprived backgrounds. Both have a history of sexual abuse, although in the case of Mrs. Ramsey that sexual abuse may not have constituted incest, in the traditional sense of that term.

Mental Illness. Forward and Buck (1978) state that mothers who incestuously victimize their daughters are "almost always disturbed" (p. 117), although they do not define that term. Presumably they are referring to mental illness, but the severity of that mental illness cannot be determined by the word "disturbed."

Neither incestuous mother in the clinical sample is psychotic. Both are very clearly unhappy, chronically depressed women, with dismally low self-esteem. Both are socially isolated and appear to be inextricably and certainly pathologically bound to their daughters. There is no history of lesbianism for either woman and no indications of latent lesbian attraction. Both vehemently denied any lesbian connotation of their victimization of their daughters.

Motivations. If a lesbian relationship was not the aim of the victimizations, what was? In exploring the answer to this question, a common motivation was discovered: both mothers identified strongly with their daughters, if for different reasons, and it was that blurring of the "I-Thou" boundaries which led to the incest.

Mrs. Webber saw her daughter as hers alone, because she was fathered by a man other than her current husband. She did not expect her current husband to care for or about Claudine, and encouraged him to spend time with "his" sons. In this way, Mrs. Webber created a kind of we-they split in the family which drew her emotionally and eventually sexually to her daughter. The split in the family became so pronounced that her husband sexually withdrew from her and even began sleeping in the dormitory style bedroom with their sons. Mrs. Webber then took Claudine into bed with her and after several months of sleeping together, began fondling and masturbating her. Claudine was ten at the time; her victimization continued for three years. In explaining why she did this to her daughter, Mrs. Webber said, "She was lonely and unhappy, just like me. I wanted us both to have some pleasure."

The physical resemblance between Mrs. Ramsey and her daughter Marcy is remarkable, and their emotional relationship was at times symbiotic because of their social isolation. Said Mrs. Ramsey, "Every time I look at her, I see me, an unhappy, beaten down little kid. All I got when I was a kid was kicked in the face. I wanted to give her love." In giving her daughter "love," Mrs. Ramsey also gave herself pleasure. Their incestuous relationship lasted seven years.

Separation. Weiner (1964) describes a case of a daughter who was reunited with her mother after a twenty year separation. The two had a consensual lesbian relationship which lasted for some time. As in any case of prolonged separation the incest taboo is weakened. Although neither of the incestuous mothers in the clinical sample had been separated from her daughter, the dynamic that Weiner explains is certainly not unusual in cases of incest.

The Daughters

Both of the daughters voluntarily sought therapy for problems in daily living. When asked to describe their reactions to the incest while it was occurring, they gave strikingly similar answers. (Claudine is now 21, Marcy 23.)

> Claudine described her reaction to the incest in the following way: "I never thought it was bad or sick, really. I thought it was kind of special; it's kind of hard to explain, really. It was like 'you and me against the world,' that kind of thing. Dad had his boys over there; mom and me had each other over here."

> Marcy states, "We just had each other. It was always just the two of us, from the start. No other people were allowed."

Effects of the Incest. Neither of the daughters had experienced any profound disruption of daily tasks during their victimization and neither had experienced any of the symptomatic acting-out so characteristic of paternal incest victims. Their problems seemed to have begun late in adolescence, when the incest already had terminated. At that time, Claudine began experiencing depression with suicidal thoughts for which her physician referred her to a psychiatrist. She was a freshman in college at the time and it was believed that the academic pressures were too much for her to bear. Marcy experienced severe psychosomatic symptoms and depression when her mother's financial situation forced her to get a job. The company's doctor had referred her to a therapist.

A possible explanation for these sudden onsets of symptomatology in late adolescence could be that pressures of their newly found independence created a kind of delayed grief reaction to the loss of their dependent relationships with their mothers. This may have occurred for the following reasons. First, neither of the daughters described the incest experiences in terms of victimization; instead, they both described it as "special," loving and warm. After all, mothers are culturally expected to be nurturing and caring, so unlike paternal incest victims, these daughters may have expected to experience nurturing and caring in that relationship. If that nurturing and caring was only, or primarily, expressed and experienced through sexual means, then the loss of that relationship would be traumatic. Second, both daughters are very dependent individuals, rendered especially so by the incest, and have not experienced any previous success with independence. Consequently, going to college for Claudine and getting a job for Marcy, were traumatically overwhelming events for which they were completely unprepared. They may have yearned for the protection of the dependent bond with their mothers. Finally, in both cases, the dependent relationship with their mothers stopped when the incest stopped. For Claudine, the incest terminated when she began menstruating at which time her mother simply said, "You can't sleep here any more." Her mother then withdrew emotionally and physically from her daughter, leaving her quite alone and isolated within their family. For Marcy, the incest stopped when she found a job. "You're grown up now," her mother had said, and then also withdrew from her daughter. The loss of that relationship for both daughters was profound and may have produced the symptoms which necessitated their referral to mental health professionals.

UNCLE-NIECE INCEST

There are three cases of uncle-niece incest in the clinical sample, a small number given the conclusion of the Kinsey study which found an extremely high rate of this type of incest in their population (Kinsey *et al.*, 1953).

The Uncles

All three of the uncles in the clinical sample are the maternal uncles of the victims. This becomes an important fact when it is understood that all three of the mothers of the victims had themselves been victims of incest. In other words, the uncles had been raised in incestuous families and the consequences of that vicarious participation in incest already have been discussed.

Browning and Boatman (1977) studied five cases of uncle-niece incest and found that two of the uncles were viewed as "problems" in the family. This kind of "black sheep" dynamic was also found for two of the uncles in the clinical sample, who were viewed by their families as irresponsible troublemakers. One of them is an alcoholic and has trouble keeping a job, while the other has been in and out of jail for a variety of minor offenses. Meiselman (1978) suggests that the "typical" case of uncle-niece incest involves an uncle who is quite distant emotionally from his niece's family and therefore plays no significant role in her upbringing. This dynamic was not found in the clinical sample, however, since all three of the uncles, all of whom are bachelors, were strongly involved with their nieces' families, as the case of Uncle Earl illustrates:

> Uncle Earl, 40, is the bachelor uncle who eats dinner every Wednesday with his sister's family and attends church with them every Sunday. His sister's family vacations at his trailer on the lake every summer. He has been very involved with his sister's family for quite some time, taking his nephews to ball games and even coaching their Little League teams. He paid for his niece's piano lessons when the family could not afford to do so. The children in the family saw him as their "second dad," and even called him that on several occasions.

Because all three uncles in the clinical sample are very close to their sisters' families, the incest dynamics are very similar to those of paternal incest. Unfortunately, that also means that the effects of their incestuous victimization on their nieces are more traumatic than in other cases that have been discussed in the sparse literature on this type of incest.

The Nieces

Browning and Boatman (1977) find that the victimized nieces are anxious individuals who are overly dependent on their mothers. This finding is somewhat confirmed by the clinical sample since all three of the nieces are quite clinging, dependent youngsters. Their average age is only 6½ years, however, and all of them were interviewed soon after the incest had been disclosed, so those two factors may have contributed more to their behavior than anything else. Browning and Boatman also find that the nieces are pseudomature, a finding not supported by the clinical sample.

All three of the nieces in the clinical sample come from patriarchal homes where adult authority, particularly male adult authority, is never questioned or challenged. The mothers of these girls, themselves victims of incest, are passive and dependent. The stage is therefore set for some kind of incest victimization to occur, and the uncles, themselves vicarious participants in incest, capitalized on that family psychology.

Effects of the Incest. The three nieces experienced a psychosomatic reaction to the incest. Again, this is probably due to their young ages since symptomatic acting out is more likely to be found in older victims. One of the nieces had been victimized steadily over a seven month period of time when her uncle had moved into her parent's house. The other two nieces had been victimized only once. All of the girls complained of stomachaches, headaches and vague psychosomatic ailments. One child seemed to have a kind of depressive reaction which caused her some school problems. In fact, in that case, the teacher of the child was the adult who discovered the incest.

No long-term studies of the effects of this type of incest have been conducted and obviously the clinical sample does not at this time lend itself to that kind of analysis. If this type of incest is as common as the Kinsey (1953) study suggests, there are certainly enough victims to study should researchers turn their attention to this type of incest.

GRANDFATHER-GRANDDAUGHTER INCEST

Two cases of grandfather-granddaughter incest are in the clinical sample. These two grandfathers are not senile, alcoholic or psychotic, as the "dirty old man" stereotype might suggest. Both, however, had incestuously victimized their own daughters, the mothers of their granddaughters.

Perhaps age had mellowed these grandfathers. Both had been brutal victimizers of their daughters, but extraordinarily gentle victimizers, if "gentle" can be used to describe any kind of victimization, of their granddaughters.

> "It was different when I had my own family, in my own home," explains Grandpa Barr. "I raised my kids my own way by the school of hard knocks. Now I'm a grandpa. I don't have no rights to raise those grandkids. That's their folks' problem."

Forced to drop some of their authoritarian control, these grandfathers also surrendered some of their brutality.

The Granddaughters

Meiselman (1978) finds that the granddaughters who are incest victims tend to blame themselves for the incest. This appears to be a common finding for all incest victims and is no less true for the granddaughters. They tend to see their grandfathers in a stereotyped way: as jolly, loving, benign and asexual old men. As such, in the eyes of the child victims, they easily can be led astray by a child.

Again, the nuclear families of these granddaughters are "typical" incestuous families: the fathers are patriarchal and abusive; the mothers, themselves victims of incest, are passive and dependent. All of this leads to the conclusion that the grandfathers, perceiving a replication of their own families, capitalized on these family dynamics and incestuously abused their granddaughters.

The granddaughters, both young at the time of the incest, did not have traumatic reactions to the incest. This may have been due to the fact that their grandfathers were gentle, that in each case they were victimized only once, and that their perceptions of their grandfathers as loving, benign and essentially asexual precluded a traumatic reaction. That is not to imply that there was no reaction to the incest. Both of the girls felt very guilty, believing that they were responsible for the incest, a belief which was not deflated by their families who tried to exonerate the grandfathers from any blame.

OTHER TYPES OF INCEST

Presumably other types of incest occur, but there are very few in the literature or in the clinical sample of these types. Barry and Johnson (1958) describe a case of grandmother-granddaughter incest in which the granddaughter had slept for several years with her physically ill paternal grandmother. The victim terminated the incest herself when she was 15 years old, went on to become a nurse, and came to the attention of therapists when she sought counseling for hostile feelings she harbored toward elderly female patients. Theirs is the only case of this type of incest reported in the literature.

Part II. Pedophilia

CHAPTER 9. AN INTRODUCTION

The German psychiatrist Richard von Krafft-Ebing coined the term "pedophilia" in the late 19th century to describe a psychosexual perversion in which an adult is erotically attracted to children. The pedophile, Krafft-Ebing recognized, could be a male or a female (the latter has rarely been recognized in modern research), and may be heterosexual, homosexual or bisexual in orientation toward children.

Literally translated, pedophilia means "love of children," an unfortunately ironic term since researchers subsequent to Krafft-Ebing have recognized that although a pedophile may be motivated by love, the impact of his or her behavior on the victimized child rarely is experienced as love. In common parlance, a pedophile is referred to as a child molester, and those two terms will be used interchangeably in this study.

The reader will soon discover that very little is known about the origin, dynamics and effects of pedophilia. Considerably more is known about the treatment of pedophilia and a special emphasis has been placed in the literature on behavior modification techniques for accomplishing that treatment. The reader may be a bit baffled about the paucity of research on this topic, especially in the light of what often appears to be society's hysterical obsession with child molestation. The author shares that confusion along with a considerable amount of frustration that so many people appear to be so content with only the most stereotypical notions of child molestation upon which to base their ideas and actions.

The research that has been conducted, however, shows remarkably consistent results, unlike the research results on incest. Therefore, the student of pedophilic behavior is likely to be spared the frustration of constantly weighing one research study against another in order to come to some truth about the behavior being studied.

THE CLINICAL SAMPLE

For the purposes of this study pedophilia is defined as sexual intercourse, attempted sexual intercourse, or sexual contact of a heterosexual or homosexual nature with a child under the age of 12 by an adult who is not related to the child. The age distinction of 12 years old or younger is important because sexual behavior with youngsters between the ages of 13 and 16 is more properly referred to as hebephilia ("love of youth") and has different origins and dynamics than pedophilia. It is also important to remember that pedophilia occurs between adults and children who are *not* related, therefore, it is nonincestuous child molestation. The large clinical sample consists of 47 offenders, two of them female, and 30 victims, 13 (43%) of them male.

The Pedophiles

The 47 child molesters in the sample ranged in age at the time of the study from 15 to 67 years, with a mean age at the time of the study of 29. Twelve (26%) of them were exclusively homosexual in their orientation towards children; the remaining 35 were exclusively heterosexual. There are no cases of bisexual pedophilia in the clinical sample.

With the exception of four cases, all of the pedophiles in the clinical sample were on the author's court caseload, since all had been convicted of sexual offenses against children. The remaining four had not been convicted and were referred to the author by a psychotherapist who was treating them. All of the child molesters were interviewed by the author. Factual data were collected on each case and checked for accuracy against the official reports contained in the court files. The interviews were also diagnostic in nature and were therefore geared towards creating a clinical profile for each pedophile. Selected demographic data for these child molesters are shown in Table 12.

TABLE 12. SELECTED DEMOGRAPHIC DATA FOR 47 PEDOPHILES

Sexual Orientation Towards Children	Number of Cases
Heterosexual	35
Homosexual	12
Bisexual	0

Ethnicity	Number of Cases
White	40
Black	2
Hispanic	5
Other	0

Religious Preference	Number of Cases
Protestant	5
Catholic	20
Jewish	0
Other	8
None	14

Occupation Group	Number of Cases
Professional	7
Skilled	6
Unskilled	4
Unemployed (includes retired)	21
Student	9

The Victims

The clinical sample also contains 30 victims, ranging in age from three years to 44 years, with a mean age at the time of the study of 17. Obviously this wide age range means that some of the victims are older and are offering a retrospective description of their victimization, while the others are younger and are just emerging from their experiences.

This component of the clinical sample was created from widely divergent sources over a three year period of time. Many of the older victims are or have been the author's students in a large community college; some of the younger victims are the children of the author's students. A few victims were referred to the author by a psychotherapist who was treating them. The remaining victims were on the author's caseload, having been convicted of felony offenses.

Demographic data for these victims can be found in Table 13.

TABLE 13. SELECTED DEMOGRAPHIC DATA ON 30 CHILD MOLESTATION VICTIMS

Sex	Number of Cases
Male	13
Female	17

Ethnicity	Number of Cases
White	26
Black	1
Hispanic	2
Other	1

Religious Preference	Number of Cases
Protestant	11
Catholic	14
Jewish	0
Other	1
None	4

PEDERASTY

A very specific type of homosexual child molestation, pederasty, is also included in this study. Pederasty is defined as the sexual contact between an adult male and a "consenting" child for the purpose of creating a mutually satisfying relationship. As so defined, it is clearly distinct from "typical" homosexual child molestation, and because it has a well defined popular culture surrounding and supporting its practice, it is considered separately from homosexual pedophilia.

There are only three pederasts in the clinical sample. All were in their early twenties at the time of the study, with a mean age of 21.6 years. All three had been on the author's court caseload, having been convicted of child molestation.

No victims — or perhaps they would be better referred to as "partici-pants" — of pederasty were available for this study. With the exception of one very large study, very little scientific research has been conducted on pederasty and its effects on youngsters.

CHAPTER 10: THE SOCIAL ORIGINS OF THE SEXUAL ABUSE OF CHILDREN

The historian Arthur N. Gilbert once wrote that "raising consciousness by demonstrating historical continuity has always been an important function of the historian's trade" (Gilbert, 1980/1981:58). That is no less an important function of those who study the sexual abuse of children. What we are experiencing now in this country—incest, child molestation, "kiddie" pornography, child prostitution and sex rings—are not new nor are they unique to this society. They are, instead, problems which evolved from a rich tradition as every society throughout history struggled to come to grips with its own sexuality and the role of its children in the expression of that sexuality.

The historical evolution of both the concepts of childhood and of sexuality is characterized by unflagging superstition, religious and medical fanaticism, incapacitating fears and overwhelming ignorance. What follows is a chronicle of that evolution. It is not intended to be a probing analysis of history but an attempt, in the words of Gilbert, to raise consciousness by demonstrating historical continuity.

ANCIENT SOCIETIES

As a continually evolving, adapting institution, clearly distinct levels of status developed within the family during antiquity. As an example, in the Roman civilization prior to the A.D. 600's, wives, slaves and children were considered to be the possessions of their masters, the male authority of the household.

There is an inherent difference in status between an owner and a possession and that difference evolved into what Newman (1978) refers to as the "obedience model of punishment" (p. 53), which was not only characteristic of the families of Roman antiquity but also persisted throughout history as a predominant attitude toward childrearing. This obedience model gave meaning to normative (nonabusive) childrearing practices while at the same time it gave structure to child abusing behavior.

Early Roman society illustrates the coexistence of a normative obedience model with an abusive obedience model. The concept of *patriae potestas*, "the power of the father," dominated Roman civil and criminal law for centuries. It gave the father of the household unlimited power and granted him the role of the punisher within the family. In so doing, the truly patriarchal family system developed in which the all-powerful father demanded of his children obedience and conformity. Newman (1978) states as an example of this that in Rome a father could take his uncontrollable child to the city gate where the elders would stone the child to death.

Certainly not every incorrigible child was in danger of losing his or her life in ancient Rome. Yet the fact remains that the obedience model also created the opportunity for child abusing behavior, and that this abusive behavior probably coexisted with normative childrearing. History records more of that abusive behavior than it does the normative. The killing of children, or infanticide, for example, was more than likely widely practiced in ancient Rome (Newman, 1978). Although the first born child of any family was usually permitted to live, other children, particularly girls, or handicapped or sickly infants, were put to death (De Mause, 1974). Some children were sold into slavery or simply abandoned by their mothers who found it more profitable to wet nurse wealthy women's babies than to feed their own. Other children were sold into prostitution rings (Bullough and Bullough, 1978). Since the practice of infanticide reduced the number of young girls, some boys were castrated in infancy to enhance their sex appeal as prostitutes (Schultz, 1980), or were put into tubs of hot water so that their softened testicles could be squeezed until they disappeared (De Mause, 1974).

Although the rate of incest within these patriarchal families of early Rome has never been calculated or even estimated by historians, Cohn (1975) gives a number of examples which seem to suggest that latent incestuous feelings may have been a feature of normative childrearing. To develop that theory he gives as examples the accusations pagan Romans made against the small Christian communities within their society. Sometime before A.D. 200, the Latin apologist for Christianity, Minucius Felix, wrote about the pagan description of Christianity: "As for the initiation of new members, the details are as disgusting as they are well known. A child, covered in dough, to deceive the unwary, is set before the would-be novice. The novice stabs the child to death.... Then, it is horrible!, they hungrily drink the child's blood and compete with one another as they divide his limbs" (Cohn, 1975:1). This initiation ceremony is then followed by an incestuous orgy lasting throughout the night. Later accusations against the Paulican sect also focused on incest, claiming that when a child was born of an incestuous relationship it was thrown from one person to another until it died. The person in whose hands the child died became the leader of the sect. The child's blood was then mixed with flour to form a heretical parody of the Eucharist (Cohn, 1975).

Cohn theorizes that these accusations of incest made against Christian communities reflected unconscious projections made by a latently incestuous society. Certainly there is a great deal of modern evidence to suggest that rigidly patriarchal families are more incest-prone (Herman, 1981) and that surely gives credence to Cohn's theory which can be used to suggest that although normative childrearing coexisted with abusive childrearing, the line of differentiation between the two indeed may have been thinly drawn.

THE JUDEO-CHRISTIAN SOCIETIES

The possession of children by their parents was also given religious sanction in the teachings of both the Talmud and the Bible. Rush (1980) states that the Talmud teaches that a girl of "three years and one day" could be betrothed through an act of sexual intercourse if the child's father gave the interested party the permission to do so. This practice, she reveals, grew out of the Semitic folklore in which a woman came before Rabbi Akiba ben Joseph and complained that sexual intercourse had been forced on her before she was three years old. The Rabbi pondered the problem and then compared the situation to that of a baby who submerges his fingers in honey: "The first time he cries about it, the second time he cries about it, but the third time he sucks it. He ultimately enjoys the experience" (Rush, 1980:18). The Rabbi therefore concluded that it is lawful to have intercourse with a child of three years and one day if her father, her possessor, gives his permission.

The Biblical female also was considered to be a possession of her father, a kind of "sexual property" in the words of Rush (p. 18), a perception which caused all heterosexual relationships to be defined in financial terms. Marriage involved the purchase of the daughter from her father for fifty pieces of silver; rape was the theft of her virginity for which her father could be compensated by a payment of fifty pieces of silver from the offender; and prostitution was the selling of her sexuality by her master.

It was normative behavior during these times for daughters to be considered the property of their fathers and for heterosexual relationships to be defined in financial terms. Ebel (1977) suggests that the Judeo-Christian societies had a more compassionate and protective attitude regarding children than did the earlier Greek and Roman societies. Using many Biblical references to support his thesis, he explains that the Jewish population explosion in the Post-Exilic period was largely due to a termination of the practice of infanticide, and that the Bible clearly and vehemently condemned the practice of sacrificing children in religious ceremonies.

Although Ebel's argument favors a view of a more humane interest in children, Gilbert (1980/1981) traces the taboo against anal sex which has permeated history directly to the spread of Christianity. The Christian religion, with its dichotomy between body and spirit, teaches that life ends in death and that the living body enacts the drama of death in its physical function. "Excrement was always the clearest and most persistent reminder of the fate of man," explains Gilbert. "It became a symbol of evil, darkness, death and rebellion against the moral order" (p. 64). It is little wonder, then, that as history has progressed from this point, the sexual abuse of boys always has been treated more seriously than has the sexual abuse of girls.

THE MIDDLE AGES

De Mause (1974) states that the reaction of adults to children during the Middle Ages was primarily projective in that children were used as receptacles for the adults' unconscious projections. Yet, before children can be so used, they first must be seen as miniature adults, subject to adult passions and desires, and this is a new perception of children.

Part of that change in perception was undoubtedly due to the burgeoning feudal society and the beginning of social reforms brewing during the Middle Ages. Sommerville (1978) hypothesizes that "when people organize for social change it is not long before they recognize that the rising generation will be crucial to their enterprise. Special efforts will be made to secure their loyalty. And the image of the child will inevitably figure in the movement's ideology, revealing its understanding of human nature" (p. 114).

There is vehement disagreement as to the nature of normative childrearing during the Middle Ages. Not a great deal of documentation about family life in the 8th through the 13th centuries exists, but the later Middle Ages produced extensive records of family life which has fueled this argument. Tuchman (1978), in her analysis of the 14th century, emphatically states that "of all the characteristics in which the medieval age differs from the modern, none is so striking as the comparative absence of interest in children" (p. 49). She further states that frequent childbearing and an infant mortality rate of one to two out of every three births contributed to an "atrophy of maternal love" (p. 50).

Kroll (1977) argues against this analysis. He points out that the first pediatric textbook was written during the Middle Ages by Soranus whose writings clearly show, in the words of Kroll, "an appreciation for the vulnerability and the value of the infant" (p. 386). In fact, Kroll argues that by modern standards babies were treated too carefully and were perceived as "inherently weak and without positive health" (p. 386).

Using the city of Venice as an example, Ruggerio (1975) found that the rape of a girl under 12 years of age would get the offender two years in jail, a comparatively lenient sentence from a modern perspective, but a sentence which was then exceeded only by that given to murderers and traitors. Rush (1980) also discovered that in medieval England the rape of a nonresisting child was treated as a misdemeanor. Although both of these examples fall short of modern legal reactions to child molestation, they do serve to demonstrate that during the Middle Ages children began to enjoy some protection under the law, an observation that gives support to Kroll's (1977) theory that the development of the legal concept of childhood paralleled the development of the law.

Normative childrearing is difficult to determine during the Middle Ages, but there is more evidence that children as a rule were protected rather than exploited or even ignored. Prostitution was widespread during the Middle Ages, for example, and frequently involved very young children, many of whom had been orphaned or had been sold to unscrupulous procurers by destitute parents (Bullough and Bullough, 1978). Reform movements directed against prostitution in general and toward child prostitutes in specific flourished as early as the 12th century when Pope Gregory IX created the Order of St. Mary Magdelene to establish convents for reformed prostitutes and orphanages for children so employed. This reform movement prevailed for centuries and reached a peak of activity during the Reformation when widespread prostitution and the spread of venereal disease imbued the movement with a moral fervor.

Although it appears that the abuse of children did not coexist with normative childrearing as a viable alternative for the treatment of children during the Middle Ages, the two did coexist in the religious culture of the times. Yet that could have occurred only after the church had created such a hysteria that rational faculties and judgment were severely impaired.

In 1484, Pope Innocent VIII issued a bull which empowered one of the judicial arms of the church, the Inquisition, to find, imprison, torture and execute heretics and witches. The medieval stereotype of the heretic and the witch can be traced back to the ancient fantasy that within the larger society exists a small, clandestine society which both threatens the existence of the larger society and which is addicted to antihuman practices (Cohn, 1975).

In this medieval version of the fantasy, witches thrived on the blood of children and used their flesh in *maleficium*, or the destruction of life and property through occult means. Much of the hysteria directed against witches was done under the guise of protecting children (Cohn, 1975); paradoxically, some children were victimized by that very hysteria. The *Malleus Malificarum*, the document which guided the activities of the Inquisition, for example, stated that children as young as six could enter into a heretical pact with the Devil through sexual intercourse. Rush (1980) relates the case of 8-year-old Loyse Mailley who was tortured for copulating with the Devil by one of the Inquisition's attorneys, Henri Bouget, who reasoned that once in Satan's clutches no child could be reformed. That was not an isolated case. In 1624 the Chancellor to the Prince-Bishop of Wurtzburg reported that 300 children between the ages of 3 and 4 had been accused of sexually consorting with the Devil. Forty years later, 15 young children were burned at the stake and 36 more were scourged weekly at the church door for entering into a sexual pact with the Devil (Rush, 1980).

The Middle Ages was a tumultuous period, at varying times characterized by unflagging superstition and religious fanaticism as well as by far-sighted reform. It appears that two things may have made the treatment of children different in the Middle Ages as compared to the treatment of children in ancient societies. First, children increasingly were seen as human beings, albeit miniature adults, yet as people deserving of all the nurturing and protection that society was able to give. Second, although the abusive treatment of children did exist during the Middle Ages, it created some anxiety in the populace and spurned some reform movements which had as their goal the eradication of that behavior. When the abusive treatment of children did coexist with normative childrearing, it did so only after the mass hysteria of the time had significantly distorted judgment and perception.

COLONIAL AMERICA

Ebel (1977) points out that "a direct line runs from the 'chosen' feelings of the Hebrews to the 'chosen' feelings manifested by the Puritans" (p. 76). That "direct line" was not only affective in nature, but encompassed the law as well.

When the Puritans codified their laws in the 1630's they relied heavily on the Old Testament for guidance. One of the capital crimes in that newly codified set of laws was sodomy; the Puritan's justification for punishing this crime with the death penalty was taken directly from Leviticus 20:13, "If a man lyeth with mankind, as he lyeth with a woman, both of them have committed abomination, they both surely be put to death" (Oaks, 1980/1981:79).

Laws regarding rape and child molestation, however, were not written in Biblical terms because they were created after sensational cases. And there were sensational sex cases in Puritan America, despite the stereotype of Puritans as a sexually repressed people living in a sexually repressive society. Actually, sex within marriage, of course, was enthusiastically and even religiously endorsed by the Puritans (Morgan, 1942). It was sex outside of marriage that enraged the Puritans, an event that was all the more possible by the presence of unattached men eager to conquer a new frontier, yet without marriage partners with whom to exercise their sexual desires.

Out of such a situation arose the development of the laws against the sexual abuse of children. In 1641 three men were discovered having molested two young sisters, ages 9 and 7. The molestations had occurred frequently over a two year period of time, apparently without the strenuous objections of the children. The colony was outraged when the molestations were discovered, and it demanded that the three offending adults be put to death. However, there was no crime of rape in the codified laws and none of child molestation either. In desparation the authorities tried to apply the recently adopted sodomy statute to the case, but a conviction of sodomy required proof of penetration which had not occurred during the molestation. After much debate, the three gentlemen in question were sentenced without having first been charged. Since they had not been convicted of sodomy they could not have been put to death, however each was whipped repeatedly and had to pay a monetary restitution to the father of the two girls. On the day they were sentenced, the court created a law which made the "carnal copulation with a woman-child under ten years" punishable by death, even if the victim "had consented to the act" (Oaks, 1980/1981).

How much sexual victimization of children occurred during the colonial period is questionable, although existing court records indicate that cases brought to trial were rare. It was certainly true that the crimes of sodomy and buggery, in that they reflected the Judeo-Christian taboo against nonprocreative sex, were considered to be much more serious than any sexual crimes with children as victims (Oaks, 1978). Prostitution existed in colonial America and the offender was punished by being stripped to the waist, tied to the back of a cart, and whipped as the cart moved through town, or "whipt at the cartstaile" in the words of the Puritans (Bullough and Bullough, 1978). One particularly notorious madame, Alice Thomas, employed young girls in her brothel, but the extent of child prostitution throughout the colonies is unknown.

The sexual abuse of children appears to have been far removed from normative childrearing in colonial America. The Puritan perception of children was that they were innocent beings, yet conceived in sin so that they were viewed as innately depraved as well. This paradoxic perception of children pervaded Puritan thinking, as illustrated by this admonition to parents by the reformer, John Dod:

> The young childe which lieth in the cradle is both wayward and full of affections, and though his body be but small, yet he hath a reat [wrongdoing] heart, and is altogether inclined to evil.... If this sparkle be suffered to increase, it will rage and burn down the whole house. For we are changed and become good not by birth but by education. Therefore parents must be wary and circumspect.... [T]hey must correct and sharply reprove their children for saying and doing ill [Illick, 1974:316–317].

To subdue this potentially destructive "sparkle" Puritan parents were admonished to strictly discipline their children and to fill them with the terrors of hell to secure their conversion. This was accomplished with the rod, appeals to the conscience, and daily discipline in diet, dress and manners. It also included a regime of self-denial and even self-mortification.

Since the physical body was the perpetual reminder of the persistence of sin in the Puritan mind, that self-denial was especially focused on sexual behavior. Greven (1977) argues that the intensity of the parent-child relationship in the early life of the child created a "psychic matrix for inner conflicts over sexuality and sexual identity" (p. 125). That conflict, only intensified by the self-denial, created a strong latent incestuous desire in Puritan families, according to Greven, who recounts in support of his thesis the emotionally incestuous relationships with their mothers described by such Puritan evangelical leaders as Thomas Shepard, Increase Mather and Jonathan Edwards. For young women, too, unconscious incestuous feelings toward their fathers were also evident, and were symbolized by the "intricate interplay between a daughter's intense love for her earthly father and her devotion to her heavenly Father" (Greven, 1977:134).

In summary, the Puritan contribution to the history of childhood is the paradoxic perception of the child as "embryo-angel and infant fiend" in the words of evangelical Puritan, Samuel Davies (Greven, 1977:28). The Puritan contribution to the history of the sexual abuse of children is a set of laws, steeped in Biblical tradition, which protected children from sexual abuse, a religious fervor in the enforcement of those laws, and a compelling latent incestuous desire spawned from a rigid family structure characterized by uncompromising self-denial.

THE VICTORIAN ERA

Advancements in medicine and nutrition during the 1800's in America assured that more children would survive infancy, while economic advancements made having children more of an asset, especially for the middle and upper classes. Advancements in the behavioral sciences created a fascination with the physical, social and moral development of children. In Victorian America the child-centered family had arrived.

Its arrival, however, was more a source of anxiety than celebration. Rapid economic changes and increased urbanization weakened traditional forms of social control, and in a rapidly changing world the family was seen as both a refuge and a conserver and conveyor of morals. To give legitimacy to that new role, the child of the family had to be perceived as weak and innocent, especially vulnerable to the influences of evil. The adolescent, in turn, was viewed as a kind of noble savage, bubbling with moral idealism and sexual precocity, a creature to be controlled and restrained rather than indulged. As Victorian parents struggled with their own sexuality they increasingly defined as sexual that evil to which their children were vulnerable, and being wholly unprepared for that reality, they turned to the burgeoning medical and behavioral sciences for advice.

The medical profession immediately warmed to the task by turning to the medical philosophies of the day for guidance. Hermann Boerhaave, a dominant figure in 18th century medicine, had written that the rash expenditure of semen produced a variety of debilitating physical and mental disorders. His words were echoed by S.A.D. Tissot who claimed that the "secret vice" of masturbation caused young people to become distracted, stupid, and indiscriminantly sexual. In order to preserve the necessary fiction that sex is for procreation not pleasure, and for adults, not adolescents, American doctors and behavioral scientists wasted no time in associating masturbation with virtually every known ailment, from acne, to epilepsy, to insanity.

Take as an example the words of Stall (1897) who described the "predictable" consequences of masturbation: "The eyes lost their luster, the skin becomes sallow, the muscles become flabby, there's indifference to exertion, work becomes distasteful, the back and head hurt, there is dizziness, cold clammy hands, poor digestion, heart palpitations, hollow chest and stooped posture, and early death" (p. 104).

To prevent this catastrophe parents were encouraged to keep careful vigil over their children and to look for signs of the secret vice: general debility, consumption, sudden changes in disposition, love of solitude, lassitude, sleeplessness, untrustworthiness, weak back, rounded shoulders, confusion of ideas, capricious appetites, use of tobacco, eating chalk, plaster or crayons (a sign for girls only), nail biting, acne and bedwetting. A sophisticated thinker may recognize that perhaps with the exception of chalk eating and bedwetting, many of these "signs" delineated by Kellogg (1877) are merely symptoms of adolescent development, but Victorians had only just discovered adolescence so they were hardly sophisticated enough to recognize its developmental signs. For them, these signs surely indicated secret masturbation, a sign in and of itself of adolescent independence, an ugly threat to a child-centered family.

For those perhaps unconvinced of the correlation between masturbation and these physical and social ills, masturbation also was considered to be an etiological factor in insanity. As the medieval belief that witches and evil spirits caused madness began to fade, a satisfactory substitute hypothesis as to the origin of mental illness had to be developed. Much of the responsibility for doing so fell on the shoulders of the medical profession which had supplanted the theologists as the "touchstones of authority" (Tyler, 1977:472) in such matters. Capitalizing on the hysteria of the day, the medical profession made an expedient connection between masturbation and insanity.

Maudsley (1863) described the progressive deterioration of this insanity. First the youngster becomes egotistical and insensitive to the needs of others, then he or she develops hypochondriasis and paranoid ideas. The youngster then refuses to work and sits listlessly, staring into space.

These sexual advice manuals, "deeply Protestant in tone, with a strong undercurrent of Old Testament vengeance" (Haller, 1972:70), portrayed sex as the basest of human desires, the aberrations of which were inexorably detected and punished with physical and mental anguish. Despite their ubiquity, it is unclear as to how much these sex manuals influenced normative childrearing during the Victorian era. Mechling (1975) argues that these manuals are the "consequents not of childrearing values but of childrearing manual writing values" (p. 53). He also argues that parents learn how to parent from imitation rather than instruction, an assumption which would lead to a rather static concept of childrearing.

Despite the objections of Mechling, it is clear that such values had deeply infiltrated the popular culture of Victorian America. Books like *Charlotte Temple* and *Tales for Fifteen* detailed the tragedies to befall young women who asserted their independence and their sexuality. Wyman (1951), in analyzing "women's fiction" of the 19th century, discovered that the "seduction novel won sanction in a moralistic America by a strict balancing of sin and retribution that left no room for the personal salvation of the sinner" (p. 167). Citing examples such as *Margret Howth*, *Hedged In*, and *John Godfrey's Fortune*, she unveils a persistent theme of independence leading to sexual degeneracy, and that, in turn, to degredation and even death. That these books were written to be read by young women is no surprise to Kett (1971) who observes that "a society which failed to provide a significant role for women outside of marriage had difficulty envisioning girls passing through a protracted period of adjustment to responsibility, but no trouble recognizing the threat to feminine virtue posed by the sudden onset of sexual maturity" (p. 296).

Boys also experienced the infiltration of their popular culture with moralistic advice. Crume (1973) analyzed boys' magazines in vogue between 1826 and 1857. He found that they emphasized Christian goodness, conservatism, self-restraint, and dependence. Although he does not see them as a tool of social control, he does recognize their pervasiveness and their power to reinforce the values being taught in the home.

What Mechling does not recognize is that these advice books extoled a consistent philosophy and in doing so caused a flurry of antimasturbation techniques which had the potential, if nothing else, of creating an unparalleled amount of sexually abusive behavior directed against children. To deter the act of masturbation doctors recommended that parents put their children into chastity belts and splints, or that they place bells on their children's hands, the ringing of which surely indicated masturbatory activity (Haller and Haller, 1974). They suggested that ice packs be placed on the genitals of children, that they be handcuffed to bedposts, and that they carry with them always pictures of their mothers to be guiltily reminded of their admonition against masturbation (Schultz, 1980). A physician recommended that girls be made to sleep in sheepskin pants with their hands tied to a collar around their neck and their feet tied to the footboard so "they could not slide down and use their heels" (Colby, 1897:206).

When such mechanical and physical restraints failed to prevent masturbation, more drastic measures were also available. In 1858 in London, Dr. Isaac Baker Brown introduced the surgical procedure of clitoridectomy for girls who habitually masturbated. Some thirty years later, Dr. Eyer in the United States advocated the same procedure, which had since fallen out of grace in Europe but which was still described as a viable surgical procedure in medical books as late as 1925 (Comfort, 1967). In between those times, Dr. E.H. Pratt founded the *Journal of Orificial Surgery*. Armed with the philosophy that "health begins below the belt," he and his group advocated circumcision for boys and clitoridectomies for girls, as well as forcible dilation of the anus for both sexes, and castration of the mentally ill (Bullough and Bullough, 1977). For those physicians uncomfortable with these procedures, various medical groups also recommended cauterization and blistering of the genitals as alternate procedures (Barker-Bensfield, 1978).

Again, it is unclear as to how much these philosophies and practices had infiltrated normative childrearing. It is clear, however, that regardless of that extent, American families during the Victorian era were strongly latently incestuous, and that fact may explain why these clearly abusive philosophies and practices could coexist with so little objection or anxiety with nonabusive childrearing patterns. Strong (1973) argues that the child-centered family of the era was characterized by mothers who turned emotionally to their children to compensate for the emotional barrenness of their roles as wives. Children, especially sons, in turn, left without alternatives to their budding sexual interests, turned to their parents for gratification. Into this "experiential bond" as Strong calls it (p. 457), both parents and children projected their individual sexual frustrations.

The sexual frustration of youngsters, particularly adolescents, has already been documented. Expected to stay chaste until marriage and sternly admonished to refrain from the "secret vice" of masturbation, Victorian adolescents were even warned against sublimating these sexual feelings through dance, theatre, and romantic literature. Their parents' frustrations, in turn, were also profound. A great deal of that frustration was experienced by Victorian women whose sexuality was perceived as virtually nonexistent. Take as an example the words of Dr. William Acton: "A majority of women, happily for them, are not much troubled with sexual feelings of any kind. What men are habitually, women are only exceptionally" (Degler, 1978:403). That frustration was a feature of Victorian men as well who were so admonished against being effeminate, sexually indiscriminate and impotent that sexual behavior in marriage was brutally overcompensatory (Rosenberg, 1973). Thus developed the frustrating Victorian attitude about sex: adolescents are asexual; women are repulsed by sex and engage in it only to reluctantly fulfill their marital obligation; and men are libidinous sex fiends restrained only, if at all, by the rules of etiquette which dictated the behavior of proper Victorian gentlemen.

American sexual morality of the Victorian era consisted of "middle class prejudices, sentimentality, romanticized expectation, the workings of Divine Providence, and pseudoscientific sophistication" (Haller, 1972:70). All of these combined to bring sexually abusive behavior directed against children within the range of viable childrearing practices for families in Victorian America.

THE PROGRESSIVE RESPONSE

The Victorian era's philosophy and sexual practices represented a kind of mercantilist image of available energy which "was not one of hoarding a surplus of stimulating growth of one's resources, but rather, of maintaining one's scarce fund of goods" (Fellman and Fellman, 1981:240). That approach put a great deal of pressure on the individual person to manage his or her resources within the limits dictated by society. Obviously not all people were capable of successfully accomplishing this task: youngsters, despite all warnings to the contrary, attended dances, read romantic novels, and engaged in the "secret vice" of masturbation; men failed to control their brute passions in their marriages and in their social relationships; and women fell from grace into promiscuity and prostitution.

There was a certain seductiveness in the simplicity of Victorian thinking. It served as an anchor in a rapidly changing society; a refuge in a world in which the traditional modes of social control had been rendered impotent. Its thesis was both simple and compelling: people are in charge of their own destinies. If people can only learn to understand and to control themselves, they can create order in a chaotic world.

Some Progressive thinkers, however, saw the influence of that chaotic world as much stronger than any individual. They worried that poverty, urbanization and modernization had more influence on people's behavior than did self-restraint and moderation. They saw as their mission the elimination, or at least the modification, of these social influences through programs of reform and change. Others remained Victorian in their thinking, attempting "to achieve a rural timelessness, to freeze a state of innocence, to stop history" (Connelly, 1980:123). Ironically, to promote their own beliefs, each group used the same cause—the white slave traffic in children for the purpose of prostitution.

White slavery hysteria had peaked in England in the late 1880's but did not become a feature of American society until 1907 when George Kibbe Turner published an article in *McClure's Magazine* which exposed the white slave trade in Chicago. In that same year a number of white slavery trials resulted in the convictions of men for that crime. The prosecutor, assistant state's attorney, Clifford G. Roe, confirmed in people's minds that a commercialized network of white slavery did exist in this country. Between 1909 and 1914, 22 white slavery tracts were published and widely disseminated throughout the country. These included such works as: "Fighting for the Protection of Our Girls: A Truthful and Chaste Account of Buying and Selling Young Girls for Immoral Purposes"; "The Cruel and Inhuman Treatment of White Slaves"; and "Graphic Accounts of How White Slaves are Ensnared and a Full Exposition of the Methods and Schemes Used to Lure and Trap Girls" (Connelly, 1980). White slavery movies were produced and dime novels recounted in purple prose the capture and treatment of young girls for the purpose of prostitution.

The scenario in all of these was basically the same: a rural girl, innocent and chaste, moves to the big city to find a job and to assert her independence. Upon arrival, she is trapped by a disreputable man, usually a foreigner, who forces her into a life of prostitution. His methods of ensnaring the girl vary from drugging her and carrying her unconscious to his lair, to threatening and physically abusing her, to exploiting her naïveté with promises of marriage. Once trapped, the girl suffers years of degradation and humiliation. If she is not saved, and she rarely was, she was condemned to an early death.

For the Victorian thinkers, accounts of white slavery only supported their belief that the city was evil, the home was sacred, and that independence at any age was premature. For the reformers, accounts of white slavery only reinforced their belief that urban poverty and disadvantage must be reduced, children must be sexually educated, and programs of social reform must be implemented. The former crusade, characterized by nativism and xenophobia, "was irrational, evangelical [and] uncompromising," while the latter was "closely associated with the temper of the social gospel, the social settlement, and the more rational humanitarian ambitions of progressivism" (Feldman, 1967:197). Despite their divergent perspectives, both campaigns to eliminate white slavery suffered from the same flaw: there was virtually no white slavery to be eliminated (Connelly, 1980; Feldman, 1967; Lubove, 1972). What at first blush appears to have been a humanitarian concern for the welfare of children was in reality only a ruse to disguise the real targets of both campaigns: urbanization, immigration, modernization and liberalization.

Both of these campaigns also served a latent function. They offered the still proper, conservative post-Victorian society a "glimpse into the id of American society, into a sexual underworld that was at the same time repulsive and attractive" (Connelly, 1980:119). In that way they had an almost pornographic function, appealing to the secret desires and fantasies of a sexually repressed society. By liberating these desires and fantasies, both campaigns prepared the way for the sexual revolution yet to come.

They also paved the way for the new role of women in society. After all, America had never had before a group of women so well educated, so enlightened and so inactive. Their attack on white slavery was passionate and well organized and was a "means of warning modern industrial and urban America to make way for the New Woman" (Feldman, 1967:206).

In that the Progressive era revolutionized sexual attitudes and roles, it prepared society for the even more drastic changes that were yet to come. The reforms of that era produced an impressive amount of legislation which in the long run did protect children from sexual abuse. As those changes occurred, the sexual abuse of children moved further away from normative childrearing (Neuman, 1975).

MODERN AMERICA

Janus (1981) states that five major social revolutions in the latter part of the 20th century have so significantly upset traditional values that children have been sexually abused as a result. He cites the sexual revolution's destruction of the age old morality that "sex and marriage are for procreation, not pleasure" (p. 22) as one of the prime causes of sexual abuse of children. He further states that the contraceptive revolution "backed up the psychological changes of the sexual revolution with the medical means to eliminate unwanted pregnancy" (p. 23), thereby making the sexual abuse of children more expedient. He then argues that the feminist and the civil rights movements have joined to free children "from the restraints of culture and its Judeo-Christian morality" (p. 26), and that the gay rights revolution has had the strongest impact on young women who now consider lesbianism the "politically correct thing to do" (p. 26).

Janus's thesis that these modern revolutions have led simply and inevitably to the sexual victimization of children is spurious, indeed. Perhaps the weakest feature of his thesis, however, is that his perspective is ahistorical; in fact, in some ways it is even antihistorical. Categorically rejecting the notion of the "eternal constant" — that there always have been certain modes of behavior in every culture — Janus refuses to recognize that children have been sexually abused from the beginning of time. And in refusing to recognize that, Janus fails to see that the social revolutions he decries have only changed the modes and the justifications for that abuse, they have not in and of themselves created that abuse.

What we see from an attempt to demonstrate the continuity of the sexual victimization of children throughout history is that normative (non-abusing) childrearing has been predominate. At various points in history abusive childrearing has existed as a viable alternative to normative childrearing, while at other points it has moved so far from normative childrearing that its presence had created anxiety within the society and had initiated widespread reforms.

What we as a modern society must struggle with is deeper and more thoroughly ingrained in our psyches than any social revolution external to us can ever be. What we must struggle with, as a modern society, is the historical continuity of the sexual victimization of children which forces us to decide whether we will allow that behavior to easily and effortlessly coexist with the humane and compassionate treatment of children.

CHAPTER 11: HETEROSEXUAL PEDOPHILIA

In the mind of the public a child molester is many things: a desperate, pitiful individual, such as Peter Lorre portrayed in the 1931 film classic, *M*; a dangerous, anonymous psychopath who snatches unsuspecting children from playgrounds and grabs headlines in newspapers; and the lecherous, "dirty old man" popularized in *Hustler* magazine's "Chester the Molester" cartoons.

Like any stereotypes, these perceptions are convenient and only partially true. They are convenient in that they reduce the anxiety people would ordinarily experience if they were to seriously contemplate the phenomenon of child molestation. For example, if all child molesters were of the Peter Lorre type, hopeless and so obviously mentally ill, then compassion might be the public's response — an emotion that may not be strong and persistent enough to motivate the action necessary to deal with that behavior. Not confronting the behavior of child molestation, of course, saves time and human energy. The stereotype of the dangerous, predatory pedophile creates so much defensiveness that the public conveniently rationalizes "that kind of thing cannot happen in this community," and therefore denies its reality. Similarly, the stereotype of the dirty old man has become an object of humor and what the public can laugh at can create only a modicum of anxiety.

These stereotypes are also only partially true since, like any stereotypes, they betray the real life experiences of the persons so characterized. Once again, it is amazing to come to realize that in a society in which the welfare of children is said to be of paramount importance, the public is willing to accept only the most clichéd perceptions of those who would seriously endanger their welfare.

Take as an example this situation, which happened recently in a local school district: A civic-minded principal insisted that all of his elementary school teachers show the film, *The Dangerous Stranger*, to their students. The film depicts one type of child molester, the stranger who uses threats, bribes and even violence to coerce the child into a sexual experience. The PTA heartily supported this plan, but when a young first grade teacher explained to them that the majority of child molesters are not strangers to the children but are friends and acquaintances whom the children are likely to trust, her plan to educate the children to this reality was vetoed on the grounds that to tell this to children would create "rampant paranoia and unhealthy distrust." Content to rest upon a convenient stereotype, the school system inadvertently endangered the welfare of its children.

The lack of research into the dynamics of pedophilia also has contributed in many ways to the popularization and promulgation of these stereotypes. Quite a great deal of research has been published on the treatment of pedophilia, but little appears as to its origins and dynamics.

THE MALE HETEROSEXUAL PEDOPHILE

Thirty-three male child molesters, ranging in age from 15 to 67 are in the clinical sample. All of them are exclusively heterosexual in their orientation toward children and all have been convicted in courts of law for their offenses. While drawing a clinical sample from a court caseload population often means dealing with defensive subjects with well rehearsed stories which have been told countless times, it also affords the unique opportunity to review court, police, and victim accounts of the molestation experience.

Family History

Although it may be more comfortable to believe that child molesters spring up in some parthenogenic fashion from the unknown, the family histories of child molesters are remarkably similar and undoubtedly play an important role in the etiology of pedophilia. Gebhard *et al.* (1965) find that 50% of the incarcerated heterosexual pedophiles they studied came from broken homes (p. 56) and that those who did not typically had very strained relationships with their parents, particularly their fathers. In the clinical sample, only four (12%) of the pedophiles came from broken homes, but virtually all of them reported poor relationships with their fathers.

A frequently overlooked feature of the childhoods of pedophiles is the physical abuse which takes place, usually at the hands of the fathers. This is suggested in a preliminary study performed by Sack and Mason (1980) in which the self-reported histories of physical abuse in the backgrounds of 112 convicted felons are compared to those of 376 randomly chosen, noninstitutionalized males. Using an abuse scale rating of 0 to 4, with zero representing no abuse during childhood and four indicating a well documented childhood history of severe physical abuse, they found that physical abuse is a much more common feature of the childhoods of felons than it is for law-abiding males. An unanticipated finding of this study is that this history of physical abuse is more than eight times more likely to be found in the childhoods of those felons who had been convicted of sex offenses (p. 213). Although Sack and Mason do not specifically define "sex offense" behavior, presumably some of their population are child molesters.

Marshall and Christie (1981) are more specific about physical abuse in the childhoods of convicted pedophiles. They studied the childrearing practices of the parents of 34 convicted pedophiles and found that only six of them had been raised in homes characterized by "acceptable levels of discipline" according to community and social service standards. The remaining 28 had experienced parental rejection, inconsistent discipline and/or physical abuse (p.

148). In fact, of those who had a father or a father-substitute in the home, 68% described them as "physically abusive, especially when intoxicated" (p. 148).

In the clinical sample of 33 heterosexual pedophiles, 21 (64%) had experienced physical abuse in their homes during their childhoods. In the vast majority of cases the father or the father-substitute was the perpetrator of that abuse. In three cases the mother also participated in the abuse, but in no case was the mother alone the perpetrator. An additional seven (21%) of the pedophiles had witnessed physical abuse directed against their mothers and/or siblings in their homes, although they themselves had not been victimized. That is a total of 85% of the 33 heterosexual pedophiles in the clinical sample who had experienced or witnessed physical abuse within their own homes during their childhood years.

Is all of this abuse an etiological factor in child molestation? Much more research needs to be conducted before that question can be answered, but some theoretical approaches would suggest that the question can be answered in the affirmative. First and most obvious, the child who grows up in such a home is exposed to a very poor adult/parent model. Consequently, as adults themselves, their interactions with children, any children, are likely to be poor. A further etiological factor is provided by Marshall and Christie (1981) who theorize that children growing up in homes characterized by physical abuse "fail to learn to discriminate different arousal states resulting in the identification of all arousal (e.g. anger as well as the arousing effects of alcohol ingestion) as sexual" (p. 156). Therefore, they are more likely to sexualize their anger or their stimulation from alcohol, and because of their inability to effectively relate to children who can so easily be a source of frustration and anger, that sexualized anger may be directed towards children.

Early Sexual Experiences

Another etiological factor in heterosexual pedophilia is the early sexual experiences of these individuals. In his study of sexual trauma in the life histories of child molesters, Groth (1979) finds that 69% of the 178 pedophiles he studied had been sexually traumatized as youngsters.

TABLE 14. EARLY SEXUAL TRAUMA EXPERIENCES
OF 15 HETEROSEXUAL PEDOPHILES

Type of Sexual Trauma	Number of Reports	Average Age at First Occurrence
Paternal incest	8	10.1 years
Sibling incest	4	11.2 years
Maternal incest	1	14 years
Molestation by adult male acquaintance	2	9.5 years
Molestation by adult male stranger	3	8.6 years
Molestation by teenage male acquaintance	1	11 years

In the clinical sample, 15 (45%) of the 33 heterosexual pedophiles had been sexually traumatized as children. Some of these individuals had experienced more than one incident of sexual victimization. The experiences of these 15 pedophiles are presented in Table 14.

In addition to those 15 who had personally experienced sexual trauma as children, six (18%) more had witnessed it in their own homes even though they themselves had not been sexually victimized. This figure attests to the long overlooked fact that nonmolested children in homes characterized by sexual victimization may be as adversely affected by their exposure to victimization as the child victim is. The types of sexual victimization these six pedophiles had witnessed as children are presented in Table 15.

TABLE 15. TYPES OF SEXUAL VICTIMIZATION WITNESSED BY
SIX NONMOLESTED HETEROSEXUAL PEDOPHILES

Type of Sexual Victimization Witnessed as a Child	Number of Cases
Paternal incest	3
Sibling incest	2
Paternal incest and sibling incest	1

The net effect of all of this is that a total of 26 or 79% of the 33 heterosexual pedophiles in the clinical sample either had been sexually victimized as children or had witnessed some form of sexual victimization within their own homes, even though they were not themselves victimized. The type of homes in which all of this occurred is of some interest as well. Goldstein (1973) finds that pedophiles tend to grow up in sexually repressive homes. That conclusion may sound blatantly contradictory to the data just presented, but it really is not. Such homes are attitudinally but not behaviorally sexually repressive. In fact, a better description of these homes is "sexually schizophrenic"; sexual victimization is taking place but no one is talking about it, or they are condemning verbally the very behavior they are performing. Such homes create a tremendous amount of anxiety and confusion for the children as the case of Mr. Gentry illustrates:

> Mr. Gentry had been the victim of paternal incest as a child. "My old man once beat the shit out of my older brother when he hustled some chick who lived in the neighborhood. He told my brother that women have to be treated with respect; then he'd turn around and beat the shit out of my mother. He was always bitching and moaning about homosexuals; then he'd turn around and force me to give him a blow job. Up is down; black is white; good is bad in that family. As a kid, I never knew if I was coming or going."

Another problem with a sexually repressive family is that it often is incapable of providing care, nurturing, protection and a framework of reality if one of its children is sexually molested by a person who is not a family member. The dynamic of a victimized child not having anyone to turn to and feeling unprotected and confused already has been discussed for incest victims, but those same feelings are experienced by children who have been molested by nonfamily persons. Without that protection, caring and framework of reality, the molestation experience is likely to be overwhelmingly traumatic and therefore may adversely affect the sexual attitudes and behaviors of the developing child.

Behavioral Dynamics

Childhood histories such as have been described for the clinical sample have a profound effect on adult behavior. As a consequence, various studies of heterosexual pedophilia have pointed out remarkably similar behavioral characteristics of their samples.

Infantile Behavior. In their comprehensive study of one pedophile named Norman, Bell and Hall (1971) conclude that an infantile character is at the root of pedophilia. This assumption is based primarily on their psychoanalytic analysis of Norman's 1,368 dreams over a three year period of time. Their analysis shows that "all of his conflicts, projections, actions and traits are expressions of an infantile character. Chronologically, Norman is an adult; psychologically he is a child, an infant, possibly even a fetus" (p. 19).

Hammer (1954) also alludes to the "childlike state" of the 34 incarcerated pedophiles he studied. He administered the House-Tree-Person projective test to his subjects and found that profound psychosexual immaturity is characteristic of these pedophiles.

Interpersonal Inadequacy. Many people, laypersons and professionals alike have problems with the concept of "infantile behavior" in adult child molesters. Consequently, a more common finding for this population is stated in terms of "interpersonal inadequacy" or "psychosexual immaturity."

The childhood histories of pedophiles have rendered them unusually awkward in interpersonal relationships, especially with adult women (Hammer and Jacks, 1955; Revitch and Weiss, 1962; Fisher, 1969; Panton, 1979). They may present a facade of adult heterosexual competence to the world: 26 (79%) of the pedophiles in the clinical sample are married and 19 of them have at least one child.

However, their perceptions of adult women belie this facade. All of the heterosexual pedophiles in the clinical sample were asked to give one word which most accurately describes most adult women. It is interesting that with all of the descriptive adjectives available for use, two types of descriptions were heard with some frequency. Five of the pedophiles described most women as "deceptive" or some synonym of that word, and six others described them as "seductive" or used some other word which had the same connotation. Both of these words indicate in their own ways a perceived difference in power between the pedophile and the adult woman with whom he is likely to interact.

Psychological tests given to pedophiles pretty much substantiate this observation. Stricker (1967) administered the Blacky Picture Test to 64 pedophiles and concluded that the test results indicate "immature, feminine approaches, not unlike the test results for young girls" (p. 38). Profile configurations of pedophiles for the MMPI show an elevation in the Social Introversion scale which indicates self-alienation, despondency, insecurity, and fear of heterosexual adult relationships (Panton, 1979). Similarly, results of the Edwards Personal Preference Schedule show high scores for pedophiles in deference, succorance and abasement, leading Fisher (1969) to conclude that such pedophiles are typically "passive, subservient, dependent, insecure, guilt-ridden, rigid, possessing low self esteem and low heterosexual drive. In addition, they are unable to make decisions, express their anger, be assertive, and to act independently and accomplish tasks" (p. 420). Hammer and Glueck (1957) administered the Thematic Apperception Test to pedophiles and conclude that they are most likely to be extremely inadequate socially and sexually.

Alcohol. One way by which a passive, inadequate person may compensate for these traits is through the ingestion of alcohol. Only two of the heterosexual pedophiles in the clinical sample are identified alcoholics, but a full 20 (61%) committed the pedophilic offenses while under the influence of alcohol, and their reasons for drinking sound remarkably similar to the reasons why many nonviolent people drink.

> "I'm no alcoholic," states Mr. Watson, "but I have to drink to get through some situations, like a party or a social gathering. I feel better about myself when I drink, you know, like I'm more confident and easier to get along with."

> "I wouldn't molest no little girls if I wasn't drinking," states Mr. Dunlap. "I can control myself when I ain't drinking but when I do the booze gets some power over me. I guess you could say I'm a mean drunk. Like when I drink I don't take no for an answer."

Marshall and Christie (1981) found that 31 of the 41 pedophiles they studied either had been drinking just prior to the offense or were drunk at the time of the offense. They conclude that alcohol potentiates the effects of any provocative stimulus, sexual or aggressive, and enhances the current emotional state, whether it be sexually aroused or angry, with consequent effects on overt behavior. Alcohol also, of course, markedly reduces the usual inhibitory effects that aggressive cues can have on sexual responses (Barbaree *et al.*, 1980).

Mental Illness. It is a common tendency to confuse our feelings about a behavior with the mental status of the person who is demonstrating that behavior. Because most people feel disgust and repulsion when they think about child molestation, they assume that the molester is mentally ill. The greater our revulsion the more likely the perception of mental illness.

There is a certain comfort in the stereotype that the pedophile is mentally ill but there is little truth. Most major studies have demonstrated clearly that mental illness, especially severe mental illness, is not likely to be found in child molesters. In his study of 25 pedophiles, Swanson (1968) found that only five showed the "vaguest signs of psychosis" (p. 679). Groth *et al.* (1978) discovered that only 12 of their sample of 148 convicted pedophiles were psychotic (p. 21). Henn *et al.* (1976) also agree that psychosis is rare in child molesters.

In the clinical sample, two of the heterosexual pedophiles are psychotic. It is interesting (and at the same time unfortunate) that both of these individuals had experienced the most trauma in their childhoods.

Ryan, 16, had a history of child molestation that dated back four years. The victims were all between the ages of one and three years old. Ryan's father is a physically and emotionally violent man who frequently beat his wife and son so severely that on several occasions they were both hospitalized. To "comfort" her son after his beatings Ryan's mother would take him to her bed. The two had an incestuous relationship for nearly five years. Soon after that relationship began, Ryan started to communicate with God, and has experienced frequent hallucinations since that time. He has periodically experienced the delusion that he is God or Satan. Each molestation experience occurred during one of these psychotic episodes.

Mr. Butler, 37, had been the victim of paternal incest for three years until his alcoholic father hung himself. Mr. Butler then lived in a series of foster homes and institutions. In one foster home he was beaten so severely by his foster father that he was in a coma for several days. Upon recovery, he began experimenting with drugs and alcohol. A religious conversion stopped further drug use but also made him extremely anxious about his own sexuality. To punish himself for "sex thoughts" he would cut his penis with razor blades. At one time he tried to castrate himself. He molested a three year old girl and attempted to molest a seven year old girl but was thwarted in that attempt

While psychosis is not often found in heterosexual pedophiles, character disorders and neuroses are. Swanson (1968) found that 68% of his sample of pedophiles suffer from character disorders (p. 680). In the clinical sample, 12 (36%) have been diagnosed as character disordered or neurotic.

Mental retardation is not a common finding in the clinical sample. Only two of the individuals in that sample are mentally impaired. The fact that this sample was created from a court caseload may have contributed to this low figure. It may be fair to assume that obviously mentally retarded molesters may be treated more informally by the criminal justice system or may be diverted into community treatment programs. This is not to imply that mentally impaired individuals are a significant risk to children, but that they may appear less frequently on court caseloads from which clinical samples of pedophiles are likely to be created.

PATTERNS OF PEDOPHILIA

The data from both research and the clinical sample suggest, then, that the "typical" heterosexual pedophile is an interpersonally awkward, psychosexually immature individual with a childhood history of physical and sexual abuse. This is a modal profile, however, since three very distinct patterns of pedophilia are identified in the literature.

Fixated Heterosexual Pedophilia

Burgess et al. (1978) describe a fixated heterosexual pedophile as a person suffering from a "temporary or permanent arrestment of psychosocial maturation resulting from unresolved formative issues that persist and underlie the organization of subsequent phases of development" (p. 6). The child molester they are describing has been, from adolescence, sexually attracted to children, and this sexual attraction has persisted throughout his adult life. Emotionally and certainly sexually he is himself still a child, therefore he is likely to be more comfortable around children than with adults, and because of that comfort, will be more likely to act out sexually with children than with adults.

How a person becomes fixated at this childlike level of functioning is highly related to the childhood histories that already have been examined. Freud, who developed the concept of fixation, stated that a person will become fixated at an early stage of development if he receives too little gratification at that particular stage so that he is too anxious to go on to the next stage of development, or if he receives too much gratification so that there is no motivation to go on to another stage of development (Hall, 1954). If either one of these happens, the person will become fixated and will try during his adult life to achieve the same type of satisfaction that was appropriate for that earlier stage of development.

The childhood histories of physical and sexual abuse among the 17 fixated pedophiles in the clinical sample suggest that these individuals received too little, rather than too much, gratification at that early stage of development. Consequently, they are emotionally and sexually children, still desperately striving to get their dependency and nurturing needs met — needs that were not simply unmet by their parents, but cruelly and rejectingly unmet.

Due to their fixations, these pedophiles are passive, dependent persons who are noticeably socially awkward with adults and heterosexually anxious with adult women (Cohen and Seghorn, 1969; Groth and Birnbaum, 1978). They are, in the words of Burgess *et al.*, "sexually addicted" to children (1978:7), not only in that they feel more interpersonally at ease with children, but also in that they dream and fantasize about children. This obsession has become such an integral part of their personalities that they are likely to entertain these pedophilic impulses with only the most transient feelings of guilt and shame.

The concept of fixation is also related to another finding in the clinical sample and that is that all 17 of the fixated heterosexual pedophiles stated in some way that they identified with their child victims. Their own passivity and dependency may lead them to identify with the female sex of the victim, and their childhood histories of abuse may lead them to identify with the perceived status of the child.

> Mr. Tufts, 27, a playground supervisor, molested a nine year old girl; previously he had molested two other young girls. In explaining his motivation for doing so, he said, "I felt sorry for her. Her clothes were dirty and two sizes too big like they were hand-me-downs or something. Once she had a big shiner and I thought for sure her old man had hit her, you know. I went through that as a kid; I know what it's like. So I wanted to show her some love, you know, just some love. The other two girls, too. I could tell nobody cared about them either, you know."
>
> Mr. Enders, 33, an elementary school janitor, had been molested by a stranger when he was nine years old and had been raised in foster homes. He molested the two daughters, age five and seven, of the woman he was

dating. "Okay, I love my girl Janet, okay, but she's not a good mother. I should know; my mother wasn't no good either. Janet's old man used to beat her and the girls too. So when she split from him she decided to have a good time, okay, and she kind of neglected her girls. Sometimes she'd hit them too, like my mother used to hit me. I like those girls and I know what it's like to be shit on as a kid. I was just giving them some comfort after their ma hit them, okay, and it just kind of got out of hand."

Both Mr. Tufts and Mr. Enders hold jobs, one as a playground supervisor, the other as an elementary school janitor. These two occupations which put these men in constant contact with children, are not coincidental. Many fixated pedophiles, because of their obsession with children, choose jobs that are very children-oriented. These types of jobs serve a dual purpose: they allow the pedophile to feel socially and interpersonally comfortable, and they allow a steady population of potential child victims. Remember that these pedophiles are not incapacitated by their fixation and they are not so child-like that they cannot assume some adult responsibilities, such as holding jobs. Many laypersons, in observing and interacting with them, would probably use such terminology as "immature," "shy," "withdrawn," or "ineffectual" when referring to them.

In their adult relationships, these pedophiles typically seek dominant or nurturing persons who gratify their needs to be dependent and protected. They may have adult sexual relationships, but they are usually passive in those relationships and do not initiate them.

They are also typically passive with their victims. These pedophiles are not inclined to use force with their victims although verbal threats are not uncommon. Because of their identification with their victims and their own immature level of psychosexual functioning, the fixated pedophiles are usually content with the fondling, kissing and caressing of their victims. The only fixated pedophiles in the clinical sample who used any amount of force in accomplishing the molestation were those who were under the influence of alcohol at the time of the offense.

These 17 fixated pedophiles are also the child molesters with the greatest number of previous molestations in their backgrounds. In other words the fixated pedophile is more likely to be a recidivist. These 17 fixated pedophiles averaged 3.5 admitted molestations prior to the one that brought them to the court caseload from which this clinical sample was created. Since this is simply a piece of information based on self-reports, there is reason to believe that this figure actually underestimates the total number of prior offenses.

Regressed Heterosexual Pedophilia

A regressed pattern of heterosexual pedophilia is defined by Burgess *et al.* (1978) as one in which a person who originally preferred age-mates turns to children for sexual gratification when peer sexual relations become conflictive. This conflict with the peers usually constitutes a challenge to the person's sexual adequacy or may involve a situational crisis of a nonsexual nature which resurrects unresolved dependency needs and anxieties.

Fourteen (42%) of the heterosexual pedophiles in the clinical sample fell into this category. All had achieved some degree of adult interactional success before they had experienced the setback that led to the molestation of a child. Those "setbacks" they had experienced are presented in Table 16.

TABLE 16. EVENTS TRIGGERING MOLESTATION EXPERIENCES
FOR 14 REGRESSED HETEROSEXUAL PEDOPHILES

Event	Number Reported
Divorce/separation/ breakup of relationship	7
Sexual problems	3
Wife's pregnancy	2
Death of family member	1
Loss of job	1

Each one of these events triggered a depressive reaction which clearly preceded by several days at least the molestation of a child. In many cases it also initiated a dissociative response in that many of the pedophiles also discussed feeling that they had committed the molestations "in a trance" or that the molestations just "did not seem real."

Why these events were so powerful in creating these pedophilic responses has to do with the modal portrait of the heterosexual pedophile. As a passive, dependent person it is clear that a divorce, separation or dissolution of a relationship would resurrect unresolved dependency needs, just as the death of a family member could. For someone who is also psychosexually immature, sexual problems which challenge his adult sexual role can also be traumatic and can thus trigger a regressive reaction. Also, for a person who feels personally incompetent, the loss of a job can certainly exacerbate a negative self-image. Hartman and Nicolay (1966) also report on the traumatic effect that a wife's pregnancy can have on such a passive, dependent person. They studied 91 men who had been arrested while their wives were pregnant and compared them to 91 men who had been arrested but whose wives were not pregnant. They discovered that 41% of the men with pregnant wives had been arrested for sexual offenses ranging in seriousness from making obscene telephone calls to raping adult women, to molesting children. Only 18% of the control group had been arrested for sexual offenses (p. 233). This data lead Hartman and Nicolay to conclude that the pregnancy of the wife creates a stress that the dependent, immature husband is not able to manage effectively, as the case of Mr. Howell demonstrates:

> "My wife was going to have her first kid," he explains. "You'd think she was the first lady ever to have a kid, the way everybody carried on about it. She didn't even want to have sex with me for fear that it would hurt the kid. Sure I felt left out and I got real uptight about it. I guess I felt kind of jealous too. So when our neighbor brought over her little girl for us to watch one afternoon when she went shopping, I just kind of started to fool around with her when I was laying her down for her nap. Next thing I remember her daddy was banging on my door telling me he was going to kill me."

The regressed pedophile is significantly less likely to be a recidivist. He may commit more than one molestation during this depressive reaction, but even that is relatively unlikely. Once he regains mastery over whatever competent coping skills he has, the regressive reaction has dissipated. Another reason why he is unlikely to repeat the molestation is because the pedophilic behavior may be inconsistent with his self-image so that he experiences guilt and shame after he has committed the molestation. These feelings are powerful deterrents to further misbehavior.

The regressed pedophile is likely to use more force, however, in gaining the cooperation of his victims. His needs take precedence over those of the child and his dissociative state may render him not fully aware of how he is treating the child.

> Mr. Van was confronted with the physical injury he had done to the child victim. She was bruised and had suffered a broken finger during the assault. "I didn't do that to her, I swear!" he explains. "I'm not saying she's lying or nothing, but maybe it happened some other way." When asked to detail his behavior during the assault, he replied, "Hell, I don't know how I was acting. I just kept thinking about how pissed off I was with my old lady for leaving me." Asked if he could remember if his child victim had struggled or screamed, he replied, "She might have. Hell, I don't know!"

Because the regressed pedophile is more adult in his behavior and because he has usually achieved some degree of interpersonal and sexual success before the molestation has occurred, he is also more likely to attempt or to complete intercourse with his victim. Six (43%) of the 14 regressed pedophiles had done so, and four (29%) more had used their fingers to forcefully penetrate the child.

Twelve (86%) of the regressed pedophiles molested children who were strangers to them. This fact may have contributed also to the issue of force since the molester does not have an ongoing relationship with his victim or with her family, a relationship in which any degree of force used against the child would surely bring retaliation of some kind by the family, even if they chose for some reason to ignore the molestation.

Sadistic Heterosexual Pedophilia

The type of pedophile for whom aggression is truly an issue is the sadistic pedophile. For him, "sex appears to be in the service of the need for power" (Groth and Burgess, 1977:259). Physical aggression becomes eroticized for this individual and sexual satisfaction is achieved only when the child has been hurt and humiliated.

Despite the fact that such cases of sadistic heterosexual pedophilia grab a great deal of media attention, true cases are thankfully quite rare. Only two such cases are in the clinical sample. Both men had histories of physical abuse as children and both had themselves experienced multiple sexual victimizations as children. Both also had been under the influence of alcohol at the time of the offense.

> Mr. Baines, 34, has an extensive prior record for assaultive offenses all of which involved adult victims. He had done time in prison for one of those assaults and had been jailed several other times. Mr. Baines had been

molested himself as a child and had been sexually victimized by his two older stepbrothers. He also had been physically abused as a child and still has scars on his face and neck from burns received when his mother deliberately splattered hot grease on him. As a child he tortured and killed animals, set fires and terrorized his neighborhood. He abducted a seven year old girl from a school playground, raped her, and cut her repeatedly with a knife. He left her bleeding and dazed in a park where she was found several hours later.

Mr. Kirk, 33, had been sexually victimized as a child by his father and later by his older stepsister. He, too, had been horribly physically abused as a child. Mr. Kirk has numerous child sexual assaults on his criminal record. Jailed on several occasions, he once spent a month in a psychiatric hospital for observation but was released because he was "untreatable." Mr. Kirk attacked an eleven year old girl who was wading in a stream in an isolated rural area. He raped her and bound her hands and feet, and tied another rope around her neck and dragged her across an open field. When the child lost consciousness he assumed she was dead and left the scene. When asked what he had felt like when he had done this, he replied, "Like Superman — strong, invincible and horny, too!"

The sadistic heterosexual pedophile sees the child victim as a representation of everything he hates about himself as well as the dreaded memories of his own childhood. Unfortunately, because of these feelings, this pattern of pedophilia can result in the death of a child. When asked if they could kill their victims, one sadistic pedophile in the clinical sample said that he did not know; the other unhesitatingly answered yes. Again, despite the fact that these types of cases grab the public's attention and its sympathy, they are actually rare occurrences, statistically speaking. Swigert *et al.* (1976) analyzed 444 homicides committed between 1955 and 1973 and found that only five of that total were sexual homicides and only one of those five had as its victim a child (p. 392).

AGE PATTERNS

In many ways, heterosexual pedophilia is an age-specific offense. It is most likely to occur when the offender is an adolescent, or in his mid-thirties, or senescent.

Adolescent Pedophiles

There are four adolescent child molesters in the clinical sample. Their mean age is 16.2 years and the mean age of their victims is 5.1 years. All of the young men in question were profoundly psychosexually immature and one was psychotic. None of them had had a sexual experience with an age-mate; in many ways their molestation of little girls represents a "rehearsal" for later adult sexual encounters.

Shoor *et al.* (1966) completed one of the most comprehensive studies to date of adolescent child molesters. They studied 80 such cases and draw the following profile of the adolescent: He is sexually naive and suffers from "panimmaturity" in that he is socially naive as well. He is a loner who prefers the company of children because he is not intimidated by them as he is by adults and peers. He is an academic underachiever and is likely to identify most with his dominant mother.

In the four cases of adolescent child molesters in the clinical sample, there is a great deal of conformity to this profile. However, it was also found that the parents of these young men were fiercely protective of their sons, even in the face of the most damaging evidence against them. The boys were obviously protected from the consequences of their behavior, especially as far as their molestation of children is concerned.

There is some reason to believe that a parental collusion process may have set up these boys for this offense in the first place. This process is very evident in one case, and only alluded to in the others.

> Alex, 15, molested a four year old girl for whom he was babysitting. He had told his father that the girl previously had acted "sexy" by taking down her pajama bottoms in his presence. His father had replied, "She's just asking to get raped." His mother who had overheard the conversation added, "Now's your big chance to be a man, Alex." That evening, while baby- sitting her, Alex molested the little girl.

Two of these young men had themselves been victims of incest; in fact, they were just emerging from the incest experiences at the time of their offenses. The other two deny having been sexually victimized, although one of those lived in a home in which paternal incest was occurring with his sister as a victim.

Mid-Thirties Pedophiles

Another age period in which pedophilia is likely to peak is in the mid- thirties. Gigeroff et al. (1968) state that between the ages of 35 and 39, marital problems as well as social and economic stresses may initiate a regressed pedophilic reaction in persons so disposed.

Mohr (1962) estimates that this age group represents the largest num- ber of heterosexual pedophiles. This assumption is certainly substantiated by the clinical sample in which 25 (76%) of the child molesters are between the ages of 27 and 40.

Senescent Pedophiles

Four of the pedophiles in the clinical sample are over the age of 60 years. They constitute the senescent child molesters. Gigeroff et al. (1968) suggest that these individuals typically have led impeccable lives and the child molestation usually occurs within the context of play and is not likely to in- volve force. This finding was basically substantiated by the clinical sample in which three of the senescent pedophiles have no prior records of any kind and have led adult lives characterized by economic and social success.

All of these three had undergone a stressful event which had triggered a depressive reaction before the molestation had actually occurred.

> Mr. McKay, 62, suffered a heart attack and was forced to take an early re- tirement from his job. He became depressed and bored. On the advice of his

physician he began taking long walks and on one of those walks befriended a seven year old girl. She would often walk with him. On one occasion he took her to a park, a regular stop on their walk, and molested her by fondling and kissing her. He then took her home and turned himself into the police.

Mr. Albert, 65, lost his wife to cancer. He had no family in his community and was suicidally depressed for months. He then began to invite neighbor children into his home "for company" and molested two of them during the course of a game they were playing.

Mr. Rose, 61, had been experiencing impotency for a year, and that sexual problem placed a severe strain on his marriage. He began drinking rather heavily and during an intoxicated state, fondled and caressed a grand-daughter of an acquaintance.

None of these three men has a history of sexual victimization, however, the fourth pedophile does. He also has several prior charges of child molestation on his criminal record and is alleged to have been incestuously involved with his daughter and stepdaughter as well.

Mr. Gifford, 67, had been the victim of paternal incest as a child and had been sexually molested by an adult male acquaintance as well. He has been investigated numerous times on suspicion of child molestation but no case had ever gone to court until he enticed a four year old neighbor girl into his home and used his fingers to violently penetrate her. He has adamantly denied guilt in this or in any other case.

Despite the violent nature of Mr. Gifford's molestation of a child, most senescent pedophiles are gentle with their victims, usually content with fonling and kissing rather than with intercourse or attempted intercourse. Their goal in molesting children is the gratification of needs for companionship and affection; the gratification of sexual needs appears to be of secondary concern.

APPROACHES TO THE CHILD VICTIM

Snatching children from playgrounds and enticing them into cars with promises of candy are two common perceptions of how child molesters approach child victims. Groth and Burgess (1977) have defined various approaches which pedophiles are likely to use in obtaining a child victim; these approaches clearly go beyond the stereotype of how child molesters operate.

Sex Pressure Approach

A pedophile who uses this approach has as his aim the gaining of the "sexual control of the child by developing a willing or consenting sexual relationship" (Groth and Burgess, 1977:257). He does so through enticement and a kind of nonviolent entrapment which typically does not place the child victim in any real danger of being physically harmed. Sexuality, in this type of approach, is in the service of dependency needs for physical contact, therefore this approach usually involves only the fondling and caressing of the child.

Fourteen (42%) of the pedophiles in the clinical sample used this type of approach with their victims. All were relatively gentle with their child victims, if child molestation can ever be accurately described as "gentle."

Mr. Albert invited children into his home and let them play with a model train set he had in his basement. While they played he busied himself by serving cookies and soft drinks to them. After most of the children had left, he invited two sisters, ages six and eight, into his bedroom to see model airplanes he had constructed. While they were looking at the models, he put his arms around them and began kissing them. Both initially withdrew, but Mr. Albert pressured them by saying, "Now the least I can expect from you is some hugs and kisses. If you give me some hugs and kisses I'll let you two play with the train all by yourselves the next time." Both of the girls acquiesed to his sexual approach which continued several times a week for over a month before the girls told their parents.

All of the 14 pedophiles who used the sex pressure approach with their child victims also tended to idealize children in general and their victims in particular. They see the children as loving, innocent, open and affectionate. That perception not only motivates their interpersonal attraction to children but also their sexual attraction to them. It is also this perception which leads to the "gentle" molestation of the children since violence is less likely to be used against the children if they are perceived in an idealistic, romanticized fashion.

It appears that in the most basic way, the pedophile who uses this sex pressure approach genuinely cares for the child victim. This is a difficult concept for most people to grasp since in the eyes of so many child molestation is the ultimate victimization of a human being. However, the dependency needs of the child molester draw him to the child, and his idealized perception of the child draws even more tightly the bond between them. Since this type of child molester usually knows the child victim, and has taken the time to establish a relationship with the child before the molestation actually takes place, he cares for the child and does not seek to harm the child.

Sex Force Approaches

Other pedophilic approaches to children involve more coercion or even physical violence than does the sex pressure approach.

Exploitative Assault. Groth and Burgess (1977) describe this approach as one in which the pedophile "uses the child as an object of sexual relief, he makes no attempt to engage the child in any emotional way" (p. 259).

Seventeen (52%) of the heterosexual pedophiles in the clinical sample used this approach in gaining the cooperation of their child victims. Approximately half of them did some physical injury to their victims, that injury usually involving bruises, scrapes and contusions. The others denied having been physically injurious but did admit to using verbal threats in the accomplishment of their goals.

The issue of physical violence often has been underplayed in studies of pedophilia. Sadoff (1975), for example, states that pedophiles are typically nonviolent in their molestation of children, an assumption supported by Kopp (1962) who adds that pedophiles are no threat to the physical safety of children. Kroth (1979), in his analysis of 24 cases of pedophilia finds that only two of the men in question used physical force in gaining their victims' cooperation (p. 52), and McCaghy (1967) finds that only one in five pedophiles use any kind of force whatsoever in achieving their sexual goals with children (p. 80).

In the light of all of these assertions that pedophiles are basically non-violent, it is interesting that over 50 % of the pedophiles in the clinical sample used some violence, albeit verbal, in their interaction with their victims. Since there is no indication that this clinical sample differs significantly from other research populations, especially in its origin, the answer to this discrepancy must lie somewhere else. Marshall and Christie (1981) may provide that answer. In their study of 41 pedophiles, they find that the pedophiles themselves frequently deny having used physical or verbal force with their victims. However, when victim reports and medical records are examined, a very different scenario develops. Using this data, they discovered that 75 % of their sample either physically injured their victims or verbally threatened to do so (p. 148). They also conclude that the degree of force used in each case exceeded that which was necessary to achieve the pedophiles' goals. In the clinical sample data about the degree of physical or verbal violence that was done to the child were gleaned from victims' reports and medical records, not from the pedophiles themselves, who tended to seriously underreport the degree of physical or verbal violence they used.

This possible discrepancy between verbal accounts of the molestation and the reality of the molestation itself is alluded to by Forgione (1976) who advocates the use of mannequins in the assessment of child molestation behavior. He finds that pedophiles tend to verbally underreport violence in accomplishing their goals, but that when they are asked to role play the molestation with the use of mannequins, the behavioral acting out of that molestation stimulates the proffering of details not previously reported. Many of these details involve the disclosure of physical force or verbal threats during the course of the molestation. All of this would suggest that physical force is used more often in child molestation than researchers have realized, and this, in turn, serves as a caution to researchers and practitioners to go beyond the pedophiles' accounts for an accurate description of what actually occurred.

Sadistic Assault. Finally a minority of pedophiles derive sexual gratification from hurting their victims who "symbolize everything the offender hates about himself and, thereby, becomes an object of punishment" (Groth and Burgess, 1977:261). Only two of the heterosexual pedophiles in the clinical sample used this approach, the dynamics of which have been examined in the presentation of the sadistic pattern pedophile.

THE FEMALE HETEROSEXUAL PEDOPHILE

In 1978, a 23-year-old housewife was charged with contributing to the delinquency of a minor in that she had sexual intercourse with a 15-year-old boy. The charges were later dismissed, however, because in the ruling of the court, "Intercourse with a young boy is nothing more than sex education, essential and necessary in his growth toward maturity and subsequent family life" (*Boston Globe*, February 10, 1978:28).

The idea that a sexual relationship between an adult woman and a young boy is acceptable and even desirable also can be found in publicized accounts of such encounters. For example, Fleming and Fleming (1975) in their book, *The First Time*, a collection of accounts of initial sexual experiences, relate the first time experience of actor Joseph Cotten who was "sexually educated" at age 8 by a 19-year-old woman. Calling that experience a "delightful shock" he then bragged that he was her "star pupil" (p. 74). Pianist Liberace lost his virginity at age 13 to "some big chesty broad" and stated that he liked the experience (p. 172); and singer Lou Rawls lost his virginity at age 13 and although he was embarrassed, he was happy he had not lost it "to a faggott" (p. 222).

This highly romanticized vision of older woman-younger boy sexual encounters may have some truth in reality since female aggressors are typically less threatening to children and their molestation of the children even may be less traumatic (Finkelhor, 1979). Yet these accounts do not accurately reflect all incidents of molestations of children by women, as the clinical sample illustrates. Two female heterosexual pedophiles are in the sample.

> Madelyn, 21, had sexually victimized a five year old boy for whom she had been babysitting. She fondled his genitals and placed Q-tips in his rectum. This occurred on several occasions because the boy's parents did not at first believe his complaints.

> Sarah, 22, a teacher's aide in an elementary school was accused of child molestation in that she had fondled the genitals of two first graders in her charge. This was not the first complaint against her, but the other charges could not be substantiated because the boys would not testify against her.

Both of the female heterosexual pedophiles in the clinical sample came from severely disorganized homes characterized by physical abuse. Both also had been sexually victimized as children.

> Madelyn had been incestuously victimized by her older brother who sodomized her over a three year period of time. Her religiously conservative grandmother with whom the children lived would abusively punish her for "sexual thoughts." The grandmother lived a double life, however. During the day she was a pious, hardworking woman; at night men paid her for sex. Some of those men found their ways into Madelyn's bedroom.

> Sarah had been a victim of paternal incest and had been molested by a friend of her father. She went through a period of lesbianism and self-enforced celibacy. She has a pathological fear of pregnancy.

There is little doubt that displaced aggression played an important role in Madelyn's offense and that the fear of pregnancy and adult male sexual behavior played similar roles for Sarah. Both women are also mentally ill and the best information would suggest that they have been for quite some time. Madelyn suffers from an endogenous depression which occasionally has psychotic features. She was first diagnosed when she was 15 and had attempted suicide. Sarah suffers from hysterical neurosis which was diagnosed several years previous to this offense.

So the much touted "sexual education" of little boys actually may be done at the hands of women whose own sexual experiences have rendered them angry, confused and frightened. If that is the case, education does not take place, victimization does.

CHAPTER 12: HETEROSEXUAL PEDOPHILIA — EFFECTS ON THE VICTIMS

In a book titled, *The Sensuous Child*, author Hal Wells concludes, "Children have a right to sexual pleasure.... [M]ost of the sexual trauma stuff is nonsense" (1978:152). Dr. Wells' conclusion is based primarily on his analysis of one of his female patients who had been gang-raped at 14 and then had been incestuously victimized by an older sibling. As an adult she had married and had raised children and, in the opinion of Dr. Wells, had experienced no observable problems as a result of her molestation.

While it is true that some youngsters can emerge virtually unscathed from a molestation experience, that is more the exception than the rule. And because it is an exception, Dr. Wells' flippant dismissal of this sexual trauma "stuff" as "nonsense" cruelly ignores the experiences of most child molestation victims.

The clinical sample contains 20 victims of heterosexual pedophilia; three of whom are male. The mean age at which the molestation occurred is 9 years. This mean age is slightly older than the 8-year-old mean age of the victims discovered by Gebhard *et al.* (1965:71), and slightly younger than the median age range of 10 to 12 years discovered by Kroth (1979:67). Ten of those 20 heterosexual molestation victims are now adolescents or adults and they will be utilized to present a distinctly longitudinal perspective on the molestation experience. The remaining 10 were just emerging from the molestation experience at the time of the study.

STRANGER VS. ACQUAINTANCE

Many of the effects of heterosexual pedophilia on the child victims are dependent on whether the child is acquainted with the offender. McCaghy (1967) found that 68% of the 181 pedophiles he studied were acquainted with their victims (p. 80); Gebhard *et al.* 1965) discovered that 60% of the pedophiles they studied were acquainted with their victims (p. 100).

In the clinical sample of 20 child molestation victims, 11 (55%) knew the offender well; three (15%) were slightly acquainted with the offender; and the remaining six (30%) had been molested by a stranger. This particular dimension of the molestation experience is perhaps more important than it initially appears in that the relationship of the child victim to the offender has a great deal to do with the effects the molestation will have on the child as well as the type of molestation experience, per se, the child is likely to have.

MOLESTATION EXPERIENCE AND EFFECTS

Stereotypical perceptions of child molesters have some truth in reality but certainly not enough to accurately describe the experiences of all victims. In actuality, pedophiles use several different techniques in gaining the co-operation of the children and each approach to the child creates a unique set of effects.

Rape

Five (25%) of the child victims in the clinical sample had been raped by the offenders. There are some factors in addition to the rape that distinguish these five children from the other children who had been molested. First they were slightly older than the other victims. The mean age of the five rape victims was 10.4 years, nearly one year older than the other victims who had been molested. Second, four of these five youngsters had been raped by strangers; the remaining youngster had been raped by a man with whom she was slightly acquainted. Third, the type of molestation, per se, involved much more force and penetration compared to the experiences of the other victims. Two of the children had experienced sexual intercourse; one had been sodomized by her attacker; and the remaining two had been violently penetrated with the fingers of their attackers. In addition to this physically violent sexual assault, three of the child victims had been physically assaulted to such an extent that they had experienced cuts, bruises, contusions, and in one case, broken bones, all of which required immediate medical attention.

Given the fact that five rape cases do not constitute a large enough sample from which conclusions can be generalized, a tentative pattern based on these cases does emerge. The child rape victim is likely to be slightly older than other molestation victims. She or he is most likely to have been raped by a stranger who is more inclined to be physically as well as sexually violent with the child.

Rape Trauma Syndrome. Burgess and Holmstrom (1974) define the rape trauma syndrome as "the acute phase and long-term reorganization process that occurs as a result of forcible rape or attempted forcible rape" (p. 982). While originally theorizing that this syndrome is predictable for adult victims of rape, the authors later suggested that this syndrome could also occur for child victims of rape (Burgess, et al., 1978).

The acute phase of this syndrome occurs immediately before, during and immediately after the rape itself. The predominant feeling the child experiences, of course, is fear, but it is a fear that is so overwhelming and at times incapacitating that it clearly surpasses in intensity any traditional description of fear. The fear is so intense that the child can only surmise that her or his life is in imminent danger. Descriptions of that reaction are provided by a child who had been raped by an adult, and by an adult woman, remembering her rape experience which had taken place thirty years before.

> Freda, 9, had been violently sexually assaulted by an adult stranger whose home she had gone to while selling candy to raise money for a class trip. The man had invited her into his home, and then grabbed her, slapped her repeatedly across the face, and pulled down her panties. He then used his fingers to violently penetrate her vagina and rectum. Her struggles were in vain since his physical size clearly overwhelmed her. The entire assault, by the molester's own account, occurred over a thirty minute period of time. When he finally let her leave the house, after threatening to kill her if she told, she tumbled down his porch steps and was found staggering down the middle of the street by a passerby who took her to the hospital. While being examined by medical personnel at the hospital she became hysterical, screaming, "Don't hurt me! Please don't hurt me!" When her parents arrived thirty minutes later she did not recognize them. She assumed the fetal position on the examining table and sucked her thumb. During her three day hospitalization she had to be force fed and diapered because she refused to attend to herself. The skillful intervention of a child psychiatrist summoned by the hospital eventually brought her out of her regressive withdrawal.

> Marilyn, 40, remembers her rape experience at age ten. "This guy came to the park. I was playing by myself because my friends had already left to go home for supper. Anyway, this guy was all frantic. He told me that my mom got hurt at home and had to be taken to the hospital and that she had asked him to come and get me and bring me to her. My folks had always warned me about getting into cars with strangers but that never even crossed my mind. I jumped right in the car, crying my eyes out, and I never even worried about myself until he drove his car into the woods behind the park and shut off the engine. At first I was worried because he wasn't bringing me to my mom. Then I thought, 'Oh God, he's going to hurt me!' He just ripped my shorts off and put his penis in me before I could even get out of the car. The pain was terrible and I was sure I was going to die. I must have passed out because the next thing I remember I was in the hospital. A nurse was stroking my head and talking to me. I thought she was an angel and I was dead. I think it was days before I really realized that I wasn't dead. For over a month afterwards I refused to leave the house. I wanted to be near my parents all of the time, even at night. In fact, for a couple of weeks I even slept in the same room with them. For months after that I had to sleep with a light on in my room."

Regressive behavior such as described by Freda and Marilyn is not at all uncommon in cases of child rape, nor is a kind of shocked numbness in which the child appears withdrawn and uncommunicative. The management of this acute phase of the syndrome is obviously very important with attention to be paid not only to the physical injuries the child has sustained, but to the emotional injuries as well.

The long-term reorganization that follows the acute reaction differs in symptomatology for each child victim, depending on her or his own psychology, the reaction of the family to the molestation, and the nature of the molestation itself. Younger children are most likely to somaticize the trauma and will complain of various psychosomatic symptoms which may persist for some time after the molestation. Of course the physical damage a rape can do to a young child is severe and may slow the emotional recovery.

The older child is more likely to behaviorally act out the fear and anxiety created by the rape. This was certainly true of the five raped children in the clinical sample. All of them experienced nightmares for as long as six months after the molestation had occurred. A phobic reaction to strangers was noted for these children, although in no case did this phobia persist for longer than two months after the molestation. Eating and sleeping disorders, documented for all five of the children, also dissipated after two months. School phobia was noted for two of the child victims; in one case it spontaneously terminated after six weeks, while in the other case prompt psychological intervention brought an end to the school phobia in a week. The experiences of these five raped children would suggest that a two month reorganization phase is predictable, although data on many more children would have to be collected before that finding can be stated as a fact.

Despite the finding from the clinical sample that a two month reorganization is predictable, some children are so traumatized by the rape that the reorganization phase of the rape trauma syndrome lasts for many months and even, in some cases, for years. No more eloquent illustration of the potential chronicity of this trauma can be found than the description the writer and poetess Maya Angelou gives of her rape at the age of 8 by her mother's boyfriend, Mr. Freeman (Angelou, 1971:60):

> And then there was the pain. A breaking and entering when even the senses are torn apart. The act of rape upon an eight year old body is a matter of the needle giving because the camel can't. The child gives because the body can, and the mind of the violator cannot.

Several weeks before the rape, Mr. Freeman had cuddled and caressed young Maya, ostensibly to comfort her when she was despondent, Then, during the trial of Mr. Freeman, Maya, alone on the witness stand, was asked by the attorney whether Mr. Freeman had ever touched her before the rape took place. Maya, fearing ostracism from her family if she told the truth, lied and answered, No. Mr. Freeman was convicted and sentenced to one year and one day in jail. Before he could be incarcerated, however, he was found in a vacant lot, beaten to death. Ms. Angelou describes her reaction (p. 73):

> To the logic of an eight year old child, "a man was dead because I lied"....
> I could feel the evilness flowing through my body, and waiting, pent up, to rush off my tongue if I tried to open my mouth.... If it escaped, wouldn't it flood the world and all the innocent people?

In the logic of the child she was responsible for the death of Mr. Freeman and she had within her the capability of flooding the world with evil by the simple act of speaking. In the logic of the child the control of that overwhelming capacity for evil was simple — she would never speak again. Maya kept that vow of silence for many months after the trial.

Katan (1973) suggests that emotional problems created by childhood rape may persist into adulthood. She theorizes that because rape closely combines aggressive and libidinal contacts, the normal fusion of these two drives is disrupted. As adults, these rape victims then become fixated at the anal-sadistic stage in which destructive aggression does not become tempered with warm, affectionate feelings. Consequently, these women have low self-esteem, are self-destructive, and also tend to identify with males.

Two of the childhood rape victims in the clinical sample are now adults, retrospectively describing their respective rape experiences. Katan's description of an adult who had experienced childhood rape holds true for one of the women, however, since she had also been battered as a child and as a wife, it may not be accurate to state that the rape alone caused her adult emotional problems.

Katan also observes that women who were raped as children also tend to expose their own children to the same experiences by not protecting them properly, and in doing so, relive their own early traumas through their own children. Both of the adult women in the clinical sample have children, and in one case the daughter of one of these women was molested.

> Celia, now 44, had been raped by a stranger when she was thirteen. She remembers few of the details of the rape and curtly dismisses any discussion about it saying, "I was tough. I got over it quick." Now she is the mother of a twelve year old who was raped by a stranger. Although Celia refuses to acknowledge any connection between her own childhood rape and that of her daughter, she does admit that she has given her daughter no sexual information "because she is too young," and virtually no supervision "because nothing will happen to her." When apprised of her daughter's rape her first response was, "She'll get over it. She's a strong kid." When it became apparent that her daughter would not quickly get over the rape, she brought her to a therapist at the urging of a friend. Soon she became so immersed in her daughter's therapy that the social worker observed, "It's hard to tell who's the patient."

It is obvious that the rape of a child will produce acute and long-term traumatic symptoms. Available evidence would suggest that there is a two month critical period during which the trauma-related symptoms are likely to peak.

ACCESSORY TO SEX

Fifteen (75%) of the victims of heterosexual pedophilia had been involved in sex pressure situations which Burgess *et al.* (1978) refer to as the "accessory to sex" type of molestation. Manipulated by threats or by promises and gifts, these children acquiese to the power of the adult making the sexual demands and engage in a sexual relationship with that adult.

Kroth (1979) found that the median duration of this type of sexual victimization is three months (p. 72). In the clinical sample, the median time could not be conveniently determined. However, the number of incidents of molestation per se could be calculated for each child and this information is presented in Table 17.

Due to the fact that these molestations are likely to occur more than once for each child, the heterosexual pedophile is typically careful not to hurt the child since any injury to the child would certainly lead to the termination of their sexual relationship. Also their sexual advances are likely to be less coercive and violent, with fondling, masturbation, and occasionally oral sex being the predominant modes of molestation. Verbal threats may be used to gain the cooperation of the child; in fact, they are often used.

TABLE 17. NUMBER OF SEPARATE MOLESTATION EXPERIENCES
REPORTED FOR 15 ACCESSORY TO SEX CHILD VICTIMS

Number of Separate Incidents	Number of Children
One time only	8
Twice	3
Three times	2
Four times	1
Five times	0
Six times	1

In 14 of the 15 cases in the clinical sample, the offending adult was a person familiar to the child victim. Therefore, the pedophile was a person who could be trusted because of his or her familiarity with the child. In the one case the pedophile was a stranger to the child but had spent several hours gaining her trust before he actually molested her.

Accessory to Sex Syndrome

Child victims of an accessory to sex type of molestation will react to that victimization in a variety of ways, "from apparent indifference to acute states of anxiety, withdrawal and depression" (Herjanic and Wilbois, 1978:333). It is understandably difficult to predict exactly how any individual child will react.

In the clinical sample, three young victims appeared to be virtually indifferent to their molestations. There were no real signs of trauma in these youngsters except for an annoyed impatience with adults in their lives who were clearly more traumatized by the molestation than were the children. Rather than using this finding as support for the theory that sexual trauma is nonsense anyway, it would be advisable to analyze the molestations of these children, since a combination of factors makes these molestations and the reactions of the children to them very unique.

First, the three nontraumatized youngsters were very young, ages three, four and six, respectively. Those tender ages may have made it intellectually impossible for these youngsters to have assimilated the reality and the repercussions of their molestation. Second, the molestations per se were gentle in that they did not involve penetration, physical battering, or verbal threats. Each child was fondled and kissed with special attention placed on the buttocks and genital area, while the pedophile masturbated himself. Third, the molestation in each case was carried out by an adult whom the child knew, liked, and trusted. Each molester had been involved to some extent in the child's life prior to the molestation. Two were babysitters and one was the boyfriend of the child's grandmother. Fourth, in many ways the molester in each case had "rehearsed" the molestation many times before it actually took place. Therefore, each of them had been able to successively approximate the actual molestation without raising the child's anxiety or fear. Finally, two of these actual molestations occurred only once; the other occurred three separate times before the child actually told her parents.

The other 12 children who were victims of this accessory to sex type of molestation showed more trauma-related symptomatology. The most profound reaction to the molestation is confusion. This is especially noted when the children are bribed or threatened into keeping the molestation secret. Children are certainly not the best secret keepers, but most of them have an intuitive sense of what is appropriately kept secret. The pressure to keep the secret of the molestation produces feelings of confusion for the child who recognizes that the furtive attempts of the adult to keep the behavior secret must mean that there is something wrong with the behavior.

That confusion develops quickly into fear in most cases. The child is frightened that more will be asked of her or him than the child is willing to give; that she or he will be hurt; that someone will find out; that she or he will not be believed if the secret should be shared. In the words of Simmel (1964): "The secret is surrounded by the possibility and temptation of betrayal; and the external danger of being discovered is interwoven with the internal danger ... of giving oneself away" (p. 334). All of this may become an overwhelming burden for a very young child who, because of her or his familiarity with the pedophile, fully expects to be engaged again at some future time into the sexual relationship. This burden, then, may disrupt the tasks of daily living.

> Luke, 5, had been sexually victimized by his female babysitter who fondled him and coerced him into fondling her. She also inserted Q-tips into his rectum as punishment for a variety of real and imagined wrongdoings. This happened on two separate occasions before he told his parents who scolded him for lying. At that point, his behavior became disruptive. He refused to go to his kindegarten class and developed psychosomatic symptoms when his parents would call the babysitter to take care of him. This victimization continued on four more occasions. By this time Luke would vomit so violently when his parents would call the babysitter that they were finally forced to take his charges against her more seriously.

The sense of betrayal the child experiences when someone she or he has trusted is the victimizer is very real indeed and may create a depressive or anxious reaction. Young children often put their trust blindly and unquestioningly in some adults so their disappointment when that trust is betrayed is likely to be profound. If parents or significant other adults in the child's life also betray that trust by refusing to believe the child's disclosure of the victimization, the trauma is compounded.

Guilt is another powerful feeling which may affect the child victim and even may persist into adulthood. This guilt is especially likely to occur if the child is molested more than one time by the same pedophile, and it unfortunately may be exacerbated by the victim-blaming techniques of so many adults.

> Elaine, 22, remembers the four times her piano teacher had molested her. "He used to bribe me with little gifts, cheap stuff, but good for kids. After he masturbated me once I asked my mom if guys were supposed to do that to kids. It was kind of a hypothetical question. She said they weren't supposed to do that. Then I asked what she would do if some guy did that to me and she said she would kill them. I gave her all kinds of hints like that, but she never picked up on them. I couldn't just outright tell her because I was too scared. So anyway, my piano teacher was doing it to some other little

kid too, and she told and it made all the papers. So then my mom asks me if he ever did it to me. I told her he did it four times, and she starts screaming that I'm a whore, that I must have liked it. God, I wonder to this day if I did.

If the molestation is made public and the child's identity in some way is revealed, the resulting stigma can be very traumatic.

Virginia, 29, had been molested at age seven by an adolescent pedophile. Since she had lived in a small community and the case had received a great deal of local attention, she was quickly identified as the victim. "There were basically two reactions to me," she explains. "Some people treated me like I was a piece of fine china. They pampered me and made all kinds of excuses for my behavior. Other people treated me like I was spoiled goods. The older kids at school were especially guilty of this. I remember walking to the swingset on the playground during recess and some junior high boy yelled, 'Hey hot stuff! How about a kiss?' Lord, it was awful! It wore out after a while, of course, but Lord it really hurt me!"

The ten victims of child molestation in the clinical sample who are now adolescents or adults show few residual effects of the molestation. Each does have occasional "flashbacks" to the experience and one woman does have a variety of sexual problems which she feels were caused by the molestation. Each victim can easily resurrect intense feelings of anger, hurt, fear and guilt when thinking about the molestation. Six of these adults have voluntarily sought therapy at one time or another, but only one of them is convinced that her problems are directly related to her molestation. The rest of them verbalized some curiosity about the possible connection between their problems as adults and their molestation experience as children, but were not convinced that this connection existed.

It should be noted that there are three boys in this clinical sample of molested children. Their reactions did not differ appreciably from those of the girl victims with one exception. They experienced a more intense initial confusion than did the girls. This intense confusion is undoubtedly a product of the fact that none of these three boys had been in any way informationally prepared for the possibility of being victimized by a child molester, let alone a female child molester. Two of them had never really heard of child molestation and one had heard of it but was under the impression that it could only happen to girls.

THE ROLE OF THE VICTIM

Much has been written and speculated upon by researchers and practitioners who want to determine the role of the child in her or his own sexual molestation. It appears that this speculation first began, at least in the professional literature, with a 1937 article by Bender and Blau who, upon examining 16 molested children, concluded that the children had generally cooperated in the molestation and in some cases even initiated it. This observation led them to conclude that the victims had "derived some fundamental satisfaction from the relationship" (Bender and Blau, 1937:514). They then summarized their findings by stating, "[F]requently we considered the possibility that the child might have been the actual seducer rather than the one innocently seduced" (p. 514). The senior author then confirmed this conclusion in a follow-up study of these children which she conducted 15 years later (Bender and Grugett, 1952).

Rogers and Weiss (1953) also suspected that some children play contributory roles in their molestation. They labeled these children "participant victims." Weiss *et al.* (1955) then studied these children in more depth. From a population of 73 molested girls between the ages of 4 and 16 years, they discovered that well over half of these youngsters were participant victims.

Weiss *et al.* find that these participant victims are more attractive and appealing than the other victims, that they frequently behave seductively, and that they had had more than one sexual experience with more than one adult. In therapy these victims tended to be "preoccupied with family conspiracies" (p. 4), a finding that should not be surprising given the fact that 15 of these victims had been incestuously victimized by a family member. It is too bad that Weiss *et al.* did not separate incest victims from molestation victims since the dynamics of the sexual victimizations are very different.

In discussing the family dynamics of participant victims, they find that their mothers tend to feel harrassed by their daughters and do not feel that they can control them. They also find that the mothers are experiencing conflicts over their daughters' emerging sexuality but at the same time are jealous of them. These findings certainly should be of no surprise for incest victims. But why should they also be true of molestation victims?

In the clinical sample only four (20%) of the child molestation victims could in any way be considered participant victims, although the distinction between participant and accidental victims is only reluctantly acknowledged in this study. The reason that it is acknowledged at all is to point out an important etiological factor in that alleged participation which other research studies have failed to recognize.

The four children in question behaved in a pseudomature, pseudoseductive fashion. Each initially had been approached by the adult molester, then each had initiated further sexual contacts with that adult. That begs the question. Why?

Three of the children had been incestuously victimized by their fathers *before* they were molested by the pedophile. Therefore, the alleged "seductive" or "participatory" behavior of these children originated within the family and was a product of the role reversal, the identification with the aggressor, the new deviant identity and the lack of protective coping skills as well as the affection-seeking behavior already discussed in detail for incest victims. Their "participatory" behavior in the molestation was nothing more than bringing into the larger world the survival skills they had taken on within the incestuous family.

The fourth child is the daughter of an incest victim who is still in the process of therapeutically working out the trauma of her own incest experience. The woman has done a great deal of flagrant sexual acting out in recent years and has been sexually victimized in many of these relationships. It is entirely possible that because of her own unresolved sexual and emotional problems, the mother was simply unable to transmit the necessary protective coping skills to her daughter, while at the same time she modeled for her daughter flagrant and victimizable sexual behavior.

When the family dynamics of the so-called participant victims of molestation are examined more critically, their role in the molestation becomes considerably less contributory. Rather than insisting that child molestation victims "may be placed on a continuum from totally accidental victimization at one end to seductive partners on the other" (Schultz, 1980:148), it may be more appropriate to envision that continuum as stretching between totally innocent victims and innocent victims.

Chapter 13: Homosexual Pedophilia

In the summer of 1976, the Dade County Coalition for the Humanistic Rights of Gays invited local political candidates to the YMCA to discuss discriminatory practices and attitudes against homosexuals. A total of 65 candidates came to the forum; 49 were endorsed by the Coalition, and 45 of those 49 were elected to their respective offices. Jubilant over its successful political clout, the Coalition next drew together a gay rights ordinance which it presented to the county's Metro Commission. The ordinance was adopted in January of 1977.

Four days before its adoption, gospel singer and orange juice spokesperson, Anita Bryant, narrowly avoided a three car crash on a Florida highway. Thankful to God that He had spared her life, she decided to serve Him by campaigning to have the gay rights ordinance repealed. She was ultimately successful in doing so on a local level; however before the ordinance was repealed, the shockwaves emanating from Anita Bryant's antihomosexual campaign would be felt throughout the country.

"Homosexuality is an abomination to the Lord," Bryant expounded, paraphrasing a passage from Leviticus, and a large portion of America's population agreed. In saying so, Bryant capitalized on a largely unconscious homophobia, or fear of homosexuality, that is prevalent in this society. For those who find the phrase "fear of homosexuality" too strong to characterize their feelings, Sagarin (1977) suggests the phrase "compassionate and sympathetic hostility" as representative of the majority of people's attitudes about homosexuality, as his case of Mr. and Mrs. Brown, a fictitious middle class couple, illustrates (pp. 450-452):

> She has read of gay bars in the big cities, and cannot possibly imagine what they are, how they function, and why they would be tolerated. She does not know that there is one in her own city, or two, depending on what group of people happens to be there at the moment when one is looking. It is just as well, her husband feels, there is no need for her to know. Though Mr. Brown no longer calls homosexuals "perverts" because he has learned that is not a nice word, he too thinks that something should be done about them.... On the rare occasion that she thinks of homosexual activity, Mrs. Brown is filled with a sense of repulsion, and because she does not understand why someone could do this, or wants to do it, she finds it difficult to believe in the numbers that she hears about. She is certain that homosexuality is on the increase and this bothers her, but all in all, her concern with the problem is small.

Although people like Mr. and Mrs. Brown may have remained mildly hostile about homosexuality throughout Bryant's campaign, it was undoubtedly becoming increasingly difficult to keep small their concern with the problem. By this time, Bryant's crusade had the active and vocal support of many politically and religiously conservative groups and individuals throughout the country. And by this time, Bryant and her followers had made the ultimate connection between homosexuality and child molestation—a connection that made even the most die-hard liberals shudder in fear.

"Because homosexuals cannot have children," explained Bryant, "they can only recruit children. And that is what they do." In a barely perceptible change, Bryant's antihomosexual campaign became the Save Our Children crusade. "Some of the stories I could tell you about child recruitment and child abuse by homosexuals," Bryant intoned, "would turn your stomachs!" She did not have to tell these stories; the fertile imaginations of people caused their stomachs to turn without ever hearing the words. People by the thousands across the country began to support, in money and in spirit, Anita Bryant's Save Our Children crusade.

The subtle shading of the practice of homosexuality between consenting adults into homosexual assaults on children did not go unnoticed by many researchers who had found the latter connection spurious at best. Even the best attempts at educating the public to the realities of homosexuality and child molestation had difficulty in penetrating the homophobia and the "compassionate and sympathetic" hostility of people who, often for the first time, were giving serious thought to what Sagarin calls "the largest American minority" (1977:452). The homosexual molestation of children, "every parent's nightmare" in the words of Anita Bryant, had become an almost tangible fear.

While few would argue that child molestation is indeed every parent's nightmare, there is actually a comparatively less reason to fear homosexual assaults on children than most people believe (Geiser, 1979). Researchers have variously estimated its occurrence as 19% of reported molestations (Revitch and Weiss, 1962), 25% (Swanson, 1968), and 33% (Swift, 1977). Even at its maximum proposed rate of 33%, from a purely statistical point of view and relying on reported cases, it is clear that a child is much more likely to be heterosexually than homosexually molested. In the clinical sample of 45 child molesters, twelve (27%) were homosexual molesters.

Anita Bryant has since mellowed in her crusade. After her own tumultuous divorce, she assumed a "live and let live" attitude. Although she feels no less strongly about the nightmare of child molestation she is, these days, less inclined to blame homosexuals for its occurrence. But the homophobia and the hostility, even if tinged with sympathy, of society remains, subconsciously perhaps, but there nonetheless, ready to be mobilized in response to another crusade or in reaction to a reported case of homosexual pedophilia.

It is remarkable that despite the fact that people are horrified and re-pulsed by the crime of child molestation so little is known about the psychology of the offender. If that observation holds true for child molesters in general, it is even more true for homosexual molesters. What little data are available hardly constitute a comprehensive portrait of the homosexual pedophile. A tentative profile can however be drawn.

Childhood

In Gebhard's *et al.* (1965) study of incarcerated sex offenders, homo-sexual pedophiles as children tended to have had the worst relationships with their parents of any of the various groups of sex offenders studied. This poor relationship is especially evident with their fathers. Although Gebhard *et al.* found that over 50% of the homosexual pedophiles came from broken homes (p. 299), a figure that is confirmed by the clinical sample in which 66% came from broken homes, the fact remains that the fathers, whether present or absent, made powerful impressions on their sons.

Often described as "cold and rejecting" the fathers are typically a source of fear for the developing son. Ten of the 12 homosexual pedophiles in the clinical sample stated that as children they had been afraid of their fathers. Frequently the father is physically abusive, often directing his anger specifically at the son who later becomes the homosexual child molester. However horrible the physical abuse or threat of it may be, the emotional rejection of the sons by the fathers has an even more devastating impact on the boys as the case of Joe demonstrates:

> Joe, 19, was arrested for molesting a seven year old mentally impaired neighbor boy. Although his parents are divorced, he has frequent contacts with his father, whom he describes as "indifferent." Joe states that his father "does not love me but does not hate me either. He doesn't feel anything for me." Joe remembers an art class project in elementary school in which he had to draw a "family portrait." In it, he and his mother and two sisters, all smiling broadly, were sitting on a sofa. His father was sitting in a chair in the far corner of the picture. He was depicted with his profile turned away from his family and with no facial features because Joe could not even remember how his father looked.

Such an emotionally and/or physically abusive father is a poor model for the son to emulate. However, equally poor is the father who is perceived by the son as possessing personal characteristics which are virtually superhuman in nature, as the two remaining sons in the clinical sample saw their fathers:

> Dennis, 21, who had molested two young brothers, states that as a child he always thought his father, a hellfire and brimstone preacher, was God. "I put him on a pedestal," he explains, "and I've never dared to take him down. Even now I worship him like he told his congregation to worship God."

> Ricky, 23, who molested a young boy on a playground, describes his father as a "prince." A politician, his father was frequently featured in newspaper

and magazine articles. "As a kid I always thought that he was the most famous person in the world. Now I'm beginning to understand that my dad is little more than a newspaper article in my scrapbook."

Whether the father is viewed by the son as rejecting or as superhuman perhaps makes little difference. The fact remains that both types of fathers are seen in a dehumanized fashion by their sons. As such, they are unapproachable and inimitable.

The fathers of three men in the clinical sample were also interviewed as to their perceptions of their sons as children. While it is certainly true that findings from this small a sample cannot be generalized, it is interesting to note that all three fathers saw their sons, in one way or another, as "different" from other children, and in all three cases, this perception appeared to have preceded by many years their sons' molestations of young boys.

Joe's father described him as a "pansy" as a child and alleged he had seen homosexual characteristics in Joe when Joe was only a preschooler. The label "pansy" was rather capriciously administered by his father who could not offer any tangible evidence that there was any truth to the label which hints at homosexual tendencies. In another case, the father saw his son as "different" because he had been born prematurely and in his father's eyes "would always be falling behind other kids" in his development and abilities. The remaining father cited his son's constant illness as a child as a sign that he would always be different from other children. It is interesting to note that Gebhard *et al.* (1965) in response to that latter observation about the constant illness of the child, found that poor health is a rather common feature in the childhoods of homosexual pedophiles.

The role of the self-fulfilling prophecy cannot be overlooked in these examples. It is also important to understand that all three sons, although adults when they molested boys, were viewed by their fathers as "different" throughout their lives. In fact, all three fathers, perhaps desperately searching for something to explain their sons' sexual assaults on children, believe that it was their sons' respective "different" qualities which lead, simply and inevitably, to their molestations of young boys.

The homosexual pedophiles' relationships with their mothers were generally considered to be better than their relationships with their fathers. They did, however, view their parent's marriage, if it was intact, as poor, but were more inclined to blame their fathers for the unhappy marriages than they were their mothers.

Childhood Sexual Experiences. Gebhard *et al.* (1965) noted that as children these pedophiles tended to have had considerably more homosexual experiences than the control group of nonmolesters. Some of these experiences occurred during the course of play with children of similar ages, an occurrence that is commonly found in the childhoods of most males. Such exploratory "homosexual" behavior is generally noncoercive in nature and is mutually pleasurable. However, Groth (1979) found that coercive sexual experiences with adults are also more commonly found in the backgrounds of child molesters in general than they are among the larger population.

Although Groth does not separate homosexual from heterosexual molesters in his study, he does note that 31% of the molesters as children had experienced sexual trauma which was "emotionally upsetting or disturbing to the subject" (p. 11). In his control group only 3% of the men had had similar experiences as children.

In the clinical sample, nine of the 12 homosexual pedophiles had experienced sexual trauma, as defined by Groth, as children. That is an alarmingly high figure in an admittedly small sample; as such, it may reflect the impact that these experiences can have on young children. The types of sexual experiences and the ages at which they occurred are varied.

TABLE 18. REPORTED CHILDHOOD SEXUAL TRAUMA
IN NINE HOMOSEXUAL PEDOPHILES.

Type of Experience	Number of Boys	Age at First Occurrence
Paternal incest	2	6 and 12 years
Molestation by adult male acquaintance	3	7, 7 again, and 14 years
Molestation by adult male stranger	2	11 and 12 years
Molestation by adult female acquaintance	2	12 and 12 again

As can be seen in Table 18, all nine of the pedophiles in the clinical sample had been molested as children by adults. That is an important observation since there is, at the very least, an aura of coercion in that type of molestation even if the child is not physically harmed. The ability of the adult to overpower, persuade, manipulate and reinterpret morality and reality lends itself to a coercive experience in the eyes of the child. When asked to rate their early childhood sexual experiences on the following scale,

1	=	very positive
2	=	positive
3	=	neutral
4	=	negative
5	=	very negative

the mean score for these nine men from the clinical sample was 4.1, indicating a significant degree of perceived trauma.

> Roger who had molested one young neighbor boy, remembered his molestation experience at age seven when his father's best friend had taken him camping and had committed fellatio on him. "I was terrified. He kept telling me that it was o.k., that I wouldn't get hurt. He was very gentle but I never stopped being scared. He bribed me into not telling my father. To this day when I think about it, I still feel helpless and powerless."

Identification with the Child Victim. "Helpless, powerless and terrified": Those words surface often when adult molesters recount their own molestation experiences as children. One may then wonder why the recall of these feelings does not deter them from molesting children. Can they not remember what it was like when they were molested as children? Groth (1979) answers those queries in the following manner: "The offender's adult crimes may be in part the repetitious actings out of sex offenses he was subjected to as a child and as such may represent a maladaptive effort to solve an unresolved early sexual trauma or series of traumas. It can be observed, especially with reference to the child molester, that his later offenses appear to duplicate his own molestation" (p. 15).

Now, as an adult, the molester is able to compensate for those childhood feelings of helplessness, powerlessness and terror. Psychosexually, he is in a position of strength and command.

> Ricky explains that process in the following way: "It's like when you go to a horror movie. The first time you see it, it scares you silly. You never know what will happen next. But if you go to the same movie a second time, you're in control. You know what's going to happen every minute. It's not nearly as frightening."

Ricky had molested a 10-year-old boy in a playground. Ricky himself had been molested at age 11 in a park by an adult who was a stranger to him. Although the compulsion to repeat the molestation experience may not always be as clearly evident as it is in Ricky's case, the molestation may be an attempt to undo the early victimization the molester himself had experienced.

All of this raises yet another question: if the molestation is an attempt to psychologically undo the experience of early victimization, then why did 11 of the 12 homosexual pedophiles in the clinical sample molest more than one boy? Should not one molestation experience have been sufficient to undo their individual childhood experiences? The answer to that latter question would be yes except for the possibility that the molester also identifies with the child victim, and through that process of identification experiences again some of the helplessness and powerlessness he himself had experienced as a child. Consequently, he may be motivated to undo these new feelings by committing yet another molestation.

All of this is rather theoretical since studies of homosexual pedophiles have not generally indicated that an identification process occurs. However, it may account for at least part of another rather unusual feature of the homosexual pedophiles in the clinical sample. Each one of them reported an increase in anxiety after each molestation experience. Curiously, none of them identified this uncomfortable feeling as guilt or shame, but as "uptightness," "fear," "worry," "discomfort," and "helplessness." Many of them dismissed these feelings at the time simply as the fear of getting caught and, while that fear may certainly have been a part of these feelings, it is also possible this anxiety represents the arousal of feelings which come with the identification with the victim. In fact, the feeling of anxiety was so strong for the homosexual pedophiles in question that all of them experienced noticeable task disruptions in their daily lives after each molestation experience. For some of them, that task disruption lasted only a day while for others it lasted several days, and for one man, it lasted nearly a week. Some of them failed to go to work while others failed to be responsible for other family and personal obligations. There was an increase in psychosomatic complaints in some of the molesters. Regardless of the individual reactions to that anxiety, it took all of them some time after each molestation experience to settle back into their daily routines.

Parents' Sexual Attitudes. One other aspect of the home environment of homosexual pedophiles must be noted. In this rather cold, rejecting home atmosphere, parental attitudes regarding sex are generally intolerant. Little discussion about sex occurs in these families, leaving the youngster to get that information from peers or to generalize from his own frequently coercive early sexual experiences.

As he gets older, the youngster has been so affected by these parental attitudes that he is considerably less likely to read or view pornographic material than are other boys his age. This conservative sexual attitude is likely to persist into adulthood as well. This observation led Goldstein (1973) to conclude: "The low exposure to erotica reported by the ... male pedophiles suggest that their sexual development was more likely to have been influenced by actual sexual contacts as a child than by erotica" (p. 216).

Types of Homosexual Pedophiles

Very little research has been done on the dynamics and origins of homosexual pedophilia. However, some types can be proposed.

Socially Inadequate. Some homosexual pedophiles are clearly socially inadequate individuals (Hammer and Glueck, 1957). Their frequently abusive and depriving early childhood experiences have rendered them dependent, passive and essentially helpless in the face of life's demands (Hammer and Jacks, 1955). In the clinical sample, two subtypes of socially inadequate homosexual pedophiles are recognizable: the withdrawn and the conforming.

The withdrawn homosexual pedophile is the most noticeably passive and inadequate of the child molesters. He is also the most likely to have experienced a significant degree of rejection and deprivation himself — childhood experiences that have rendered him withdrawn and ineffectual as an adult, as the case of Benny demonstrates:

> Benny, 20, was arrested for molesting a seven year old boy for whom he was babysitting. Benny is the eleventh of fifteen children born to an alcoholic father who frequently beat his wife and his children, and a passive, devoutly religious mother. Benny's father was a sharecrop farmer who drank away most of the family's meager income. In fact, the family was so poor that they had to rely on handouts from other farmers and from the church just to survive. Benny dropped out of school in the 8th grade after an unspectacular educational career. He is so socially inadequate that he has never held a job except for the occasional babysitting he did for neighborhood children. When he applied for a janitorial job, he had such an anxiety attack that he fled from the interview. He lives with his aunt and uncle and has no friends. He rarely leaves the house and watches television most of the day.

In addition to Benny, two other men from the clinical sample are withdrawn, socially inadequate homosexual pedophiles. Like Benny, they came from cruelly depriving and rejecting home environments which rendered them so inadequate that they could not hold responsible jobs for any period of time if at all nor could they maintain adult relationships. They see adult women as particularly threatening, maintaining this perception by vesting them with all kinds of seductive, manipulative powers which would clearly render them helpless and inadequate should they be forced to interact with these women.

> Ray believes that women can read men's minds and cause men to do things they ordinarily would not do. "Women got power men don't have. They make men think things that they don't think about otherwise and they can make a man do things he ain't supposed to do. I don't like to be near them cause of the power they have. You can't trust them because they know they got the power, too."

Even female children are perceived as powerful by these pedophiles. Consequently their sexual attraction is channeled towards young boys. They do not, however, see themselves as homosexuals, and are actually very unlikely to engage in homosexual relationships with men their own age. That is probably true because any adult, regardless of gender, is perceived as too threatening to them. Perhaps they are best referred to as asexual, a term that some may reject or resist because of the sexual experiences with young boys. However, it may be possible that these sexual experiences are less sexual than they initially appear. They may more likely represent the expression of dependency and affection needs which are directed towards young boys because of the socially inadequate, withdrawn pedophile's identification with the child victim.

If this small clinical sample is indicative of the "typical" withdrawn, socially inadequate homosexual pedophile, then very young children are most likely to be the targets of their sexual behavior. The average age of the victims of the three young men in this category from the clinical sample was 5.5 years. Perhaps this reflects the observation that very young children are the safest victims of all; their tender age making them unlikely to resist, belittle, or challenge the molester.

It is interesting that all three young men who fall into this subtype accomplished the molestation while babysitting for their victims. The average age of this molester was 19 years old. Since babysitting is not conventionally considered to be a responsibility for males, particularly not teenaged males, it is evident that these three young men were attracted to a job that is characterized by low pay, little social interaction and considerable isolation. These job characteristics are certainly commensurate with the personal characteristics of the molester. This observation may also suggest that the withdrawn molester is too socially isolated and too personally inadequate to aggressively seek a victim. He is more likely to have met his victim through a job and to have established at least a tentative relationship with the victim before the molestation actually occurred.

This type of homosexual pedophile is not very inclined to hurt his victim. Perhaps because he identifies with the child or because he is fixated himself at the child's level of psychosexual functioning, he is usually gentle and appears to be content with fondling and mutual masturbation rather than fellatio or anal intercourse as means of achieving sexual satisfaction. Of course hurting the child, or even engaging in more active forms of sexual behavior requires a certain degree of assertiveness and power that may be inconsistent with the dynamics of this molester's personality.

All three of the homosexual molesters in this subtype were also mentally impaired to a certain degree. One was very clearly mentally retarded while the other two were borderline in their intellectual functioning. This particular type of impairment may contribute to the molester's social isolation and withdrawal.

It may also contribute to the molester's apparent inability to cover up the molestation. It is interesting to note that none of these molesters even tried to convince the victim to keep the molestation a secret. Each of them molested the child and then went about his duties as babysitter. They did not threaten the children, nor did they bribe them, nor did they communicate with them in any way in an attempt to dissuade them from telling someone about the molestation. Their lack of social skills, so evident in the traits of their personalities and in the nature of their sexual interactions with their victims, is also reflected in their postmolestation behaviors.

One would expect that mentally ill homosexual pedophiles would also fall into this subtype. Hammer (1955) states: "[A]n increase in distance from an appropriate sex object goes hand-in-hand with an increase in the likelihood of serious psychopathology. The homosexual pedophiles, who deviate from the norm in both age and sex of partner chosen, are then viewed as the most emotionally crippled subgroup of the sex offenders studied" (p. 68). Although this conclusion is certainly logical, Henn *et al.* (1976) could find few psychotics among the 159 child molesters they studied. There were no psychotics in the clinical sample, but one could reasonably assume that any psychotic homosexual pedophile would most likely be of the withdrawn, socially inadequate type.

The conforming, socially inadequate homosexual pedophile is another subtype. This homosexual pedophile has a patina of acceptability which may be initially misleading. He is usually a slightly older molester, in his twenties or thirties, is married, may have at least one child, and is employed.

Three homosexual pedophiles in the clinical sample fall into this category and all three lead what is rather melodramatically referred to as a "double life." Although their behavior, from all outward appearances, is socially acceptable, they are under closer scrutiny seen to be isolated individuals:

> When John was arrested for molesting a twelve year old boy, many people were initially shocked. His wife stated that he is such a "responsible husband and father" that he could not have possibly molested the boy. His employer called him a "loyal employee" and his minister referred to him as a "faithful churchgoer." But when John admitted to having molested the boy as well as several other young boys, the assessments of his personality began to take on a different tenor. His wife admitted that she had no idea what John did in his spare time and did not even know "what was going on in his head" most of the time. His employer stated that he was "quiet and polite but a real loner." The minister confessed that he saw John in church every Sunday, but when pressed could give no testimony as to John's character.

The clinical sample suggests that this type of homosexual pedophile also is not inclined to hurt his victim. His sexual behavior is likely to be more sophisticated than that of the withdrawn, socially inadequate type, in that he is more likely to engage in fellatio and attempted anal intercourse. All three of these pedophiles first met their victims and established a superficial relationship with them before the molestation actually occurred. They were considerably more careful about not getting caught than were the withdrawn types. Two of them bribed the boys with gifts and money to keep the molestation secret; one verbally threatened the victim and later gave him gifts when it was apparent that the threat alone was insufficient to deter the child from telling someone about the molestation.

Intrusive. The intrusive homosexual pedophile is an individual who surrounds himself with young boys. In three of the cases in the clinical sample, the molesters were active participants in the lives of young boys. Two were Little League coaches and the other was a children's choir director. In these types of roles they hold trusted positions in the perceptions of both the youngsters and of the youngsters' parents.

This is the pedophile who knows how to communicate and interact with boys and because of these skills is able to persuade the boy to engage in a sexual act with him. It does appear that persuasion is the primary tact used to accomplish the molestation since force is rarely used. Since the victim has an on-going, trusting relationship with the molester, he usually does not initially resist the sexual advances and does not immediately disclose the sexual experience to another person. The desire to maintain that premolestation relationship and the loyalty often felt to the molester usually constitute a significant motivation for the youngster to keep the molestation a secret. This type of pedophile knows that and capitalizes on it, as the case of Manny demonstrates:

> Manny, 27, was a Little League coach and was for a short time previously, a Boy Scout troop leader. In his role as a coach he was popular and trusted by the boys and their parents. When he persuaded one of his Little Leaguers to become sexually involved with him, the boy was frightened and confused but did not resist. Manny later convinced him to not tell anyone about the encounter. "I told him that I'd lose my job as a coach and that I would go to jail. I reminded him of our friendship and our team loyalty. I told him I knew he wouldn't let me down." The boy was involved sexually with Manny for several months, but finally told his parents when a teammate confided in him that he, too, was sexually involved with Manny. The boy felt jealous and confused and told his parents about the sexual relationship.

The intrusive type of homosexual pedophile does appear to engage in homosexual behavior with consenting adults more frequently than does the socially inadequate type. He is also more likely to label himself a homosexual, a label which, curiously enough, most homosexual pedophiles actively resist. None of the three molesters in this subtype appeared to have any great anxiety about being labeled a child molester, a label which is undoubtedly one of the most reprehensible labels that can be applied to a person. McGaghy (1967) explains this observation in the following manner: "It appears that many homosexual molesters have previously accepted a homosexual role, which in itself represents a drastic departure from the sexual norms of conventional society. Being accused of molesting does not constitute a threat to their present self-concepts as sexual deviants" (p. 82).

One man in the clinical sample was more passively intrusive than the men just described. He did surround himself with young boys but did not participate in their activities. This individual, in his early fifties, had a swimming pool in his backyard which he made available to the children in the neighborhood. He also had a large yard convenient for baseball and football games. He, too, was a popular, trusted figure in the neighborhood and used that role position to persuade young boys to engage in sexual acts with him.

Aggressive. Three men in the clinical sample were aggressive homosexual pedophiles in that sexual satisfaction was achieved through the use of aggression. By these characteristics they conform to the stereotyped perception of the homosexual pedophile but they do not appear to represent the "typical" homosexual molester. In fact, violence is infrequently a feature of homosexual molestation (Groth, 1978; Geiser, 1979).

These individuals are more likely to be strangers to the victims and are more likely to attempt or to achieve anal intercourse. Since the aggression is a predominant feature of their personalities, they are also more inclined to threaten the victim or even physically harm the victim after the molestation itself. Usually these threats are in vain because the violent effect of the molestation precludes any motivation to keep the assault a secret.

In those cases of aggressive homosexual molestation the primary motivation of the molester may be to undo the sexual trauma of his own childhood molestation. Two of the men from the clinical sample who could be characterized as aggressive homosexual pedophiles had been molested themselves as children by male adult strangers. Both had also been physically battered children. The third man was a victim of paternal incest and was by all accounts emotionally battered during his childhood.

This homosexual molester gains some satisfaction from the violence itself. In that capacity, he is truly sadistic. But he gains the most satisfaction from the feeling of power he has over the child, attesting to the earlier observation that this type of molestation can be a way of compensating for childhood feelings of helplessness and powerlessness.

> George has molested many young boys over the past several years. He abducts the boys from parks and playgrounds, threatens them, beats them and has anal intercourse with them. "I like how I feel when I do this," he explains. "It's sexually like a rush, but mostly I feel strong and powerful. You know, I got that kid's life in the palm of my hand. I call all the shots and he knows it. I'm the boss; I'm in control."

All three aggressive homosexual pedophiles had extensive records of violent behavior in their backgrounds. Much of this violent behavior could be traced to childhood, with fighting, aggressive firesetting and cruelty to animals most noticeable in their backgrounds. When asked if they could kill the children they molest, two stated that they would not go that far in their violence, but the third did not rule that out as a possibility. All three showed impulsive behavior with very weak ego controls and a remarkable lack of conscience. In that way they typify chronically violent people, not necessarily chronic homosexual pedophiles.

Geiser (1979) defines a pederast as an "eternal adolescent in his erotic life. He becomes fixated upon the youth and the sexual vitality of the adolescent boy.... Pederasts love the boy in themselves and themselves in the boy" (p. 83). Pederasts are boy-worshippers who are often deeply involved in a pederast underground group and who have a code of ethics which governs their sexual behavior with boys. Their boys are willing partners in the sexual relationship. As such, pederasts perhaps are not really best classified as homosexual pedophiles. The history of pederasty is rich in details and, thanks to the significant contribution of Rossman (1976), the dynamics of the pederast and of the underground to which he belongs are clearly delineated. For these reasons, pederasty will be considered as a category separate from other homosexual pedophiles. Three additional cases from the clinical sample will be used to illustrate its dynamics.

History

During early Greek times, "the system of pederasty basically was an accepted socially endorsed emotional and sexual relationship between an older man and a youth" (Ungaretti, 1978:292). With its roots in the warrior/hero tradition of classical Greece, in its ideal form pederasty represented a hierarchial relationship which afforded the adult male, known as the "inspirer," the intellectual and sexual company of an attractive youth, "the listener," who in turn admired and learned from his adult lover. Pederasty was thought to produce both brave men and good citizens.

The custom of pederasty may have been derived from the divine precedent established in the myth of Zeus and Ganymede. Zeus was so entranced with the beautiful boy Ganymede that he transformed himself into an eagle and swept the boy to Mount Olympus where he became Zeus's lover and servant.

Among mere mortals, however, the suitor would consult with his intended boy's father and once permission was received to establish a sexual relationship with the boy, there would be a public announcement of their intentions. Then, in keeping with mythology and custom, a mock abduction of the boy was staged with family and friends feigning anger and pursuit. The suitor would take his boy to a place secluded from the community and would teach him the "manly" arts of love, liberty and courage (Rush, 1980).

Love, liberty and courage were eminently homosexual traits in classical Greece, and pederasty was considered an enviable relationship. Karlen (1971) states that if a boy did not have a lover by the age of 12, he and his family would live in shame. Some of the pederasts in classical Greece, Socrates, Plato and Pindar, were the most eminent figures in Greek society. That their behavior was socially and even historically acceptable is reflected in an observation by Karlen: "Even today it is difficult for people to think of Plato's and Agathon's buggery as the same act that is performed by two 42nd Street 'queers' " (p. 38).

Classical Greece was not the only period during which pederasty was praised. Taylor (1976) documents the works of such notables as Oscar Wilde, Aubrey Beardsley and Algernon Swinburne as examples of "the uses of artistry as a motive-forumlation resource for the justification and possible enactment of guilt-free sex" (p. 100). He also examines the works of the so-called "Uranian poets," those overtly and covertly pederastic poets whose name is an epithet applied to Aphrodite, and whose verses "justify and motivate the enactment of that love" (p. 101).

Taylor found five predominant themes in the verses of the Uranian poets, themes that may underlie pederastic practices to this very day. The first is the "transience of boyhood" theme, in which the pederast laments the passage of boyhood to manhood. An F.E. Murray (1923:5) poem illustrates it:

> In trousers now my boy's arrayed,
> And in my heart I'm sore afraid
> That manliness will interfere
> With what to me has been so dear —
> My hand upon his bare knee laid.

The transience of boyhood is a concern of the pederast when he looks at the boy to whom he is attracted; it is also a concern to him personally when he ponders his own passage into manhood. A "lost youth" theme was also predominant in the poetry of the Uranians, as a poem by W.D. Nesbitt (1924:5) demonstrates:

> The boy-days, the boy-days — when comes
>   the thread of grey,
> You may live in tomorrow, but you dream
>   of Yesterday;
> You may look in the mirror but the
>   only face you see
> Is one that has the semblance of the
>   boy you used to be;
> And musing, you may stumble on a
>   broken bit of song
> That wanders from the boy-days
>   in cadence sweet and strong.

Another theme which Taylor identifies in the poetry of the Uranians is the "divine sanction" theme. Perhaps alluding to the almost mystical nature of pederastic relationships in classical Greece, the divine sanction theme allows pederasty to transcend the usual connotation of homosexual relationships. A verse by Ralph Chubb (1934:4) exemplifies this theme:

> I announce a secret event as tremendous and mysterious as any that has occurred in spiritual history of the world. I announce the inauguration of a Third Dispensation of the Holy Ghost on earth, and the visible advent thereof on earth in the form of a Young Boy of 13 years old, naked, perfect and unblemished.

The "class sanction" theme of the Uranian poets is also identified by Taylor. Here the royal status of pederasty is extolled by J. F. Bloxham (1894):

> Then suddenly the shades of night took wing,
> And I saw that love was a beautious thing
> For I clasped to my breast my curl-crowned King,
> My sweet boy-king.

The final theme which threads through the writings of the Uranian poets is the "erotic superiority of pederasty" theme. Since even the most persistent pederast conforms to a code of ethics in his sexual encounters with young boys, pederastic love is often viewed as erotically superior to any other form of love. The poem of John Gambril Nicholson (1892:11) illustrates this final theme:

> You have had your predecessors
> Of whom you've scarcely heard,
> There was Ernest; and there was Alec;
> And you, my Victor, are the third.

In these days when the poetic expression of love is often considered trite, it may be easy to dismiss the verses of the Uranian poets as the products of the excesses of poetic license. Yet the twentieth century has its own version of pederastic poetry, which can be found now in pornographic material that in its own way, although less dramatically of course, appeals to the same needs and desires of the pederasts. In his study of 215 pederasts, Rossman (1976) found that a vast majority of them regularly peruse pornographic material specifically designed to spark the desires of the men with pederastic impulses. Magazines with the titles of *The International Journal of Greek Love, Hermes, Better Life* and *Puberty Rites* appeal to pederastic desires. Rossman found that 50,000 American men are on the mailing list of a European publishing house which prints books and photographs of young boys engaging in sexual acts with adult males. The *National Review* (1977) reported the existence of an English organization known as PIE (Pedophile Information Exchange) which keeps pederasts in contact with young boys and with each other throughout the country. Another English organization, PAL (Pedophile Action for Liberation) has been advocating the lowering of the age of consent to four years.

This country is certainly not immune from these types of organizations. The Childhood Sensuality Circle (CSC) promotes child-child love as well as adult-child love. Both Better Life and Better Love advocate homosexual relationships between boys and men. The North American Man/Boy Love Association, or NAMBLA, was formed in 1979 to promote pederastic relationships and to defend the civil rights of "boy lovers" throughout the country. The organization was formed in response to the disclosure of the so-called "Revere Ring," a homosexual child sex ring made up of some prominent professional men and over 60 young boys which operated in the Boston area for many years.

Poets may no longer be extoling the virtues of pederasty in verse, but the ode to pederasty lingers in social clubs and pornography.

Characteristics of Pederasts

Who are the pederasts? Rossman (1976) calculates that one out of every eight adult men has at least occasional pederastic inclinations (p. 3). The typical pederast appears to be a male adult in his middle years, single, with a college or professional level educational background, and a well-paying job.

He is not particularly likely to label himself a homosexual although he has been attracted to boys since his own adolescence.

He is rarely a violent individual, nor does he have any desire to be emotionally coercive with the young boys with whom he becomes sexually involved. In those ways, he does not fit the profile of the "typical" homosexual pedophile. He is not seeking a victim; he is seeking a companion. He is not stimulated by the power he has over a young boy; he seeks mutuality. He is not reliving the sexual trauma of his youth, but the sexual pleasure.

Rossman (1976) found that to make pederasty transcend homosexual pedophilia, the true pederast conforms to a code of ethics in his behavior and in his interaction with young boys (p. 192):

1. Boys should not be treated as sex objects to be used at the whim of the pederast.
2. Pederasts should know the boy's feelings and interests before a sexual relationship is initiated.
3. A pederast must not cruise to pick up strange boys because that encourages boys to hustle.
4. Protect both your reputation and the reputation of the boy.
5. At all times be truthful and honest with the boy.
6. Any photographs taken of the boy are for your own use.
7. The boys must consent to the sexual relationship.
8. No alcohol or drugs may be given to the boys.
9. Encourage the boys to initiate and maintain heterosexual relationships.
10. Encourage the boys to stay in school and to avoid crime.
11. Teach the boys a code of behavior conducive to respectable social living.
12. Do not share your boys with other pederasts.
13. Never harm the boy.

The Pederast Underground

Pederasty may have been an exalted, enviable behavior in classical Greece, but in today's times it is barely distinguishable, in the minds of most people, from mere homosexual child molestation. Due to society's negative reaction to this behavior, Rossman (1976) concludes that pederasty has become an "underground movement." He defines an underground as "one step below a subculture. It is the secret life of persons in rebellion against society and its institutions. They do what society forbids and what society fails to do" (p. 33).

There are several components to the pederast underground. An acquaintance network is an informal group of pederasts who provide support and understanding for each other.

> Chad, Don and Tim provided an informal support group for each other. When Chad's boy moved out of town, Tim convinced his boy to find another boy for Chad. When Don had a quarrel with his boy, Chad and Tim sat up all night consoling him and offering him advice. "We understand each other," Tim explained. "There is no one else who could know how we really feel."

On a more formal level, newsletters and publications such as *Straight to Hell* carry personal columns through which a pederast can advertise for boys. These columns also provide a means through which these pederasts can contact each other to form their own acquaintance networks.

Another component of the pederast underground is what Rossman refers to as the "Pederast Apologists" (p. 37). These individuals take responsibility for promoting the pederast philosophy and practice through newsletters and magazines, and undertake social and legal activism through the preparation of legal briefs as well as through testimony before various subcommittees and task forces. Rush (1980) summarizes that component in the following manner: "Fortified by history, tradition and experts, pederasts have organized to find kindred spirits and, encouraged by our sexual revolution, have lobbied to rescind legislation which prohibits sex with minors, to lower or eliminate the legal age of consent and to halt the apprehension and imprisonment of boy-lovers" (p. 172).

Rossman (1976) estimates 74% of all pederasts collect photographs of young boys (p. 38). Consequently, the photographers and pornographers constitute a sizeable component of the pederast underground. The phenomenon of "kiddie porn" certainly deserves much more scientific scrutiny than it has yet received. Baker (1980) states that child pornography began to cautiously appear in an "under-the-counter" fashion in adult bookstores in the late 1960's. It consisted of little girls posing nude in magazines titled *Lollitots* and *Moppits*. As the sexual appetites of pedophiles increased, so did the demand for child pornography, so that by 1976 child pornography had become a featured item among dealers, displaying youngsters age 3 to 16 in every conceivable heterosexual or homosexual pose. For those with purely homosexual impulses, the pornography market has responded with magazines such as *Boy Howdy*, "for those who think young," *Boys Will Be Boys*, *Legend of Paradise*, *The Boy*, *Chicken*, and *The Asbestos Diary*. There is no doubt that the photographers and pornographers are providing services both ardently demanded and extraordinarily profitable.

A considerably smaller component of the pederast underground consists of the pederast underworld. That underworld is composed of those pederasts with a history of criminal behavior who are hiding from the police.

The final component of the pederast underground is the sex ring. Burgess *et al.* (1981) define a sex ring as one in which "at least one offender is simultaneously involved with several victims, all of whom are aware of each other's participation" (p. 111). In their examination of six child sex rings, three of which were exclusively homosexual, the authors found that the pederasts gained access to children because their presence with them was never questioned. In this special role, the pederast held some legitimate power with both the child and with the child's parents. For example, two of the pederasts in their study were Boy Scout Leaders who, from positions of trust and authority, first approached the children through an indirect, nonthreatening sexual manner. Then gradually and carefully so as not to frighten the youngsters, the men initiated sexual behavior with them. They then relied on the children's loyalty and respect so their secret would not be betrayed.

Sex rings may be more predominant than society or researchers and practitioners are willing to recognize (Rush, 1980). The 1972 case of Dean Corll's murders of 27 young boys who were part of a sex ring of nearly 300 children shocked the nation. But in that same year, child sex rings were discovered in upstate New York and on Long Island. A year later, a homosexual pederast ring in Los Angeles was exposed and 14 adults were charged with 90 separate crimes against boys between the ages of 6 and 13 (Lloyd, 1976). The infamous Revere ring in Boston set off a wave of homophobia nearly unparalleled in recent history. The ring involved 17 men, many of them prominent professionals, using over 60 boys between the ages of 8 and 13 as partners for homosexual activity and as models for pornographic pictures and movies (Geiser, 1979).

EFFECTS OF HOMOSEXUAL PEDOPHILIA
ON THE VICTIMS

Swift (1977) believes that "homosexual attacks on children carry a double stigma since they violate the heterosexual norm as well as the prohibition of the use of a child as a sex object" (p. 326). This renders the homosexual pedophile a "double deviant"; it also renders the child a "double victim."

Perhaps society's homophobia or its "compassionate and sympathetic hostility" has prevented the study of the effects of homosexual pedophilia on the child victim. The prevalent attitude in regard to the child tends to be one of, "just forget about it and he'll get over it." Unfortunately, the stigma that holds for the offender is also applied to the child.

In the clinical sample, ten victims of homosexual pedophilia were studied. Eight of them were just emerging from the molestation experience at the time of the study. Their average age was 11.8 years. The two remaining victims, one 25 years old, and the other 32 years old, provide a retrospective interpretation of their victimization.

Psychological and Physical Trauma

Geiser (1979) reports that a child victim of homosexual pedophilia may show some psychological trauma after the victimization but did not elucidate as to the type of trauma that may be expected. In the clinical sample, all eight young boys experienced some disruptions of a psychological nature as a result of the experience. Most of them became quite clinging and dependent, seeking protection from their parents. Two became sullen and withdrawn, but the withdrawal was short-lived.

Nightmares were reported in three of the boys and one youngster complained of vague physical problems that were undoubtedly psychosomatic in nature. Beyond these relatively minor and predictable traumatic reactions, little symptomatology was discussed or discovered.

Is there something about little boys that makes them particularly

resilient after such experiences? Probably not, but their lack of symptomatology may be related to other issues. First, in the vast majority of cases, the
homosexual pedophile is acquainted and at times even friendly with the child.
The child trusts him, and if the pedophile is gentle, and he usually is, the
sexual experience itself may not be traumatic. Second, most boys have not
been educated about the possibility of such an experience. Consequently, they
may not have the reality context in which to place this experience and this
may diminish the trauma. Landis (1956) found that although 44% of the girls
who had been molested had been educated by their parents as to the realities
and the consequences of being a victim of child molestation, only 27% of the
boys had been similarly educated (p. 98). More recent data on the differential
education of boys and girls are not available but Swift (1977) assumes that a
great difference still prevails.

Of the ten victims from the clinical sample, only two had ever been
told by their parents about the possibility and the consequences of homosexual child molestation. All ten had heard about homosexuality, of course,
but most of them subscribed to the clichéd perception of a homosexual as a
weak wristed, effeminant person. If their molester did not fit that stereotype,
the youngsters often did not perceive their molestation as a homosexual
assault. Two of the boys from the clinical sample were worried that they
might have "feminine" characteristics because in their perception "only girls
get molested." Neither one of the boys had shared this concern with their
parents. One may wonder if other boys, similarly unprepared for the reality
of homosexual molestation, may also be wondering about this very thing, and
may also be too frightened and embarrassed to share this concern with their
parents.

Rush (1980) proposes a different reason as to why the sexual abuse of
males appears to be less traumatic in its impact on the victim. She suggests
that a boy may identify with this male molester and therefore suffer no loss of
masculine esteem through the encounter. However, if the boy feels
"feminized" by the molestation he will undoubtedly experience humiliation.
Yet in a "culture where male sexuality represents strength, superiority,
dominance and success, in a world where the desired image is a male image,
the molested boy will mature into a man who will be able to compensate for
his childish helplessness" (p. 176). Such a man could then look back on the incident with amused indifference, as the case of Steve, 25, illustrates:

> "This guy who molested me was the owner of this mom-and-pop grocery
> store by my house. He used to stick his hands in my pants when I'd go there
> for candy. Then one day he offered me candy if I would put his penis in
> my mouth. I figured, what the hell, I'd do it. Then he put my penis in his
> mouth. No big deal. You call that molestation? I call it some sad sicky
> getting his jollies with a little kid. No big deal."

One observation may be contrary to the proposed explanation of the
lack of symptomatology in male molestation victims. That is the fact that
parents, particularly fathers, may react extremely negatively to their sons'
molestations. Since the reaction of any child to a molestation experience is
largely dependent on his or her parents' reactions, one would expect to see
more symptomatology in young boys. Geiser (1979) states: "Admitting to the

rape of his son is far more humiliating for a father [than admitting] to the rape of his daughter" (p. 76). The father may feel that his son's masculinity may have been diminished by the molestation and that, coupled with the rampant homophobia among the male population, may lead to an extremely adverse reaction on the part of the father.

This was certainly true in the clinical sample. The fathers had an extremely negative reaction to their sons' molestations but in all cases the mothers served as buffers between their husbands and their sons. In other words, the sons were not really aware of their fathers' feelings and reactions to the molestation.

Perhaps that "humiliation" that is characteristic of the father applies to other people who interact with the child. Their reluctance and embarrassment to bring up and discuss the molestation may be felt by the child as a pressure to keep quiet about the molestation experience While it would be logically expected that this pressure would force the child to repress feelings about the molestation and that the repression, in turn, would create an increase in symptomatology, it would also be logical to assume that this same pressure would force the child to keep quiet about the symptomatology as well:

> Mike, 32, remembers his molestation by a neighbor and his family's reaction to it. "No one would talk about it. Whenever I would walk into a room, they would stop talking, smile and pat me on the back. Really forced, you know; really fake. I remember thinking I wasn't supposed to talk about the molestation. So when I started having bad dreams, I thought that I wasn't supposed to talk about them, either."

The two older victims did not report any long-range effects of the molestation. In fact, neither of them thought about the molestations except on rare occasions, and when they did, they thought about it in a rather detached fashion.

Effects of Pederasty on Victims

The effects of pederasty on the victim, or participant, as pederasts would prefer to call the youngster, have been more carefully examined and documented. The Los Angeles Police Department has also offered a profile of the youngster who is likely to engage in pederastic relationships (*Chicago Tribune*, May 15, 1977). The boy is typically between the ages of 8 and 17, an underachiever in school, living in a home in which the parents are physically or emotionally absent, poorly sociologically developed but having a warm personality, and without strong moral or religious affiliations. The boy is unlikely to have a history of either homosexuality or delinquency. Rossman (1976) essentially agrees with that profile; however, based on his interviews with 300 boys, he adds the following features to the profiile: self-confidence and willingness to take risks, above average I.Q., and having more freedom than other boys his age. Rossman also concludes that the youngster does not see himself as a homosexual and is primarily motivated by the need for money, adventure, affection, friendship and sexual intimacy.

Short-Term Effects. Because by definition the boy willingly and voluntarily enters into a pederastic relationship, a traumatic reaction to the sexual behavior is not generally expected, and has not been documented. However, Burgess *et al.* (1981), in examining children who voluntarily participated in sex rings, discovered that some symptomatology was recognizable during their participation and immediately after their participation was discovered. They found the children experienced physical symptoms such as headaches and anorexia and psychological symptoms like nightmares, mood swings and anxiety. Some social symptoms such as fighting and school problems were also observed. Family problems were also noted. The fathers of the boys typically reacted angrily to their involvement and both parents rationalized and minimized the sexual aspect of their children's involvement in the rings.

Schoettle (1980) also documents some short-term effects of involvement in pornography on children. Since pornography is a predominant feature of the pederast underground, it could be assumed that these effects would be characteristic of youngsters who participated in that experience. However, Schoettle documents only one case and that is of a 12-year-old girl. Consequently not all of his findings can easily be generalized to young boys. He does conclude, however, that "involvement in pornography leads to psychic trauma if the ego is threatened by the amount of anxiety aroused. Massive acute anxiety may be aroused, especially in initial sexual encounters, because of the closeness of the external event to unconscious fantasies. Chronic anxiety results when there are repeated sexual experiences of a similar nature, all tending to interfere with the resolution of developmental tasks" (p. 296). It would be logical to assume that this reaction to participation in pornography would hold true for boys as well as it does for girls.

Long-Range Effects. Tindall (1978) did a longitudinal study of nine boys who had had pederastic experiences. Observations were made in the second, third, and fourth decades after the pederastic relationships had terminated. In all cases, there were no remarkable long-range effects of the pederasty and none of the nine became a homosexual in his adult life. No other longitudinal studies have been conducted.

Part III. Conclusions

CHAPTER 14: SUMMARY AND CONCLUSIONS

After spending three years researching incest and pedophilia and interviewing hundreds of offending adults, child victims, and nonparticipating family members, some features of the sexual victimization of children appear to be so important that they deserve special attention.

First, it is all too apparent that even after fifty years of scientific research, myths about the sexual victimization of children still abound (Groth *et al.*, 1978; de Young, 1981c). In a supposedly sexually liberated society, the subject of the sexual victimization of children is no less taboo than it was a half century ago when the first cautious, tentative reports began appearing in the scientific literature. Content to rest upon half-truths, many scientists, practitioners, and laypeople alike have chosen to be blissfully ignorant of the reality of child sexual abuse.

There are prices to be paid for this ignorance. The first is that because this ignorance has served as a foundation upon which many legal and social practices have been built, sexually victimized children are being constantly revictimized by a system and a society unwilling to confront their problem. Consider the case of the child who discloses to her teacher that she is an incest victim, and the teacher pats her on the hand and suggests that she somehow learn to live with it, and then turns her back on the child. Consider the case of the prosecuting attorney who strikes a lenient plea bargain with a chronic child molester to spare himself or herself the inconvenience of trying him in court. Or how about the male therapist who takes an adult incest victim who is his patient into his bed to "treat" her for her sexual hang-ups? Or consider the case of a youngster who is placed in a series of foster homes and institutions while her incestuous family is allowed to remain intact by a protective service agency that finds it more expedient to punish the child than the offending parent.

One may argue that these are merely isolated cases, and as such do not represent the typical response of adults to child sexual victimization. That may or may not be true; however the argument presented is not that this ignorance is more prevalent than knowledge about sexual victimization, but that when it infiltrates the legal and social structures which affect all of our lives, its damage to children already victimized is inestimable.

The second price to be paid for this ignorance is that those who are concerned and are vocal in their opposition to child sexual abuse are for the first time in history facing an opposition which at times appears to be more

161

vocal and powerful than they. Part of that opposition comes from our ranks — researchers who insist that there is nothing at all harmful about adult sexual relationships with children, that in fact these relationships may even be beneficial to the child. De Mott (1980) has taken these "proincest" researchers to task, and a recent *Time* article (September 7, 1981) has demonstrated that this cavalier attitude about sexual relationships with children also includes the nonincestuous victimization of children.

These researchers have formed a peculiar alliance with groups which just a few years ago would have been considered crackpot. Such groups as The Childhood Sensuality Circle, the Rene Guyon Society, and the North American Man–Boy Love Association have been actively advocating that the age of consent be lowered or eliminated, and that criminal penalties for sexual relations with children be abolished. A decade ago these groups were quoting outdated and spurious studies by such diverse persons as Freud and Guyon to substantiate their claims; today they are quoting more modern and credible authorities like John Money, Mary Calderone, Wardell Pomeroy and Fritz Bernhard. In the face of this organized and vocal support of adult sexual relations with children, even the most concerned and articulate researchers often come off sounding defensive, weak and unsure. No child can be protected from sexual abuse and no society can be educated to its reality until those who oppose all sexual behavior with children become as organized, vocal and powerful as those who support it.

Second, the research in this study shows conclusively that child sexual abuse is harmful and that its negative effects are likely to persist into adulthood. For those who would argue that these experiences for children are dull, neutral or even positive, the challenge placed before them is to conduct unbiased, comprehensive studies of victims, offenders and nonparticipating family members *before* they insist again that child sexual abuse is not harmful.

While it is true that a causal relationship between child sexual assault and any postassault behavior cannot be proven, a correlative relationship certainly can be and is demonstrated. And that correlation is only overlooked by those researchers whose biases interfere with their objectivity.

Third, a frequently overlooked feature of child sexual abuse has shown itself in the present study to be an important factor. The physical abuse of incest victims by offending adults occurs much more frequently than most researchers have ever realized. In the clinical sample of 60 victims of paternal incest, 40 (67%) were also victims of physical abuse within their families, and many more than that had vicariously experienced physical abuse by witnessing that violence as it was perpetrated on their mothers and/or siblings.

Another role that physical abuse plays in child sexual abuse is an an etiological factor in that abuse. In the clinical sample of 51 incestuous fathers and stepfathers, 22 (41%) had been physically abused by their own fathers. The role that physical abuse plays in the etiology of other types of incest is less clear. However, of the 47 heterosexual and homosexual pedophiles in the clinical sample, 31 (66%) had been physically abused as children, and several more had witnessed physical violence against their mothers or siblings.

Fourth, the intergenerationally transmissable phenomenon of incestuous child sexual assault cannot be overlooked. The data demonstrate over and over that fathers victimized in childhood are likely to victimize their own children; that mothers who collude in setting up their own children for victimization are frequently incest victims themselves. The same holds true for child molesters, the vast majority of whom were themselves sexually victimized as children.

In fact, those youngsters who had vicariously participated in child sexual assault by witnessing its occurrence in their own families run a greater risk as adults of perpetrating that very behavior on a youngster.

Fifth, the data from this study indicate that sexually victimized children run a great risk of being revictimized sexually by another person. Early child sexual assault and the family dynamics which accompany it seem to rob a child of the necessary self-protective coping skills needed to avoid further victimization. In many ways, especially sexual, these children become eternal victims.

Taking all of these data into consideration, the only logical conclusion to be reached is that child sexual assault, whether incestuous or nonincestuous, is prevalent, harmful and transmissable. To treat it as anything less than that is to deny sound scientific evidence and to discount the experiences of countless victims. And that is its own form of child abuse.

UNANSWERED QUESTIONS

So much more needs yet to be known about child sexual victimization. Some clinical samples in this study are really too small to generate any wide-sweeping conclusions. As the taboo is lifted from this type of research, the way will be opened to examine more thoroughly types of child sexual victimization which at the present time are considered to be rare.

Perhaps the greatest task of concerned, compassionate researchers and practitioners is to break through the taboo that prevents the study of child sexual assault, the treatment of its victims and offenders, and the publicizing of its occurrence, origin, dynamics, and effects.

That responsibility is ours. Children are depending on us.

BIBLIOGRAPHY

Adams, M.S., and Neel, J.V. "Children of Incest." *Pediatrics*, 40, 55–62, 1967.
Allen, D.M. "Young Male Prostitutes: A Psychosocial Study." *Archives of Sexual Behavior*, 9(5), 399–426, 1980.
Angelou, M. *I Know Why The Caged Bird Sings*. New York: Bantam Books, 1971.
Awad, G.A. "Father-Son Incest: A Case Report." *Journal of Nervous and Mental Disease*, 162, 135–139, 1976.
Baker, C.D. "Preying on Playgrounds: The Sexploitation of Children in Pornography and Prostitution," in L.G. Schultz (ed.), *The Sexual Victimology of Youth* (Springfield, Ill.: Charles C. Thomas, 1980), pp. 292–334.
Barbaree, H.E., *et al.* "Alcohol Intoxication and Inhibition of Sexual Arousal to Rape Cues." Paper presented to the Annual Convention of the Ontario Psychological Association. Toronto: February, 1980.
Barker-Benfield, G.J. "The Spermatic Economy: A 19th Century View of Sexuality," in Michael Gordon (ed.), *The American Family in Social-Historical Perspective*, 2d ed. (New York: St. Martin's Press, 1978), pp. 374–402.
Barnhouse, R.T. "Sex Between Patient and Therapist." *Journal of the American Academy of Psychoanalysis*, 6(4), 533–546, 1978.
Barry, M.J. "Incest," in Ralph Slovenko (ed.), *Sexual Behavior and the Law* (Springfield, Ill.: Charles C. Thomas, 1965).
———, and Johnson, A.M. "The Incest Barrier." *Psychoanalytic Quarterly*, 27, 485–500, 1958.
Bell, A., and Hall, C.S. *The Personality of a Child Molester*. Chicago: Atherton, 1971.
Bender, L., and Blau, A. "The Reactions of Children to Sexual Relationships with Adults." *American Journal of Orthopsychiatry*, 7, 500–518, 1937.
———, and Grugett, A.E. "A Follow-Up Report on Children Who Had Atypical Sexual Experience." *American Journal of Orthopsychiatry*, 22, 825–837, 1952.
Berry, G.W. "Incest: Some Clinical Variations on a Classical Theme." *Journal of the American Academy of Psychoanalysis*, 3, 151–161, 1975.
Bettelheim, B. *The Uses of Enchantment*. New York: Vintage Books, 1977.
Bigras, J., *et al.* "On Disappointment and the Consequences of Incest in the Adolescent Girl." *Canadian Psychiatric Association Journal*, 11, 189–204, 1966.
Bloxham, J.F. *The Chameleon*. London, England, 1884.
Brant, R.S.T., and Tisza, V.B. "The Sexually Misused Child," *American Journal of Orthopsychiatry*, 47, 80–90, 1977.
Brown, W. "Murder Rooted in Incest." In R.E.L. Masters (ed.), *Patterns of Incest* (N.Y.: Julian Press, 1963).
Browning D.H. and Boatman, B. "Incest: Children at Risk." *American Journal of Psychiatry*, 134, 69–72, 1977.
Brownmiller, S. *Against Our Will*. New York: Simon & Schuster, 1975.
Brunold, H. "Observations After Sexual Traumata Suffered in Childhood." *Excerpta Criminologica*, 11, 132–149, 1964.
Bullough, Vern and Bullough, Bonnie. *Prostitution: An Illustrated Social History*. New York: Crown, 1978.

_____ and _____. *Sin, Sickness and Sanity*. New York: New American Library, 1977.

Burgess, A.W. and Holmstrom, L.L. "Rape Trauma Syndrome." *American Journal of Psychiatry*, **131**, 981–986, 1974.

_____, *et al. Sexual Assault on Children and Adolescents*. Lexington, Mass.: Lexington Books, 1978.

_____, *et al.* "Child Sex Initiation Rings." *American Journal of Orthopsychiatry*, **51**(1), 110–119, 1981.

Cavallin, H. "Incestuous Fathers: A Clinical Report." *American Journal of Psychiatry*, **122**, 1132–1138, 1966.

"Child Pornography: Sickness for Sale." *Chicago Tribune*, May 15, 1977.

Chubb, R. *The Heavenly Cupid*. Newbury: Privately Published, 1934.

Cohen, M., and Seghorn, T. "Sociometric Study of the Sex Offender." *Journal of Abnormal Psychology*, **74**(2), 249–255, 1969.

Cohn, Norman. *Europe's Inner Demons*. New York: Basic Books, 1975.

Colby, C.D.W. "Mechanical Restraint of Masturbation in a Young Girl." *New York Medical Record*, **52**, 1897.

Comfort, Alexander. *The Anxiety Makers*. London: Nelson & Son, 1967.

Connelly, Mark Thomas. *The Response to Prostitution in the Progressive Era*. Chapel Hill: University of North Carolina Press, 1980.

Cormier, B.M. "Psychodynamics of Father-Daughter Incest." *Canadian Psychiatric Association Journal*, **7**(5), 203–217, 1962.

Crume, John B. "Children's Magazines: 1826–1857." *Journal of Popular Culture*, **6**(4), 698–706, 1973.

Davies, R.K. "Incest and Vulnerable Children." *Science News*, **116**, 244–245, 1979.

De Francis, V. *Protecting the Child Victim of Sex Crimes Committed by an Adult*. Denver: American Humane Association, Children's Division, 1969.

Degler, Carl. "What Ought to Be and What Was: Women's Sexuality in the 19th Century," in Michael Gordon (ed.), *The American Family in Social-Historical Perspective*, 2d ed. (New York: St. Martin's Press, 1978). pp. 403–425.

DeMause, Lloyd. *The History of Childhood*. New York: Psychohistory Press, 1974.

_____. "Our Forebears Made Childhood a Nightmare." *Psychology Today*, 85–88, April 1975.

De Mott, B. "The Pro-Incest Lobby." *Psychology Today*, **13**(10), 11, 1980.

de Young, M. "Incest: The Broken Taboo." *Wonderland*, 30–32, March 9, 1980.

_____. "Promises, Threats and Lies: Keeping Incest Secret." *Journal of Humanics*, **9**(1), 61–71, 1981a.

_____. "Siblings of Oedipus: Brothers and Sisters of Incest Victims." *Child Welfare*, **60**(8), 561–568, 1981b.

_____. "Incest Victims and Offenders: Myths and Realities." *Journal of Psychosocial Nursing and Mental Health Services*, **19**(10), 37–79, 1981c.

_____. "Innocent Seducer or Innocently Seduced? The Role of the Child Incest Victim." *Journal of Clinical Child Psychology*, **11**(1), 56–60, 1982a.

_____. "Case Reports: The Sexual Exploitation of Incest Victims by Helping Professionals." *Victimology*, in press, 1982b.

_____. "Self-injurious Behavior in Incest Victims: A Research Note." *Child Welfare*, in press, 1982c.

Dietz, C., and Craft, J.L. "Family Dynamics of Incest: A New Perspective." *Social Casework*, **61**(10), 602–609, 1980.

Dixon, K.N., *et al.* "Father-Son Incest: Underreported Psychiatric Problem?" *American Journal of Psychiatry*, **135**(7), 835–838, 1978.

Dreikurs, R. *Coping with Children's Misbehavior*. New York: Hawthorn Press, 1972.

Ebel, Henry. "The Evolution of Childhood Reconsidered." *Journal of Psychohistory*, **5**(1), 67–80, 1977.

Eist, H.I., and Mandel, A.U. "Family Treatment of Ongoing Incest Behavior." *Family Process*, **7**, 216–232, 1968.

Fast, I., and Cain, A.C. "The Stepparent Role: Potential for Disturbances in Family Functioning." *American Journal of Orthopsychiatry*, 36(3), 485–491, 1966.

Feldman, Egal. "Prostitution, the Alien Woman and the Progressive Imagination, 1910–1915." *American Quarterly*, 19(2, pt. 1), 192–206, 1967.

Fellman, Anita C., and Fellman, Michael. "The Rule of Moderation in Late 19th Century American Sexual Ideology." *Journal of Sex Research*, 17(3), 238–255, 1981.

Finch, S.M. "Sexual Abuse by Mothers." *Medical Aspects of Human Sexuality*, 7(1), 191, 1973.

Finkelhor, D. *Sexually Victimized Children*. New York: Free Press, 1979.

_____. "Sex Among Siblings: A Survey of the Prevalence, Variety and Effects." *Archives of Sexual Behavior*, 9(3), 171–194, 1980.

Fisher, G. "Psychological Needs of Heterosexual Pedophiliacs." *Diseases of the Nervous System*, 30(6), 419–421, 1969.

Fleck, S., *et al.* "The Intrafamilial Environment of the Schizophrenic Patient." in J. Masserman (ed.), *Science and Psychoanalysis*, vol. 2 (New York: Grune & Stratton, 1959).

Fleming, K., and Fleming, A.T. *The First Time*. New York: Simon & Schuster, 1975.

Forgione, A.G. "The Use of Mannequins in the Behavioral Assessment of Child Molesters: Two Case Reports." *Behavior Therapy*, 7(5), 678–685, 1976.

Forward, S., and Buck, C. *Betrayal of Innocence*. Los Angeles: J.P. Tarcher, Inc., 1978.

Fox, J.R. "Sibling Incest." *British Journal of Sociology*, 13(1), 128–150, 1962.

Frances, V., and Frances, A. "The Incest Taboo and Family Structure." *Family Process*, 15, 235–244, 1976.

Freedman, A.M., *et al*. *Modern Synopsis of Psychiatry*. Baltimore: Williams and Wilkins, 1972.

Gebhard, P.H., *et al*. *Sex Offenders: An Analysis of Types*. New York: Harper & Row, 1965.

Geiser, R.L. *Hidden Victims*. Boston: Beacon Press, 1979.

Gigeroff, A.K., *et al*. "Sex Offenders on Probation: Heterosexual Pedophiles." *Federal Probation*, 32, 17–21, 1968.

Gilbert, Arthur N. "Conceptions of Homosexuality and Sodomy in Western History." *Journal of Homosexuality*, 6(1/2), 57–68, 1980/1981.

Glick, P.C. "A Demographer Looks at American Families." *Journal of Marriage and the Family*, 37, 15–26, 1975.

Gligor, A.M. "Incest and Sexual Delinquency." doctoral dissertation, Case Western Reserve University, 1966.

Goldstein, M.J. "Exposure to Erotic Stimuli and Sexual Deviance." *Journal of Social Issues*, 29(3), 197–219, 1973.

Gordon, L. "Incest as Revenge against the Preoedipal Mother." *Psychoanalytic Review*, 42, 184–292, 1955.

Greenland, C. "Incest." *British Journal of Delinquency*, 9, 62–65, 1958.

Greenwald, H. *The Call Girl*. New York: Ballentine, 1958.

Greven, Philip. *The Protestant Temperament*. New York: New American Library, 1977.

Groth, A.N. "Sexual Trauma in the Life Histories of Rapists and Child Molesters," *Victimology*, 4, 10–16, 1979.

_____, and Birnbaum, H.J. "Adult Sexual Orientation and Attraction to Underaged Persons," *Archives of Sexual Behavior*, 7(3), 175–181, May, 1978.

_____, and Burgess, A.W. "Motivational Intent in the Sexual Assault of Children." *Criminal Justice and Behavior*, 4(3), 253–264, 1977.

_____, *et al*. "A Study of Child Molesters: Myths and Realities." *LAE Journal of the American Criminal Justice Association*, 41(1), 17–22, 1978.

Gruber, K.J. "The Child Victim's Role in Sexual Assault by Adults." *Child Welfare*, 40(5), 305–311, 1981.

Gundlach, R.H. "Sexual Molestation and Rape Reported by Homosexual and Hetero-
    sexual Women." *Journal of Homosexuality*, 2(4), 367–384, 1977.
————, and Riess, B.F. "Birth Order and Sex Siblings in a Sample of Lesbians and
    Nonlesbians." *Psychological Reports*, 20, 61–62, 1967.
Hall, C.S. *A Primer of Freudian Psychology*. New York: World Publ. Co., 1954
Halleck, S.I., "Victims of Sex Offenses." *Journal of the American Medical Association*,
    180(4), 273–278, 1962.
Haller, John S., Jr. "From Maidenhood to Menopause: Sex Education for Women in
    Victorian America." *Journal of Popular Culture*, 6(1), 49–69, 1972.
————, and Haller, Robin M. *The Physician and Sexuality in Victorian America*.
    Urbana: University of Illinois Press, 1974.
Hammer, E.F. "A Comparison of H-T-P's of Rapists and Pedophiles: III. The 'Dead'
    Tree as an Index of Psychopathology." *Journal of Clinical Psychology* 11(1), 67–69,
    1955.
————, and Gleuck, B.C. "Psychodynamic Patterns in Sex Offenders." *Psychiatric
    Quarterly*, 31(2), 325–345, 1957.
————, and Jacks, I. "A Study of Rorschach Flexor and Extensor Human Movement
    Responses." *Journal of Clinical Psychology*, 11(1), 63–67, 1955.
Hartman, A.A., and Nicolay, R.C. "Sexually Deviant Behavior in Expectant Fathers."
    Journal of Abnormal Psychology, 71(3), 232–234, 1966.
Heims, L., and Kaufman, I. "Variations on a Theme of Incest." *American Journal of
    Orthopsychiatry*, 33(2), 311–312, 1963.
Henderson, D.J. "Incest: A Synthesis of Data." *Canadian Psychiatric Association Jour-
    nal*, 17, 299–313, 1972.
Henderson. D.J. "Incest" in A.M. Freedman *et al.* (eds.), *Comprehensive Textbook of
    Psychiatry*, 2d ed. (Baltimore: Williams & Wilkins, 1975).
Henn, F.A., *et al.* "Forensic Psychiatry: Profiles of Two Types of Sex Offenders."
    American Journal of Psychiatry, 133(6), 694–696, 1976.
Herjanic, B., and Wilbois, R.P. "Sexual Abuse of Children: Detection and Manage-
    ment." *Journal of the American Medical Association*, 239, 331–333, 1978.
Herman, Judith. *Father-Daughter Incest*. Cambridge: Harvard Press, 1981.
————, and Hirschman, L. "Father-Daughter Incest." *Journal of Women in Culture
    and Society*, 2(4), 735–756, 1977.
Howard, H.S. "Incest: The Revenge Motive." *Delaware State Medical Journal*, 31,
    223–225, 1959.
"I Married My Sister." *Newsweek*, 94, 36, 1979.
Illick, Joseph E. "Childrearing in 17th Century England and America," in Lloyd De
    Mause (ed.) *The History of Childhood* (New York: Psychohistory Press, 1974),
    pp. 303–350.
James J., and Meyerding, J. "Early Sexual Experiences as a Factor in Prostitution."
    Archives of Sexual Behavior, 7(1), 31–42, 1978.
James, K.L. "Incest: The Teenagers' Perspective." *Psychotherapy*, 14(2), 146–155, 1977.
Janus, Samuel. *The Death of Innocence*. New York: Morrow, 1981.
Justice, B., and Justice, R. *The Broken Taboo*. New York: Human Sciences Press, 1979.
Karlen, A. *Sexuality and Homosexuality*. New York: W.W. Norton, 1971.
Katan, A. "Children Who Were Raped." *Psychoanalytic Study of the Child*, 28,
    208–224, 1973.
Kaufman, I., *et al.* "The Family Constellation and Overt Incestuous Relations Between
    Father and Daughter." *American Journal of Orthopsychiatry*, 24, 266–277, 1954.
Kellogg, J. Harvey. *Plain Facts about Sexual Life*. Battle Creek, Mich.: Office of the
    Health Reformer, 1877.
Kent, M.O. "Remarriage: A Family System Approach." *Social Casework*, 61(3),
    146–153, 1980.
Kett, Joseph F. "Adolescence and Youth in 19th Century America." *Journal of Inter-
    disciplinary History*, 11(2), 283–298, 1971.
Kinsey, A.C., *et al. Sexual Behavior in the Human Female*. Philadelphia: Saunders, 1953.

Kirstein, L. "Sexual Involvement with Patients." *Journal of Clinical Psychiatry*, **39**(4), 366–368, 1978.

Kopp, S.B. "The Character Structure of Sex Offenders." *American Journal of Psychiatry*, **16**, 64–70, 1962.

Krieger, M.J., *et al.* "Problems with the Psychotherapy of Children with Histories of Incest." *American Journal of Psychotherapy*, **34**(1), 81–88, 1980.

Kroll, Jerome L. "The Concept of Childhood in the Middle Ages." *Journal of the History of the Behavioral Sciences*, **13**(4), 384–393, 1977.

Kroth, J.A. *Child Sexual Abuse: Analysis of a Family Therapy Approach.* Springfield, Ill.: Charles C. Thomas, 1979.

Kubo, S. "Researches and Studies on Incest in Japan." *Hiroshima Journal of Medical Sciences*, **8**, 99–159, 1959

Landis, J.T. "Experiences of 500 Children with Adult Sexual Deviation." *Psychiatric Quarterly* (supplement), **30**, 91–109, 1956.

Langsley, D.G., *et al.* "Father-Son Incest." *Comprehensive Psychiatry*, **9**(3), 218–226, 1968.

Leo, J. "Cradle to Grave Intimacy." *Time*, **69**, September 7, 1981.

Lester, D. "Incest." *Journal of Sex Research*, **8**, 268–285, 1972.

Lindzey, G. "Some Remarks Concerning Incest, The Incest Taboo and Psychoanalytic Theory." *American Psychologist*, **22**, 1051–1059, 1967.

Lloyd, R. *For Love or Money.* New York: Ballentine Books, 1977.

Lubove, Roy. "The Progressives and the Prostitute." *The Historian*, **14**(3), 308–330, 1962.

Lukianowicz, N. "Incest I: Paternal Incest; Incest II: Other Types of Incest." *British Journal of Psychiatry*, **120**(556), 301–313, 1972.

Lustig, N., *et al.* "Incest: A Family Group Survival Pattern." *Archives of General Psychiatry*, **14**, 31–40, 1966.

McCaghy, C.H. "Child Molesters: A Study of Their Careers as Deviants," in Clinard and Quinney (eds.), *Criminal Behavior Systems* (New York: Holt, Rinehart & Winston, 1967), pp. 75–88.

McEwan, I. *The Cement Garden.* New York: Berkley Books, 1978.

Machota, P., *et al.* "Incest as a Family Affair." *Family Process*, **6**(1), 98–116, 1967.

Magal, V., and Winnick, H.Z. "Role of Incest in Family Structure." *Israel Annals of Psychiatry and Related Disciplines*, **6**, 173–189, 1968.

Maisch, H. *Incest.* New York: Stein and Day, 1972.

Malinowski, B. *Sex and Regression in Savage Society.* London: Routledge & Kegan Paul, 1927.

Malmquist, C.P., *et al.* "Personality Characteristics of Women with Repeated Illegitimacies." *American Journal of Orthopsychiatry*, **36**(3), 476–484, 1966.

Marcuse, M. "Incest." *American Journal of Urology and Sexology*, **16**, 273–281, 1923.

Marshall, W.L., and Christie, M.M. "Pedophilia and Aggression." *Criminal Justice and Behavior*, **8**(2), 145–158, 1981.

Masters, R.E.L. *Patterns of Incest.* New York: Julian Press, 1963.

Masters, W. and Johnson, V. *Human Sexual Inadequacy.* Boston: Little, Brown, 1970.

Maudsley, Henry, "Illustrations of a Variety of Insanity." *The Journal of Mental Disease*, 1863.

Mechling, Jay E. "Advice to Historians on Advice to Mothers." *Journal of Social History*, **9**(1), 44–63, Fall 1975.

Medlicott, R.W. "Parent-Child Incest." *Australia and New Zealand Journal of Psychiatry*, **1**, 180–187, 1967.

Meiselman, K.C. *Incest.* San Francisco: Jossey-Bass, 1978.

Middleton, R. "Brother-Sister and Father-Daughter Marriages in Ancient Egypt." *American Sociological Review*, **27**, 603–611, 1962.

Miller, J., *et al.* "Recidivism among Sex Assault Victims." *American Journal of Psychiatry*, **135**(9), 1103–1104, 1978.

Mohr, J.W. "The Pedophilias: Their Clinical, Social and Legal Implications." *Canadian Psychiatric Association Journal*, **7**(5), 255–260, 1962.

Molnar, G., and Cameron, P. "Incest Syndromes: Observations in a General Hospital Psychiatric Unit." *Canadian Psychiatric Association Journal*, **20**, 373–377, 1975.

Morgan, Edmund S. "The Puritans and Sex." *The New England Quarterly*, **15**(4), 591–607, 1942.

Morgan, L.H. *Ancient Society*. Chicago: Kerr, 1877.

Muldoon, L. (ed.) *Incest: Confronting the Silent Crime*. St. Paul: Minnesota Program for Victims of Sexual Assault, 1979.

Murdock, G.P. *Social Structure*. New York: Macmillan, 1949.

Murray, F.E. *Rondeaux of Boyhood*. London: Privately Published, 1923.

Nasjleti, M. "Suffering in Silence: The Male Incest Victim." *Child Welfare*, **49**(5), 269–275, 1980.

Nesbitt, W.D. *The Trail to Boyhood and Other Poems*. Indianapolis: Bobbs-Merrill, 1924.

Neuman, R.P. "Masturbation, Madness and the Modern Concepts of Childhood and Adolescence." *Journal of Social History*, **8**, 1–27, 1975.

Newman, Graeme. *The Punishment Response*. Philadelphia: J.B. Lippincott, 1978.

Nicholson, J.G. *Love In Earnest: Sonnets, Ballades and Lyrics*. London: Eliot Stock, 1892.

Nobile, P. "Incest: The Last Taboo." *Penthouse*, 50–65, Dec. 1977.

Oaks, Robert F. "Defining Sodomy in 17th Century Massachusetts." *Journal of Homosexuality*, **6**(1/2), 79–83, 1980/1981.

————. "Things Fearful to Name: Sodomy and Buggery in 17th Century New England." *Journal of Social History*, **12**(2), 268–281, 1978.

Panton, J.H. "MMPI Profile Configurations Associated with Incestuous and Non-Incestuous Child Molesters." *Psychological Reports*, **45**, 335–338, 1979.

Parsons, T. "The Incest Taboo in Relation to Social Structure and the Socialization of the Child." *British Journal of Sociology*, **5**, 101–117, 1954.

Peters, J.J. "Children Who Are Victims of Sexual Assault and the Psychology of the Offender." *American Journal of Psychotherapy*, **30**, 398–421, 1976.

Rascovsky, M.W., and Rascovsky, A. "On Consummated Incest." *International Journal of Psychoanalysis*, **31**, 42–47, 1950.

Raybin, J.B. "Homosexual Incest: Report of a Case of Homosexual Incest Involving Three Generations of a Family." *Journal of Mental and Nervous Disease*, **148**, 105–109, 1969.

Reich, J.W., and Gutierres, S.E. "Escape/Aggression Incidence in Sexually Abused Juvenile Delinquents." *Criminal Justice and Behavior*, **6**(3), 239–243, 1979.

Revitch, E., and Weiss, R.G. "The Pedophiliac Offender." *Diseases of the Nervous System*, **23**(2), 73–78, 1962.

Rhinehart, J.W. "Genesis of Overt Incest." *Comprehensive Psychiatry*, **2**, 338–349, 1961.

Riemer, S. "A Research Note on Incest." *American Journal of Sociology*, **45**, 566–575, 1940.

Rogers E., and Weiss, J. "Study of Sex Crimes Against Children," in *California Sexual Deviation Research*. California: Langley Porter, 1953.

Rosen, D.H. *Lesbianism: A Study of Female Homosexuality*. Springfield, Ill.: Charles C. Thomas, 1974.

Rosenberg, Charles E. "Sexuality, Class and Role in 19th Century America." *American Quarterly*, **25**(2), 131–153, 1973.

Rossman, P. *Sexual Experiences Between Men and Boys*. New York: Association Press, 1976.

Ruggerio, Guido. "Sexual Criminality in the Early Renaissance: Venice 1338–1358." *Journal of Social History*, **8**, 18–33, 1975.

Rush, F. *The Best Kept Secret*. New York: Prentice Hall, 1980.

Sack, W.H., and Mason, R. "Child Abuse and Conviction of Sexual Crimes." *Law and Human Behavior*, **4**(3), 211–215, 1980.

Sadoff, R.L. "Treatment of Violent Sex Offenders." *International Journal of Offender*

Therapy and Comparative Criminology, **19**, 75–80, 1975.

Saffer, J.B., *et al.* "The Awesome Burden upon the Child Who Must Keep a Family Secret." *Child Psychiatry and Human Development*, **10**(1), 35–40, 1979.

Sagarin, E. (ed.) *Deviants: Voluntary Actors in a Hostile World.* New York: General Learning Press, 1977.

Schull, W.J., and Neel, J.V. *The Effects of Inbreeding on Japanese Children.* New York: Harper & Row, 1965.

Schultz, L.G. "The Child Sex Victim: Social, Psychological and Legal Perspectives." *Child Welfare*, **52**(3), 147–157, 1973.

_____ (ed.) *The Sexual Victimology of Youth.* Springfield, Ill.: Charles C. Thomas, 1980.

Schoettle, U.C. "Child Exploitation." *American Academy of Child Psychiatry*, **19**(2), 289–299, 1980.

Seemanova, E. "A Study of Children of Incestuous Matings." *Human Heredity*, **21**, 108–128, 1971.

Segner, L. and Collins, A. "Cross Cultural Study of Incest Myths." Unpublished manuscript, 1967.

Sgroi, S.M. "Child Sexual Assault," in Burgess *et al.* (eds.), *Sexual Assault of Children and Adolescents* (Lexington, Mass.: Lexington Books, 1978).

_____. "The Sexual Assault of Children." In Community Council of Greater New York (ed.) *Sexual Abuse of Children* (New York: The Council, 1979).

Shelton, W.R. "A Study of Incest." *International Journal of Offender Therapy and Comparative Criminology*, **19**, 139–153, 1975.

Shoor, M., *et al.* "Syndrome of the Adolescent Child Molester." *American Journal of Psychiatry*, **122**(7), 783–789, 1966.

Simmel, G. "Secrecy." In Wolff (ed.) *The Sociology of Georg Simmel* (New York: Free Press, 1964).

Sloane, P., and Karpinsky, E. "Effects of Incest on the Participants." *American Journal of Orthopsychiatry*, **12**, 666–673, 1942.

Sommerville, C. John. "English Puritans and Children: A Social-Cultural Explanation." *Journal of Psychohistory*, **6**(1), 113–133, 1978.

Spainer, G. "Sexual Socialization and Premariatal Sexual Behavior." Doctoral dissertation, Northwestern University *(Dissertation Abstracts International,* 1979, University Microfilms NO. 73–30, 729), 1973.

Spencer, J. "Father-Daughter Incest: A Clinical View from the Corrections Field." *Child Welfare*, **57**(9), 581–590, 1978.

Spivak, B. "Incest Histories Among Alcoholic Women." Paper presented at the Michigan Alcohol and Addiction Association conference, Bellaire, Mich., October, 14, 1980.

Stall, Sylvanus. *What A Young Boy Ought to Know.* Philadelphia: Vir Pub. Co., 1897.

Stinnett, N., and Walters, J. *Relationship in Marriage and Family.* New York: Macmillan, 1977.

Stone, A.A. "The Legal Implications of Sexual Activity Between Psychiatrist and Patient." *American Journal of Psychiatry*, **133**(10), 1138–1141, 1976.

Stricker, G. "Stimulus Properties of the Blacky to a Sample of Pedophiles." *Journal of General Psychology*, **77**, 35–39, 1967.

Strong, Bryan. "Toward a History of the Experiential Family: Sex and Incest in the 19th Century Family." *Journal of Marriage and the Family*, **35**(3), 457–466, 1973.

Summitt, R., and Kryso, J. "Sexual Abuse of Children: A Clinical Spectrum." *American Journal of Orthopsychiatry*, **48**, 237–251, 1978.

Swanson, D.W. "Adult Sexual Abuse of Children." *Disease of the Nervous System.* **29**(10), 677–683, 1968.

Swift, C. "Sexual Victimization of Children: An Urban Mental Health Center Survey." *Victimology*, **2**(2), 322–26, 1977.

Swigert, V.L., *et al.* "Sexual Homicide: Social, Psychological and Legal Aspects." *Archives of Sexual Behavior*, **5**(5), 391–401, 1976.

172 Bibliography

Szabo, D. "Problems of Socialization and Sociocultural Integration: A Contribution to the Etiology of Incest." *Canadian Psychiatric Association Journal*, 7, 235–252, 1962.

Taylor, B. "Motives for Guilt-Free Pederasty: Some Literary Considerations." *The Sociological Review*, 24(1), 97–114, 1976.

Taylor, B.J., and Wagner, N.N. "Sex Between Therapists and Clients." *Professional Psychology*, 7(4), 593–601, 1976.

Thomas, J.N. "Yes, You Can Help a Sexually Abused Child," *RN*, 43(8), 23–29, 1980.

Tindall, R.H. "The Male Adolescent Involved with a Pederast Becomes an Adult." *Journal of Homosexuality*, 3(4), 373–382, 1978.

Tompkins, J.B. "Penis Envy and Incest." *Psychoanalytic Review*, 27, 319–325, 1940.

Tormes, Y. *Child Victims of Incest*. Denver: American Humane Association, 1968.

Tsai, M., et al. "Childhood Molestation: Variables Related to Differential Impacts on Psychosexual Functioning in Adult Women." *Journal of Abnormal Psychology*, 88, 407–417, 1979.

———, and Wagner, N.N. "Therapy Groups for Women Sexually Molested as Children." *Archives of Sexual Behavior*, 7, 417–427, 1978.

Tuchman, Barbara W. *A Distant Mirror*. New York: Ballantine, 1978.

Turner, G.K. "The Daughters of the Poor." *McClure's Magazine*, 34, 1909.

Tylor, P. "Denied the Power to Choose the Good: Sexuality and Mental Defect in American Medical Practice, 1850–1920." *Journal of Social History*, 10, 472–489, 1977.

Ungaretti, J. "Pederasty, Heroism and the Family in Classical Greece." *Journal of Homosexuality*, 3, 291–300, 1978.

Vischer, E.B., and Vischer, J. *Stepfamilies: A Guide to Working with Stepparents and Stepchildren*. New York: Brunner, Mazel, 1979.

Wahl, C.W. "The Psychodynamics of Consummated Maternal Incest." *Archives of General Psychiatry*, 3, 188–193, 1960.

Warner, C. *Rape and Sexual Assault*. Germantown, Md.: Aspen Systems, 1980.

Weeks, R.B. "The Sexually Exploited Child." *Southern Medical Journal*, 69, 848–850, 1976.

Weinberg, S.K. *Incest Behavior*. New York: Citadel, 1955.

Weiner, I.B. "Father-Daughter Incest: A Clinical Report." *Psychiatric Quarterly*, 36, 607–632, 1962.

———. "On Incest: A Survey." *Excerpta Criminology*, 4, 137–155, 1964.

Weiss, J., et al. "A Study of Girl Sex Victims." *Psychiatric Quarterly*, 29, 1–27, 1955.

Wells, H.M. *The Sensuous Child*. New York: Stein & Day, 1978.

Westermark, E. *The History of Human Marriage*, 5th ed. New York: Allerton, 1922.

White, L.A. "The Definition of the Prohibition of Incest." *American Anthropologist*, 50, 416–435, 1948.

Wyman, Margaret. "The Rise of the Fallen Woman." *American Quarterly*, 3, 167–177, 1951.

"Yes, Virginia, There Is a PIE." *National Review*, 29, 1221–1222, 1977.

Yorukaglu, A., and Kemph, J.P. "Children Not Severely Damagegd by Incest with a Parent." *Journal of the American Academy of Child Psychiatry*, 5, 111–124, 1966.

INDEX

5